The Effective Teaching of History

THE EFFECTIVE TEACHER SERIES

General editor: Elizabeth Perrott

THE EFFECTIVE TEACHER SERIES

The Effective Teaching of History

Ron Brooks
Mary Aris
Irene S. Perry

Longman
London and New York

Pearson Education Limited
Edinburgh Gate, Harlow,
Essex CM20 2JE, England
and Associated Companies throughout the world.

*Published in the United States of America
by Addison Wesley Longman Inc., New York*

© Longman Group UK Limited 1993

First published 1993
Fourth impression 1999

ISBN 0-582 05915-1 PPR

British Library Cataloguing-in-Publication Data

A catalogue record for this book is
available from the British Library

Library of Congress Cataloguing-in-Publication Data

Brooks, Ron, 1930–
    The effective teaching of history / Ron Brooks, Mary Aris, Irene Perry.
        p. cm. -- (The effective teacher series)
    Includes bibliographical references (p.) and index.
    ISBN 0-582-05915-1
    1. History--Study and teaching (Higher)--United States. I. Aris, Mary, 1946– .
    II. Perry, Irene, 1948– . III. Title. IV. Series.
D16.3.B76 1993
907'.1'073--dc20   92-44657
                                                                CIP

Set by 7E in 10/11.5 Times

Transferred to Digital Printing 2005

Printed and bound by Antony Rowe Ltd, Eastbourne

CONTENTS

SERIES EDITOR'S PREFACE

This well-established series was inspired by my book on the practice of teaching (*Effective Teaching: a Practical Guide to Improving your Teaching*, Longman, 1982), written for trainee teachers wishing to improve their teaching skills as well as for in-service teachers, especially those engaged in the supervision of trainees. The books in this series have been written with the same readership in mind. However, busy classroom teachers will find that these books also serve their needs as changes in the nature and pattern of education make the in-service training of experienced teachers more essential than in the past.

The rationale behind the series is that professional courses for teachers require the coverage of a wide variety of subjects in a relatively short time so the aim of the series is the production of 'easy to read', practical guides to provide the necessary subject background, supported by references to guide and encourage further reading, together with questions and/or exercises devised to assist application and evaluation.

As specialists in their selected fields, the authors have been chosen for their ability to relate their subjects to the needs of teachers and to stimulate discussion of contemporary issues in education.

The series aims to cover subjects ranging from the theory of education to the teaching of mathematics and from primary school teaching and educational psychology to effective teaching with information technology. It looks at aspects of education as diverse as education and cultural diversity and pupil welfare and counselling. Although some subjects such as the legal context of teaching and the teaching of history are specific to England and Wales, the majority of the subjects such as assessment in education, the effective teaching of statistics and comparative education are international in scope.

Elizabeth Perrott

PREFACE

We live and teach in the age of the National Curriculum. The old order has gone and gone forever; with it, by a swift stroke of the legislative pen, went a generation and more of books of practical guidance on history teaching, made obsolete by the new requirements. Moreover, the days are gone (even if they ever existed) when a single author could offer sensible, practical advice for history teaching from the first year of the primary school to the last year of the sixth form (or its equivalent). That kind of range of professional expertise and experience is beyond most authors. With that in mind, the present volume in the Effective Teacher series has been written by three people, each with a different background in teaching. Mary Aris is an author, archivist and teacher who has prepared resource packs for use by students of all ages. Ron Brooks has taught in secondary schools, has acted as a chief examiner at GCSE and A levels, trained teachers and lectured in history. Irene Perry is a practising teacher, former head of department, project leader on GCSE and National Curriculum schemes and is a deputy headteacher.

Ron Brooks

LIST OF FIGURES

ACKNOWLEDGEMENTS

We are grateful to the following for permission to reproduce copyright material:

the Controller of Her Majesty's Stationery Office for extracts from *National Curriculum History Working Group Final Report* by DES and The Welsh Office (HMSO, 1990), an extract from the press release *History is a key subject for all students* by Keith Joseph, 10.2.84 (1984), an abridged extract from *Aspects of Primary Education – The Teaching and Learning of History* (HMSO, 1989), an extract from *History in the National Curriculum* (NCC/HMSO, 1990) and an extract from *Education Pamphlet No 54 – Archives and Education* by DES (HMSO, 1968); Curriculum Council for Wales for extracts from *History in the National Curriculum: Non-Statutory Guidance for teachers* (CCW, 1991); Ewan MacNaughton Associates for an abridged extract from the article 'History Teaching "could be dropped" ' by John Clare from *Daily Telegraph* newspaper 20.6.90, © The Telegraph plc, 1990; The Historical Association and the authors, J B Coltham and J Fines for extracts from *Educational Objectives for the Study of History* (The Historical Association, 1971); National Curriculum Council for extracts from *Non-Statutory Guidance for History* (NCC/HMSO, 1990), an extract from *Schools Council Working Paper No 5* by The Schools Council (HMSO, 1979) and an extract from *History Commissioned Group Report on N and F Syllabuses* by The Schools Council (HMSO, 1976); Talysarn School for a response by an unidentified pupil read at the HMI conference, North Wales, July 1990; Welsh Joint Education Committee for an adapted question from a past A Level History examination paper; Gwynedd Archives and Museum Service for 'The Master Race' photograph; Michael Holford for two illustrations of the Bayeux Tapestry on page 84.

We have been unable to trace the copyright holders for Figures 1.2, 5.8, 5.9 and the Allateif Mardiny cartoon and would appreciate any help that would enable us to do so.

Selling history in the schools and colleges of the 1990s

Ron Brooks

The definition of what constitutes an effective history teacher is not fixed and immutable. It must inevitably reflect the aims and objectives of the history syllabus and the age in which they operate. In the era of the first national curriculum, which came to an end in 1926, both the history syllabus and the task of the history teacher were defined in six lines.

History should include the lives of great men and women and the lessons to be learnt therefrom, and in the higher classes a knowledge of the great persons and events of English History and of the growth of the British Empire. The teaching need not be limited to English or British History, and lessons on citizenship may be given with advantage in the higher classes.[1]

The effective teacher of history was the person who could elicit clearly the moral messages to be gleaned from studying the lives of the great and the good; the age demanded that this should be interpreted mainly within an imperial context with the emphasis upon citizenship and service. There was no need to sell the subject, constituting as it did, a core element of the compulsory curriculum. History sold itself in the schools of interwar Britain. Even after the first national curriculum was quietly abandoned, elementary schools remained under the general regulations of the Board of Education, which meant in effect, continuing to teach history. The secondary school regulations drawn up in 1904 stipulated that 'not less than 4½ hours per week must be allotted to English, Geography and History'. The dropping of the detailed prescription of hours a few years later did not disturb history's dominant position among the core subjects of the liberal, grammar tradition. Only querulous pupils and awkward governors at interviews asked for some justification for studying it. However, therein lay both history's strength and its weakness. After the demise of the first national curriculum, the priority given to history in schools was dependent upon the continued dominance of the liberal academic tradition in education. When the second national curriculum was being formulated in the 1980s, this tradition was in retreat. The Labour Prime Minister, James Callaghan, attacked it in his Ruskin

College speech in 1976 and successive Conservative governments in the 1980s poured resources into technical and vocational education. The decline in the position of history in many of our schools is signified by the fact that it failed not only to be ranked as a core subject in the National Curriculum reinstated under the Education Reform Act of 1988 but was struggling hard for its survival on the list of foundation subjects as schools in the early 1990s tried to pour the National Curriculum quart into the school timetable pint pot. Even the strenuous attempts made by historians over two decades to make their subject more relevant to the needs of late twentieth-century Britain seemed to be overshadowed by the debate over empathy. As the following brief extract from a newspaper article at the beginning of the 1990s shows, history led the descent of the humanities from its secure position in the first national curriculum to the point of possible abandonment during the implementation of the second. To those who hold the view that 'the more liberal a subject is, the more useless it is', history must have appeared as the jewel in the non-utilitarian crown.

The history teacher as publicist and salesperson

HISTORY TEACHING 'COULD BE DROPPED'

by John Clare, Education Editor

History could be dropped from the national curriculum because of 'all the ink being spilled' over how it should be taught, 18 eminent historians claimed yesterday...

The 18 included, on the Right, Sir Geoffrey Elton, former Regius Professor of modern history at Cambridge, and Lord Blake, the historian of the Conservative party; and on the Left, Prof. Eric Hobsbawm and Dr Raphael Samuel[2]. (*The Daily Telegraph*, 20 June 1990)

Many history conferences in the 1970s and 1980s took as their theme the defence of the subject. As the headline suggests, it will no longer be sufficient in the 1990s to mount a defence. The effective teacher of the 1990s must be the skilled publicist and salesperson if the subject is to survive the new age of market forces. A strategy based simply upon warding off attack will be inadequate to guarantee its survival. Teachers must be prepared not only to defend their subject but positively to advance its cause in a hostile climate if history is going to stand a chance of surviving. The effective teaching of history requires first and foremost a healthy environment in which to flourish. A marginalised position on the school timetable with dwindling numbers of pupils and the possible threat of enforced merger with other subjects will not provide that. The history teacher must sell the subject in a highly competitive and possibly unfriendly market place as never before. Teachers in the independent sector have long been used to doing this. Teachers in state schools must adopt some of these selling techniques if history is to flourish in the state sector.

With the publication of the interim and final reports of the National Curriculum History Working Group in 1989 and 1990 'the history debate' finally went public, no longer being confined to in-house shareholders; that is to teachers and students. History is no longer a limited partnership or enterprise between these two groups. It is now History plc. The 1988 Education Reform Act and earlier legislation has altered entirely the political context in which history teaching operates. Parents are now full shareholders, no longer limited to voting by proxy through giving their children advice about subject choice. They have a full say in selecting schools for their children, on governing bodies where the allocation of resources is decided, and whether or not a school should opt out of local authority control, a decision which could affect the status and position of history in a school. Directly and indirectly, they have a great deal of influence over curricular matters. The meetings of the new shareholders of History plc may well be stormy; some indeed may wish to wind up the company or favour a merger with other subject areas to preserve its share of a declining pupil market. Some, who have experienced only the old-style rote learning of facts and dates, may well believe that the subject is already educationally bankrupt and will take a great deal of persuading that history is not only educationally solvent and viable but is vital to the balance and well-being of the curricular economy of the 1990s. The problem is that many shareholders and the public at large may not appreciate that the nature of the history business has changed. History plc no longer deals in the old bankrupt stock of rote learning. Historical literacy today encompasses a wide range of skills as well as the acquisition of and understanding of knowledge.

History plc is not in the theme park business, that is the immediate and shallow enjoyment of a series of short-lived and random experiences. Pupils soon grow weary of a parade of historical topics selected solely because they appear to have a popular appeal or relevance. Hitler's Germany taught *solely* as a series of brutal persecutions and bloody deeds soon galls. Such an approach is history without integrity. The crux of the Final Report of the National Curriculum History Working Group was stated in its introduction (point 1.3):

1.3   To have integrity, the study of history must be grounded in a thorough knowledge of the past; must employ rigorous historical method – the way in which historians carry out their task; and must involve a range of interpretations and explanations. *Together, these elements make an organic whole; if any one of them is missing the outcome is not history.*[3]

This idea of historical study as the rigorous combination of knowledge and method is central to any defence of a key position for history in the curriculum of the 1990s, and may best be summed up in the term 'historical literacy'. But a key problem for those wishing to engage in such a defence is history's poor image. It is often seen as a subject with very limited aims, usually the acquisition of knowledge and information about ages remote from our own, and whose teaching is restricted to dictated notes, copying from textbooks and rote learning. The preface to any argument for giving history an important position in the school curriculum of the 1990s must be an examination of the way in which history has developed into a multi-skilled discipline which has immense relevance to the general and vocational education of students.

In short, the value of history as a school subject must be constantly and publicly argued because:

(1) history may lose out in any modification to the National Curriculum;
(2) in the implementation of the existing national curriculum it may be marginalised in the scramble for resources and timetable space;
(3) a rigorous projection of the value of the subject is important to the well-being of the school in the face of competition from other schools and possible closure;
(4) students have a choice at Key Stage 4 and in the sixth form and it is essential for the integrity of the subject that single-subject history should have a good representation at both levels;
(5) above all history has much to offer to the student of the 1990s.

Developing positive attitudes and approaches

This chapter suggests a three-stage approach to promoting history in our schools. The first stage is to develop wholehearted, *positive attitudes* and approaches to selling the subject in the curricular market place of the 1990s. The second is to develop the *promotional materials* which can assist in conveying the main, general arguments for teaching history. The last stage is to *elaborate the case* carefully for presentation to specialist audiences whether they be parents, students, employers, governors or other interested groups.

While history teachers would wish to eschew the more brash sales methods they may nevertheless welcome some guidance on appropriate methods and strategies for promoting their subject. The inclination of historians may be to begin with their stock-in-trade, the arguments, but this is unlikely to be the best starting point for many, especially those who are new to the profession. What the experienced communicator recognises is that the effectiveness of what is said is as dependent upon how it is said and perceptions and impressions others have of the person presenting the argument as it is upon the quality of argument itself. From school to university level students often choose subjects to study and options within a subject on the basis of their own (or other people's) emotional response to the teacher. Impressions and perceptions are not dispassionate. In schools, in particular, the emotional response of students may well outweigh rational argument when it comes to selecting subjects to study. The preferences of individual students may be determined in whole or part by the collective feeling about the teacher rather than about the subject itself. This may be no less true of the views of parents, employers and school governors who will respond initially to the presenter not to the argument. The first task then is not to examine the arguments themselves but to consider those aspects which will assist a favourable response to the arguments.

Positive attitudes: some basic considerations

Be yourself
Avoid 'role modelling' for the successful models are rarely what they appear. Taking on a new persona is in any case impossible but it is possible to adopt and adapt some of the methods of effective presentation which others employ.

Develop your own strengths
Classroom teaching is about communication. Teachers have already developed considerable expertise within the classroom to provide a good basis upon which to build effective communication outside.

Look critically at the views of the staffroom cynic
He or she may argue that the task is impossible, because you are not skilled enough or because you have never tried to sell the subject to other than students before. Ask yourself why they hold such negative attitudes. Could it be that your success may remove much of the justification for their having done nothing, often for many years?

Develop a positive approach
Think about how history can be promoted as a school subject, instead of jumping straight in with a myriad of reasons why it can not. People who think negatively are often proved right. If they think that they can't achieve a goal, they can't.

Don't believe that you can convince everybody at once
A majority will do but even less will be acceptable on some occasions. Do not let failure to please all dent your self-confidence when it is really impossible to do so.

Be enthusiastic
This applies in your efforts to convince others, but don't be dour.
Some humour can be a valuable aid.

Be receptive to feedback
Be receptive to feedback from your audience and be willing to reduce
the length and detail of argument if interest and attention begin to
drift. Introduce new material (e.g. examples of students' work) at sag
points or more often just listen to what others have to say.

Personal appearance matters
Those whom we seek to persuade have certain expectations of
teachers. In a buyer's market we ignore these at our peril. One
expectation is that we should look like professionals. What we say will
count very little if we look wrong to the particular group or individual
to whom we are talking.

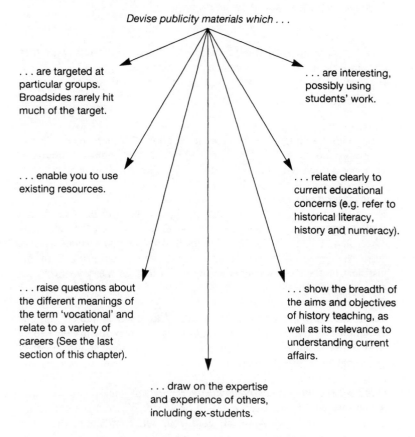

Devise publicity materials which . . .

. . . are targeted at particular groups. Broadsides rarely hit much of the target.

. . . are interesting, possibly using students' work.

. . . enable you to use existing resources.

. . . relate clearly to current educational concerns (e.g. refer to historical literacy, history and numeracy).

. . . raise questions about the different meanings of the term 'vocational' and relate to a variety of careers (See the last section of this chapter).

. . . show the breadth of the aims and objectives of history teaching, as well as its relevance to understanding current affairs.

. . . draw on the expertise and experience of others, including ex-students.

Figure 1.1 Positive approaches: some general considerations

Two further points when devising and implementing aims:

(1) give adequate scope to show your skills;
(2) put yourself in the position of those making the decisions from which you hope to benefit. What are their main concerns and how can you best meet them? What back up materials will you require to persuade them (e.g. exam results, students' work, textbooks)?

Promotional materials: their value, design and use

Much of the argument for teaching history can best be conveyed in attractively designed departmental brochures. These have several advantages.

(1) They show the history department to be forward thinking and concerned about its students and their varied interests.
(2) They allow students to play a part in their design and content, thus providing valuable consumer perspectives. Student participation in the project including its costing and possible in-school publication also provides a valuable learning experience.
(3) They enable the department to include particularly attractive features, e.g. photographs of students engaging in GCSE fieldwork or involved in other historical activities.
(4) They provide basic information in advance of meetings with interested parties.
(5) They provide a basis for discussion and elucidation at meetings so that they appear less like lectures to convey information and more like collaborative discussion.

But many of the advantages of using brochures can be achieved only if two types are produced, a general brochure conveying basic information and general argument and specialist brochures targeted at particular groups, e.g. parents, parent-governors, governors, local employers and of course potential students. General brochures may well include:

(1) a statement of the learning experiences which history courses offer. These may relate generally to vocational skills to impart the idea that history and vocationalism are not antithetical. Perhaps a brief reference to some of the careers in which former students have found historical skills and knowledge useful would not go amiss. History is not taught just to produce future generations of history teachers and history graduates!
(2) course descriptions which indicate particular areas of interest;
(3) the staff, their interests and teaching methods;
(4) photographs highlighting special features which show students at work;

(5) course results;
(6) other departmental activities and involvements;
(7) cross-references to specialist brochures.

The specialist brochures should be designed to elaborate on particular features for particular consumer groups, and may contain more diagrammatic and other illustrative material to do this. The increased costs of including a greater number of photographs and other illustrations in the specialist brochures may be offset in part by the fact that fewer of this type are required. The specialist brochures should have a suitable front page which relates to the interests of the target group.

However, brochures may be of varying kinds and history found within them in a variety of guises. The following are two examples from brochures in the early 1990s which were distributed to parents and local businesses, and were even to be found in doctors' and dentists' waiting rooms. They used no more than two sides of A4 to provide a basic outline of courses, being part of a large information pack. The following general curricular statement can be modified to suit a school's needs.

Example One: a general brochure

Purpose
Humanities teaching seeks to encourage and promote an enthusiasm for the past which has shaped our heritage and culture; a respect for the meaning and diversity of human values; and an awareness of people living in different places under different physical and human conditions.

National Curriculum
All pupils entering year 1 in September 1991, and thereafter will come under the requirements of the National Curriculum in history and geography. Religious education is compulsory for all ages.

Studying humanities
The study of humanities will promote interest in the nature and quality of life and understanding of the major economic, social, environmental, technological and political factors which have shaped and are shaping the contemporary world.

Teaching groups
Pupils are taught in mixed ability groups across all age ranges.

Methodology
A variety of formats is used including individual and group work, role plays, computer assisted learning and discussions. In addition off-site visits and fieldwork are arranged.

continued

Homework
Homework is allocated usually at least once per week. It may be set written work, answers to questions set in classes or in a pamphlet or writing up investigational work. On other occasions it may be reading set texts, finding out information or completing diagrams and/or maps.

Programmes of study
Years   Choice of four modules from 10 plus one additional
4 and 5   Six modules on offer at present are:
          People technology and change
          People in towns and cities
          Pollution and the quality of life
          The superpowers
          People in authority
          Population issues

Year 3   Revolution
          Diversity
          Power
          Democracy

Year 2   Changes in time and settlement
          People's changing needs
          Worship and celebration
          Exploration and pilgrimage

Year 1   Evidence and investigations
          Early society
          Roman conquest
          Pioneers-wagons west!
          Local community studies

[These details will require updating in line with the national curriculum]

Assessment
In addition to the cross-curricular skills, subject specific skills assessed by Humanities are knowledge, understanding, enquiry, interpretation and evaluation. In years 1–3 end of unit tests are set. In years 4 and 5 an assessment item is completed at the end of each module and is worth 10 per cent of the final examination.
[These details will require updating in line with the national curriculum]

Curriculum links
Humanities serve most cross-curriculum themes including equal opportunities, cultural diversity, Welsh context, economic and industrial understanding, environmental awareness and information technology capability. Its links with the community and industry are fostered by off-site visits to workplaces and by fieldwork.

continued

GCSE
4th and 5th Year pupils are being taught to the WJEC humanities course (Track 2)
[These details will require updating in line with the national curriculum]

A Level
A Level students are being taught to:
WJEC economics, history, geography and religious studies[4]

Example Two: a specialist brochure

The following statement about advanced level history provides an outline of the aims and content of history courses, and entry qualifications. Programmes one and two (not included here) were business studies courses and prevocational courses; the third covered advanced level history:

History 'A' Level

Aims
The course leading to the examination should stimulate interest in and promote study of history by seeking to achieve the following:

1. an understanding and sound knowledge of the period selected;
2. a consideration of the nature of historical sources and historians' methods;
3. an acquaintance with different interpretations and approaches to periods;
4. an understanding of historical concepts;
5. an understanding of the development over time of social and cultural values;
6. the development of essential study skills and empathetic awareness;
7. a sound basis for further study and the pursuit of personal interest.

Assessment
Candidates will be required to take *two* papers. Each paper will be of three hours duration and of equal weighting.

Paper A1
'An Outline of the History of Wales and England 1815–1914'

a. 15 areas of study will be identified,
b. each area of study will be linked with a question format,
c. there will be 3 sections in the paper:
   A – Structured questions
   B – Case studies
   C – Essay type questions

continued

Requirements
(1) A 'C' pass or better at GCSE.
(2) An interest in and commitment to the course.

Applications
The acquisition of an 'A' level history qualification says much about the holder in terms of analytical ability and competence of expression. These two skills among many acquired through the course give a training of the mind which is transferable to all facets of study in further education, a pre-requisite for effective industrial commercial management, invaluable in any branch of the civil service and not least a basis for informed and responsible citizenship in the future.
For further information contact Mrs I.S. Perry[5]

Promotional materials: their use in overcoming misconceptions

One of the problems confronting a teacher who wishes to present effective arguments for maintaining or expanding the teaching of history in a school or college is the way in which many people perceive the subject. Those who were educated prior to the mid-1970s may well believe that history has little to contribute to education in the 1990s because they believe it still to be predominantly concerned with narrative chronology with much copying down of dictated notes. As such people may well be school governors it may be best to preface specific arguments with a brief exposition of modern developments in the teaching of history. This can be done with one of the most attractive arguments at the teachers' disposal, students' work; a contrast can be made with the kind of work which students undertook in the 1960s and 1970s, an example of which is included in Figure 1.2. This may be introduced by some initial reference to earlier ideas about history teaching. Such a presentation could thus be structured as follows:

1. History teaching at the time of the first national curriculum in the 1920s

The history syllabus as defined in the first national curriculum which ended in 1926:

History, which should include, in the lower classes, the lives of great men and women and the lessons to be learnt therefrom, and in the higher classes a knowledge of the great persons and events of English History and of the growth of the British Empire. The teaching need not be limited to English or British History, and lessons on citizenship may be given with advantage in the higher classes.

Points for emphasis:

Content: predominantly British. British often seen as synonymous with English.
Setting: usually imperial, with history taught as a pageant of the greats.
Aim: emphasis upon the responsible citizen, and the idea of service.
Points for developments with audience involvement: how far did the content and aims of history teaching in the 1920s differ from those of their school days?

2. History teaching in the 1960s: a typical lesson

See figure 1.2 opposite.

3. Changes in the study and teaching of history since 1970

The third set of presentation materials could be examples of your own pupils' work which show how the aims and objectives of history teaching have changed considerably since the 1960s and 1970s. Before turning to the individual arguments for teaching history it would be worthwhile emphasising the professional integrity of history teachers. The broadening of aims and objectives has not been a sudden panic measure to the market forces of the 1990s but has been part of a professional and careful reassessment which has been in progress since at least the late 1960s. The following list of skills and abilities taken from Educational Objectives for the Study of History written in 1971 by Jeanette Coltham and John Fines bears out this point.

The Coltham–Fines list of skills and abilities involved in the study of history (1971)[6]

1. *Vocabulary acquisition.* Since history is a discipline of a highly verbal nature, a grasp of its terminology is obviously an important objective, contributing to achievement in all aspects of its study...
2. *Reference skills.* These are required for obtaining, checking and retrieving specific facts and pieces of information, particularly but not entirely from secondary sources...
3. *Memorisation.* The retention of some of the information encountered cannot but be expected...
4. *Comprehension.* The behaviour referred to here is that required in the first stages of an encounter with any new material. It is the result of examination at the surface or literal level – attention to the immediately observed features without any depth of cognitive treatment – resulting in an understanding of the general nature of the material.

Analysis of 35 minute lesson in terms of pupil activity.

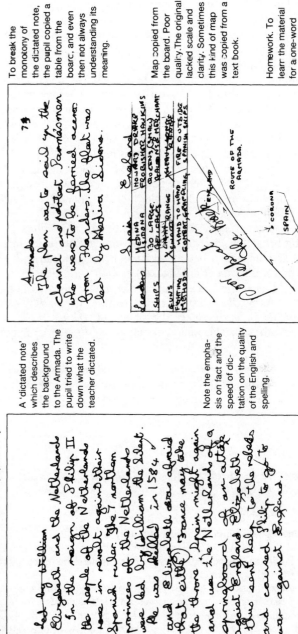

A 'dictated note' which describes the background to the Armada. The pupil tried to write down what the teacher dictated.

Note the emphasis on fact and the speed of dictation on the quality of the English and spelling.

To break the monotony of the dictated note, the pupil copied a table from the board, and even then not always understanding its meaning.

Map copied from the board. Poor quality. The original lacked scale and clarity. Sometimes this kind of map was copied from a text book.

Homework. To learn the material for a one-word answer test the following lesson.

Issues for discussion:

How far do the lesson activities bear out the pupil's view of history teaching?
How different was history teaching when the members of the 'audience' were at school?
Was this lesson, with its restricted activities, typical of their experience?

Figure 1.2 An analysis of a typical history lesson of the 1960s

5. *Translation.* The material of history is available in a variety of forms and the ability to turn information received in one form into some other form...

6. *Analysis.* As the heading of the category indicates, the cognitive behaviour intended here is that of separating a whole into its elements or component parts...

7. *Extrapolation.* In this cognitive behaviour, what is already apprehended is used as a taking-off point for some idea which is rooted but not present in the evidence being examined. 'Since I know this, then it might be that...' is the kind of thinking involved, and it represents a more positive and adventurous mental behaviour than that of comprehension...

8. *Synthesis.* The 'putting together' signified by the heading to this category is a skill which may be needed at all or several stages of study, from the formulation of plans or an enquiry up to the creation of a product...

9. *Judgement and evaluation.* The practice of any judging or evaluating behaviour implies the use of some frame of reference; a conscious comparison has to be made between features of the material and a criterion or criteria...

10. *Communication skills.* ... the products of study of history can take a variety of forms. Each different form requires the mastery of its specific skills if, as is surely the object of the enterprise, the product is to be available and to communicate to all who may be interested.

The final stage in preparing the ground for the elaboration of particular arguments for specific groups is to put forward the broad arguments presented by the National Curriculum History Working Group in their formal report in April 1990.

Extract from the final report of The National Curriculum History Working Group[1]

The purposes of school history

1.7 We consider that the purposes of school history are:

   i)   to help understand the present in the context of the past. There is nothing in the present that cannot be better understood in the light of its historical context and origins;

   ii) to arouse interest in the past. History naturally arouses curiosity, raises fundamental questions, and generates speculation;

   iii) to help to give pupils a sense of identity. Through history pupils can learn about the origins and story of their family and of other groups to which they belong, of their community and country, and of institutions, beliefs, values, customs, and underlying shared assumptions;

iv) to help to give pupils an understanding of their own cultural roots and shared inheritances. No standard, uniform culture can be imposed on the young in so culturally diverse a society as exists in Britain, yet much is shared in common. Although questions about the origins and nature of British culture are complex, school history can put shared inheritances in their historical context;

v) to contribute to pupils' knowledge and understanding of other countries and other cultures in the modern world. Education in British society should be rooted in toleration and respect cultural variety. Studying the history of other societies from their own perspectives and for their own sake counteracts tendencies to insularity, without devaluing British achievements, values and traditions;

vi) to train the mind by means of disciplined study. History relies heavily upon disciplined enquiry, systematic analysis and evaluation, argument, logical rigour and a search for the truth;

vii) to introduce pupils to the distinctive methodology of historians. Historians attempt to construct their own coherent accounts of the past by the rigorous testing of evidence which is often incomplete; the skills involved in doing this have benefits beyond the study of history;

viii) to enrich other areas of the curriculum. History draws on the record of the entire human past; it is a subject of immense breadth which can both inform, and draw upon, other areas of the curriculum;

ix) to prepare pupils for adult life. History gives pupils a framework of reference, opportunities for the informed use of leisure, and a critically sharpened intelligence with which to make sense of current affairs. History is a priceless preparation for citizenship, work, and leisure. It encourages pupils to approach them from angles not considered by other subjects or forms of study in the curriculum.

Elaborating the case for history for specialist audiences

The promotional materials outlined in stage two were concerned largely with *general* changes in the aims and methods of history teaching. Increasingly, however, teachers of history are expected to present their case in greater detail, and often to audiences of specialists such as employers or educationists. They need therefore to elaborate the case for history with such audiences in mind. This is the third stage in promoting the subject. The final part of this chapter offers guidance on how this task can be approached.

The argument for balance and breadth

There is a danger that the problems of finding sufficient timetable space for the key stages of the core subjects will weaken two basic principles of the National Curriculum, balance and breadth. By the time that Key Stage 4 of history is introduced in 1994 with the first reported assessment in 1996 there is the possibility that its position as one of the main elements providing balance and breadth will be undermined by lack of an adequate number of hours for teaching the subject. One of the key arguments in defending its position on the school timetable must be the 1988 Education Reform Act itself which should not be lost sight of among the more immediate problems of implementation. It states that the curriculum should be balanced and broadly based, and should

(a) promote the spiritual, moral, cultural, mental and physical development of pupils at school and in society; and

(b) prepare such pupils for the opportunities, responsibilities and experience of adult life.[8]

Two things are worth emphasising in this connection. First, it reiterates and extends the list of central purposes of the curriculum as outlined in the 1944 Education Act; secondly, it establishes the priority of individual and social needs over the economic, the needs of pupils as pupils rather than as future wage-earners. While history has much to contribute to the employability of young people it also has, without establishing a rigid dichotomy, much to contribute to personal and social education.

The words of Sir Keith Joseph, Kenneth Baker's immediate predecessor at the DES, and an architect of the National Curriculum are worth quoting in this context. One of his basic beliefs was that,

In the study of history, and nowhere else, the chief objective is to enable pupils to gain an understanding of human activity in the past and its implications for the present.[9]

History is essentially to do with personal development in that it takes as the object of study the roots and origins of groups and those of individuals and examines how they have changed over time. It provides in Sir Keith's view the evidence for understanding what we were and thus of what we are. This could be developed by reference to the following arguments:

(1) History is a social necessity.

(2) History is one of the essential elements of a humane education in that it informs us about man in his various activities and environments and thus helps us to understand our fellow human beings.

(3) A knowledge of history equips us to deal with the vast range of problems confronting the contemporary world.

(4) History has a vital part to play in helping pupils to understand shared attitudes. To quote Sir Keith:

'One of the aims of studying history is to understand the development of the shared values which are a distinctive feature of British society and culture and which continue to shape private attitudes and public policy. But values are shared only in a broad sense. We disagree among ourselves about much, and that is as it should be in an open society. And it is not only values that are broadly shared. There is, in our society, also much shared understanding and shared knowledge.'

It is possible to add several other arguments to the list of those which focus upon the realisation of group (a) (on page 16) National Curriculum aims. These relate particularly to a pupil's 'mental... development'.

(5) History is part of a sound general education in that it develops communication skills, as well as literacy, numeracy and graphicacy.
(6) History assists intellectual development in that it depends on rational argument and discussion, and provides practice in the skills necessary to argue a case. It assists critical judgement and the systematic presentation of a variety of arguments.

The citizenship argument

Popular education developed in the wake of the extension of the franchise. It is perhaps not surprising, therefore that from the early days when the state became involved in the education of the masses one of the principal aims of the curriculum enunciated by successive Presidents of the Board of Education, Ministers of Education and Secretaries of State for Education has been that of the preparation for citizenship. Sir Keith Joseph echoed the view of his predecessors and successors when he declared in 1984,[10] 'History, properly taught, justifies its place in the curriculum by what it does to prepare all pupils for the responsibilities of citizenship.' History has been seen by politicians of all parties as being vital to informed citizenship. The importance of shared values, not in a narrow sense, has been a constant theme of generations of educationists and politicians. Often the emphasis on shared values has been at its greatest in time of war or other national crisis. It was thus all the more interesting to see Sir Keith outlining the importance of citizenship as an aim of any agreed curriculum in the relative tranquillity of the 1980s. He defined shared values in the 1980s in the broadest sense,[11]

But I maintain not only that it is valid to speak about shared values in that sense, but also that it is that commonality that defines us as a society. It is mercifully the case that almost all the people of this country subscribe, in general terms, to the values of liberty for the individual under the law, and believe that this liberty is least insecure in a parliamentary democracy.

Clearly, there is more to being an informed citizen than an understanding of fixed shared values. The history teacher ought to go beyond the generalities of support for parliamentary democracy and liberty to help young people understand the changing nature of society, with its changing patterns of employment and unemployment, its multi-cultural and multi-ethnic nature with the changing status of women, and the ways in which moral attitudes and beliefs are being affected by science and technology. However as the open society is one which confronts its citizens with choices, it would be helpful in an age which emphasises skills to spell out to target groups the 'skills contribution' which effective history teaching can make to education for citizenship. These are of course the history teacher's daily stock in trade, often taken for granted but when we are publicly called upon to justify the spending of taxpayers' money on our subject, the most obvious may well be one of the strongest arguments for the teaching of history to *all* young people to the age of 16.

At the heart of the study of history is the question, 'How do I know this is true?' This question immediately brings history into the field of skills, including discussion, the examination of assumptions, and the justification of conclusions with evidence. Such skills are essential to the maintenance of an open society. The very language which historians use raises questions about value judgements ('rising' or 'rebellion', 'terrorist' or 'freedom-fighter', 'massacre' or 'conquest', etc). History, taught effectively, imposes the obligation to examine subjective reactions, especially our own, through employing the academic rigour of the historians' method. However, this, of necessity, raises questions about issues which are controversial and politically sensitive; it is these issues which will confront the future citizen.

The argument from leisure

In an age where employability is the keynote the idea of educating for leisure may seem an anathema; however, even job application forms ask questions about leisure interests, presumably on the grounds that it tells employers something about potential employees. To young people who are concerned more with the immediate needs of finding employment than with their leisure interests as adults, this argument may well be a powerful one. However, the general argument about the need to develop a range of leisure interests is also an important one for teachers to deploy. A small minority may find jobs in the heritage industry, but all may well find general references to historical interests useful in that section of job application forms labelled 'general interests'. All can benefit, to a greater or lesser extent, from being introduced to history as a potential leisure interest. This may simply mean a better understanding of historical sites, including those abroad in this age of mass foreign travel; it may lead to active participation of an archaeological nature; it may mean a better guide by which to judge or understand the paperback or so-called 'historical novel' or the historical play on television. One thing is certain in an age of commercialism, history is a very saleable commodity. The study of history can help to create a more discerning or aware market which can distinguish the more superficial theme park approach from the more rigorous attempts at historical reconstruction, as can be found in places such as Coalbrookdale and York. Of equal importance is the ability to understand what can be seen at some historical sites where there is little attempt at historical reconstruction to assist understanding – perhaps a burial mound in the middle of a field or a ruined castle. Creating an informed awareness of the historical environment as part of a broader programme of historical literacy must rank high in the order of the aims of history teaching.

Increasing job opportunities and opening doors

The history teacher should not shy away from the contribution which the study of history can make to the vocational and technical education of young people. It is worth emphasising that the technical and vocational aims and objectives are not simply by-products of history teaching and study but are an essential part of the historical method. Indeed, so integrated are such aims that, as the previous sections have shown, the so-called 'vocational argument' is difficult to distinguish from others. However, in an age which demands the separate definition of the vocational argument it would be unwise to merge all the arguments in favour of teaching history. Some thirty years ago the Henniker–Heaton report on Day Release made several pertinent observations about vocational training and education. In particular it distinguished two forms of such training and education:

We stress the range of educational provision that is relevant to vocational training in the broadest sense and to the developing needs of young people. Vocational education is often thought of as the acquisition of knowledge and skills directly applicable to the job; but in most posts what is required is not so much the acquisition of a skill as progressive development in the fields of human relations, of judgment, and of general educational standards. These are important over a wide range of ability and level of work. There are many posts of such a nature, for example, in junior grades in retail employment, among operatives in industry, and at all supervisory and managerial levels.[12]

History has much to contribute to vocational education in both its narrower and broader definitions. Its variety of evidence demands that students have a broad familiarity with literary and statistical sources. The communication of the results of historical enquiry requires the effective use of basic skills of graphicacy, literacy and numeracy. With the development of computer-based resources, many schools are now able to offer a full computer-across-the-curriculum approach to teaching. It would be appropriate at this point for teachers to provide examples of students' work and the resources they use. However, the Henniker–Heaton emphasis of 'the progressive development in the fields of human relations, of judgment' is one which the history teacher could accept as having a high priority in history teaching.

But how do we know that it is vocationally advantageous to study history or to put it the other way round, that to study history is not vocationally disadvantageous? The answer to this may well be found in the careers taken up by history graduates. If it is vocationally disadvantageous to study history at school, it must be vocationally suicidal to study the subject at university. But this is not the case as Figure 1.3, a diagram illustrating careers taken up by history graduates, shows. Studying history at university extends the range and depth of skills relevant to the workplace without closing doors. It explodes the myth prevalent among pupils at school that history graduates mainly become history teachers. At school and university level history helps to keep career opportunities open while providing a valuable training in vocationally valuable skills.

The spectrum of jobs history graduates enter has widened and is widening. Eyebrows were raised when history graduates began to enter the police force, accountancy, insurance, banking and large retail organisations but these, like many other occupations, need versatile people capable of managing change. Any campaign to attract students to history should emphasise how its study can open many doors while closing few. Historical study is rigorous. It also encourages people to become articulate, especially through group discussion, and places great emphasis upon the basic skills. As Figure 1.3 shows, those who study history are eminently trainable for a wide variety of occupations.

History in the National Curriculum

The effective teacher of the 1990s cannot simply be the skilled, classroom practitioner; the evolution of the National Curriculum and the dominant consumer ideology mean that history teachers should be as careful and professional in the presentation of the case for history as they are in their curricular activities. This may well mean developing the range of presentational skills which have been part and parcel of effective classroom teaching for generations. In particular, this may mean the preparation of promotional materials for specifically targeted groups, including students, parents, governors and employers, but it *will* mean the careful enunciation of arguments for particular groups. In any case it is not unreasonable to expect history teachers to justify

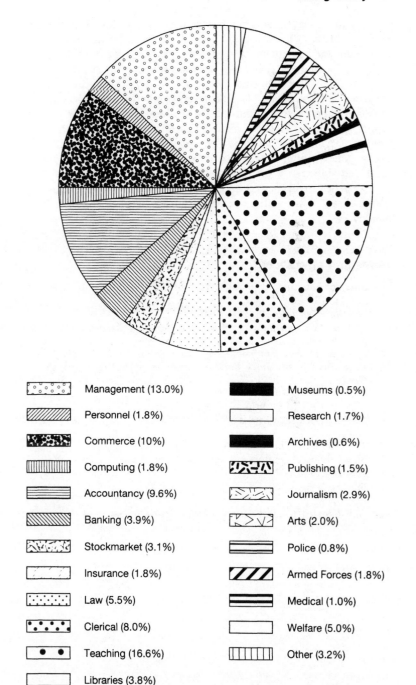

Management (13.0%)		Museums (0.5%)
Personnel (1.8%)		Research (1.7%)
Commerce (10%)		Archives (0.6%)
Computing (1.8%)		Publishing (1.5%)
Accountancy (9.6%)		Journalism (2.9%)
Banking (3.9%)		Arts (2.0%)
Stockmarket (3.1%)		Police (0.8%)
Insurance (1.8%)		Armed Forces (1.8%)
Law (5.5%)		Medical (1.0%)
Clerical (8.0%)		Welfare (5.0%)
Teaching (16.6%)		Other (3.2%)
Libraries (3.8%)		

Figure 1.3 History graduates' career choices at the beginning of the 1990s

publicly to tax-payers and rate-payers why money should be spent on teaching history. It is also important to be able to make out a continuing and convincing case to young people. History students who appear to be confused about why they are studying the subject do little to encourage others to study it as a full GCSE subject or at an advanced level. Convinced students make good ambassadors for the subject, whom even governing bodies (often including their parents) cannot ignore. An effective platform for history should not shy away from the argument about increased employability, but it should place this argument within the twin contexts of specific skills and general skills and abilities. At the end of the day it will be extremely difficult for a teacher of history to be and remain effective if the subject is marginalised in the curriculum and the teaching groups dwindle in number.

Notes and references

1. Board of Education, Statutory Rules and Orders 1922, No. 1433, HMSO, 1923, p. 13.
2. *The Daily Telegraph*, 20 June 1990.
3. *National Curriculum History Working Group Final Report*, 1990, HMSO, p. 1.
4. Ysgol Bryn Elian, *Information for Parents* (pack) 1989–90, Colwyn Bay.
5. Ysgol Bryn Elian, *Guide Book for Sixth Form Students*, 1989, Colwyn Bay.
6. Coltham, C. and Fines, J., *Educational Objectives for the Study of History*, The Historical Association, 1971, pp. 16–21.
7. National Curriculum History Working Group, *Final Report 1990*, HMSO, pp. 1–2.
8. The 1988 Education Reform Act, Section I, HMSO, 1989.
9. Sir Keith Joseph, History is a key subject for all students. Press release 10 February 1984, p. 2.
10. Ibid., p. 1.
11. Ibid.
12. *Day Release* (Henniker–Heaton Report), HMSO, 1964, p. 11.

History teaching in the primary school (Key Stages 1 and 2)

Mary Aris

Beginnings – National Curriculum History at Key Stage 1

The recommendations of the National Curriculum working groups on History in England and Wales stressed the importance of history for *all* pupils. For the first time, every pupil at Key Stage 1 is expected to cover some history (see Box 1).

Box 1
Key objectives at Key Stage 1

(1) To encourage an interest in the past and an appreciation of human achievement.
(2) To begin to develop a sense of chronology and an understanding of the way time is measured.
(3) To develop an awareness of change. To realise that things in the past were often very different.
(4) To begin to investigate cause and consequence.

Before the introduction of the National Curriculum, very little history was studied in the majority of infant schools. At the same time, it must be stressed that the work of John Fines, Sallie Purkiss and Joan Blyth, among others, had publicised the fact that excellent historical work was certainly feasible at infant level. A Department of Education Survey of primary education commenting on the teaching of history in 1978 highlighted the absence of history teaching at infant level 'in any form': 'In first schools the subject is now wholly non-existent.'[1]

The situation had improved only slightly by the end of the 1980s. An HMI survey in 1989 confirmed 'In the majority of schools history was underemphasised in the curriculum. ... In two out of three infant schools history received little or no attention.'[2]

Young children have a very real need to place themselves in time and in a wider social context, and at a very basic level they need to explore the past before they were born and to begin to share the collective human memory.

As a man without memory and self knowledge is a man adrift, so a society without a memory (or more correctly without recollection) and self knowledge is a society adrift. Arthur Marwick[3]

Understanding the past is a developmental process. While younger pupils cannot be expected to have great depth of understanding and indeed will not reach a mature conceptual level of historical understanding until their mid-teens, none the less the initial building bricks in the process can be laid from the very beginning of the pupil's school career.

Teachers of history will be helped in this process by children's natural curiosity and their need to explore and understand the world around them. History as a method of enquiry is particularly suitable for the primary school where the pupil-centred, enquiry based approach has such an important role.

Children ... are not vessels waiting to be filled up with knowledge, but rather active seekers of solutions to problems.[4]

The teacher in the infant school can start by capitalising on the interests and the innate curiosity of the children aged 5 or 6. Young children's appetite for stories can lead to the introduction of some stories of a historical nature into the curriculum. Young children's natural curiosity and need to investigate the things around them, will lend itself to historical work investigating historical artefacts and simple historical evidence, and using oral history, asking questions of older members of the community. Above all the teacher at Key Stage 1 should capitalise on the known and familiar world of the child, by concentrating on home, family, school, and the local area, and on themes closely related to the child's own experience.

The programme of study at Key Stage 1

Although the history unit prescribed for Key Stage 1 is untitled, its subject matter is essentially 'the Past'. This programme of study begins to introduce young children to the concept of 'the Past'. The 'otherness' of the past (the contrast between life today and life in the past) is something that will come into sharp focus. History at Key Stage 1 can fit easily into topic work. The programme of study for Key Stage 1 is unstructured and content-free. This is an advantage which allows the teacher full freedom to respond to local circumstances. However the lack of any structure may initially pose problems for teachers who have not covered history before.

The teacher could begin with the child's own brief life history, moving on to the history of their family. Alternatively work could begin by looking at how time can be measured. Whatever approach is adopted, much of the work will be based on the child's own direct experience. Much of the work in the first two years of school will concentrate on looking backwards at the relatively recent past (life 50–80 years ago), using oral history, photographs, objects, and looking at the locality, the family, home and school. Earlier periods will be introduced mainly through stories, pictures and artefacts. Children between 5 and 7 also need to begin to distinguish between reality and fiction.

Understanding time

The best starting point for understanding time and its measurement will be the children's own experience and the landmarks in their own very short life such as birthdays, going to school, the birth of brothers and sisters, etc. Family history and the history of the local community offer logical extensions of this process. At Key Stage 1 teachers should work backwards from the present (before I was born, 20 years ago, 50 years ago, 100 years ago etc., relating this to different generations of parents, grandparents, great-grandparents). Initially generational time ('When my grandfather was a little boy; when my grandmother's mother was a little girl') will be far more meaningful than dates. But generational time can gradually lead on to an appreciation of dates and time-lines. For example, topic work with time as its theme could offer scope for looking at ways in which we measure time, and would have many cross-curricular possibilities (see Boxes 2 and 3).

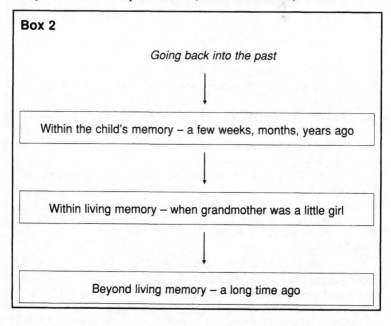

Box 2

Going back into the past

↓

Within the child's memory – a few weeks, months, years ago

↓

Within living memory – when grandmother was a little girl

↓

Beyond living memory – a long time ago

Box 3
A project on time

(1) *Measuring time*
  • Seconds, minutes, hours, days, months, years
  • Decades, centuries
  • The seasons
  • BC AD (the birth of Christ), Regnal years of Kings

(2) *Devices for measuring time*
  • Sundial (used in ancient Egypt)
  • Coligny Calendar (a Druid Calendar)
  • Water clock (used in Roman times)
  • Hourglass
  • Burning a candle (burns at a certain rate)
  • Early clocks
  • Grandfather clocks
  • Pocket watches and wrist-watches
  • Electric clock
  • Digital watch
  • Diaries, calendars
  • Time-lines
  • Speaking clock

(3) *Personal time*
  • Birthdays, anniversaries
  • Family events
  • Keeping a diary
  • Landmarks in a person's life

Cross-curricular links for a project on time
(1) *Music*
  • Beating time; metronomes; the conductor
  • Performing rhythmic music; beat music

(2) *Sport*
  • Olympic records; speed records
  • breaking their own previous speed record in swimming or running

(3) *Technology*
  • Investigating clocks and clockwork devices, followed by simple experiments with cogs, springs and levers; making their own egg timer; measuring how long things take to cook

(4) *Maths*
  • Telling the time; calculations about time; using a stopwatch

(5) *English*
  • Poems about the seasons; poems about time passing; stories e.g. about birthdays; writing a diary; listening to readings from a diary

(6) *Science*
  • The seasons; simple astronomy

(7) *Learning a foreign or second language*
  • Asking and telling the time in a foreign language

Learning how we measure time is something that could link effectively with cross-curricular work on telling the time, learning about the calendar and the seasons. Gradually children learn to give precision to events, and, through mastery of the simple mathematics involved, begin to work out dates and construct time-lines.

While very young children can differentiate the past from the present, many have considerable difficulty in differentiating between two periods in the past, or giving precision to the concept of chronology. They need to progress from 'a long time ago' to a more precise appreciation. Joan Blyth suggested sequencing as one approach to chronology. Initially young pupils were asked to decide whether one thing came before or after another, without reference to precise dates. At a later stage dates were introduced, leading on to consideration of centuries and the reference points that we measure time from, BC, AD, and so on.

In spite of much previous research to the contrary, the last ten years have shown that young children can begin to develop a sense of time . . . By the age of 9, children should be able to cope with the concept of about 1,000 years in time.[5]

Time-charts and time-lines should become important visual aids. Some teachers or museum educators have interpreted the idea of a time-line quite literally, stringing a washing line across the classroom and encouraging children to peg on key dates and photos, pictures and sometimes objects in chronological sequence.

Understanding time: the transition to Key Stage 2

Limitations in children's understanding of time need to be considered when delivering National Curriculum History. The transition from Key Stage 1 to the more structured and prescribed history curriculum for Key Stage 2 needs particularly careful handling. Stories and legends may have offered some sort of introduction to the more distant past, but it may well be necessary to use one of the school designed local history units as a 'bridging' unit to work backwards in time, in a series of leaps, in order to bridge the chasm between history within living memory (which will have been the natural focus for much work at Key Stage 1) and distant periods such as the age of Ancient Egyptians or Romans. One of the thematic optional units (perhaps even taught backwards) could serve the same purpose. Some teachers might even choose to teach the entire history syllabus by working backwards from the present. Whatever method is adopted, there should be regular reference to time-charts or time-lines.

Methods and techniques at Key Stage 1

Stories and history teaching

Interest in the past is often fired by one imaginative experience or story well told[6]

Young children have a natural appetite for stories. Storytime is a regular feature in the school timetable, and stories about the past can slot naturally into this framework. The distant past can be introduced through stories. Myths and legends can also be introduced at storytime. However, it is also important to begin to distinguish what is real from what is fictional. 'Is it true? Did it really happen? Was X a real person?' These are questions which pupils should be encouraged to ask. In order to ensure that the history requirements are fully covered there should be follow-up discussion and questioning. Questions that will help to develop a historical approach will include: Why did he say that? What happened when she did that? Is this true? How long ago did this happen? What were things like then? Why did they have to do their cooking on a fire? This need not detract from the magic of listening to a story or require any re-scheduling of the traditional story hour. For example storytime might take place at an established time towards the end of the school day, but in a follow-up session the next day questions could be asked to see how much they remember of the story, or one child could be asked to retell the story they heard yesterday (see Boxes 4 and 5).

As well as listening to historical stories and talking about historical stories, young children should also be encouraged to re-tell stories in their own words. Pupils may well find this difficult at first, but it is a skill that will come with practice. It offers a check that pupils have understood the salient points. The fact that different pupils will highlight different features in retelling a story will help children to

---

Box 4
Storytime

Storytime offers a useful way of delivering many of the requirements of National Curriculum History at Key Stage 1:

(1) Stories about famous people in the past, e.g. Florence Nightingale. (It is important to counter gender bias; stories of famous men and women must be included).
(2) Myths and legends, e.g. Robin Hood, or the story of Excalibur and the death of King Arthur.
(3) Stories about historical events, e.g. the Gunpowder plot.
(4) Fictional stories with a historical setting.
(5) Stories offering a link with artefacts or places, e.g. the tale of a penny.

Box 5
Telling of the story

Discovering copper on Parys Mountain
It was raining hard and the men digging with picks and shovels on the mountainside were wet. Their hair was wet. Their thick wool coats were heavy and clinging, and the rain streamed into their eyes so they could hardly see. The rain formed big pools in the deep holes they were digging. Their job was to dig for traces of copper in the rocks in the mountain – not that they'd found any yet. All that they'd seen was just rocks and soil and heather and of course the rain. And they'd been digging for months and months there...

Suddenly, through the sheets of rain they could see something moving. Up the mountain path towards them plodded a grey pony. Like everything else the pony's grey dappled coat was wet. Water was streaming down its dark grey mane, and the clothes of its rider were sodden with the rain. But the men looked pleased when they saw the pony and its rider. It was the Master. He went off to the bank once a month to fetch their wages. He would carry the money back in a big leather bag. and he'd count out the shillings and pennies into their hands. But the Master seemed to be coming more slowly than usual, today, and where was the leather bag with their wages? There was no sign of it!

As soon as they saw his face they knew something was wrong. 'I'm sorry lads' said the Master 'I know you've worked hard all this month. You are good workers. But I just can't pay you. I've run out of money. The bank won't lend me any more, because we haven't found any copper. I've already spent everything I've got all these months. I'm ruined.' The men gazed at him as the news sank in. They weren't going to be paid. The rain seemed to be coming down even harder now. 'I know there's copper on this mountain somewhere. There's got to be. Copper mountain they'll call this one day. If only we could find it we'd be all rich. I'm asking you lads to work for me one more month. Will any of you stay on here, without pay, to try to find the seam of copper? We haven't dug that bit of mountain over there yet ... I can't pay you. But I am begging you to stay on. What do you say lads?'

Almost any story can lend itself to this technique, with the pupils taking up the story and deciding what happened.

appreciate that there can be different versions of an event and help to ensure coverage of Attainment Target 2. Utilising the help of visiting students or parents and helpers to listen to pupils retelling stories can be very constructive.

Another useful extension of telling and retelling stories is the technique of telling only half a story leaving the pupils themselves to determine what happened next. The potential of this ingenious device was ably demonstrated by John Fines. Working with a group of trainee student teachers and a class of 6 year olds, he began a graphic story of a fictional medieval knight living in a castle who could not be bothered to lock the postern gate one dark, cold, rainy night. The class had to complete the rest of the story themselves. Of course, robbers got in and stole his jewels! In the follow-up work, which continued for several weeks, the class worked on the design of castles inventing all manner of ingenious devices to prevent unwanted intruders or attackers getting in, went on a site visit to a castle, produced drawings and models and carried out a great deal of oral work, all inspired by the original story.

Oral history at Key Stage 1

Oral history has an important role at Key Stage 1. It is particularly useful at a stage when pupils have very limited reading skills. Projects like 'How Granny and Grandpa used to live' can be extremely rewarding. The 'granny' or 'grandpa', of course, does not have to be a relative, but can be any elderly person.

One great advantage of oral history is that pupils can carry out interviews themselves. Practitioners like Sallie Purkiss[7] have stressed the importance of preparing in advance a checklist of the topics pupils want to cover and the questions they want to ask, even though, in the interview itself, children need not adhere rigidly to the list. Because older people often relate events to 'When I was six' rather than to a given date, there is a need to build up a framework of background dates and information (a time-line) about the person interviewed and his family, and the places he or she has lived in. The class may also need to know about important background dates like the date of the Second World War, and so on. Oral history can be a means of helping pupils to build up a meaningful framework of chronology for the last 80 years.

In addition to its value for historical purposes, and the fact that it involves learning through doing, the practice of oral history offers many bonuses in respect of personal and social skills (especially the skill of learning to listen). Teachers can also capitalise on visitors who are prepared to come into school to talk to the class. People who have helped could also be invited into the school at the end of the project to see the results of the children's work.

When carrying out interviews, artefacts or old photographs can sometimes provide useful stimulus. Showing an old photograph or object to an elderly person may be a means of jogging the memory, or breaking the ice, and may well prompt them to reminisce. The elderly person interviewed may take a delight in explaining to the children exactly how certain things were used or how they worked. It is also likely that interviews will generate further material (old photographs, or old objects),which may be loaned to the school for the duration of the project. All material received should be carefully labelled with the owner's name and returned with a thank you (which can be written by the children) when the project ends.

Using artefacts

At a time when the child's reading ability is extremely limited the use of historical artefacts provides an important strategy for history teachers.

An artefact from the past can be used to engage interest and awaken curiosity. Objects can be used in a whole class session or in group work. Many fairly recent objects can be found at home, bought cheaply in second-hand shops or borrowed from local people. Often pupils will bring to school some object from home. Since much of the work at Key Stage 1 will centre on quite recent times, such artefacts will not usually be rare or valuable or difficult or expensive to obtain. Museum loan services can also be useful, and visits to the local museums can be extremely valuable. Many museums providing an education service will offer object handling sessions. These allow close and direct contact with a limited number of artefacts. Some museum education services also loan items.

Small touches like presenting objects wrapped up, or putting them inside a 'feel bag' and asking pupils to guess what they are can add spice to the exercise. Pupils should have opportunities to handle and investigate objects for themselves at close quarters. A lesson focused on artefacts will probably begin with observation, gathering simple information about the object, noting its characteristics, what it is made of, how it is put together, and so on. This may include drawing the object, an exercise which in itself encourages very close observation. 'How was it made?' is a very important question which may sometimes lead on to experiment or to further research. From this pupils can go on to consider what this tells us about society in the past. Sessions with historical objects will require pupils to examine the artefact closely for clues about how it was made. They may speculate about how it may have been used and what it was for, and perhaps begin to consider how old it is, whether it is genuine or a replica. The look and feel of the object may be important. For example, examining an old iron horse-shoe could give rise to many lines of enquiry (see Box 6).

Comparing artefacts

More in-depth work may involve comparing two or more objects, noting differences, asking questions and discussing. For example, pupils could be shown a simple solid flat iron, a box iron with a

---

Box 6
Examining an old horse-shoe

(1) Asking questions

- What is it made of? Why did they make it of iron? (Links with Science and Technology – properties of materials.)

- What was it for? (Pictures of horses and horses being shod could be introduced.) What are the holes for? How exactly did they fasten it on? Did this not hurt the horse?

- How was it made? (This could include looking at pictures or videos of blacksmiths at work; examining blacksmith's tools at the museum, etc.) The class could investigate the stages in making a horse-shoe, starting with heating and bending the bar of iron. (There are many useful links with Science, e.g. how metals behave when heated.) The importance of the village craftsman and his skills could be stressed.

- Is it real? The class could look at rust (further links with Science); signs of wear, etc.

- Why did horses need shoes? Why do we need shoes? Is it an effective way of saving wear on the horse's hooves? Did the horses do a lot of travelling that would wear out their hooves?

(2) Further enquiry

- The class would also need to begin to understand the total dependence on animals for riding and for traction, in an age before motors and steam engines. They could learn about the wide range of tasks that horses were used for.

- They could look at the role of horses in their own area in the past. Where was the smithy? How many blacksmiths were there? From looking at the artefact they would go on to further investigation.

---

separate iron shoe, and an electric iron. (These might be available from a museum loan service or there might be opportunities to see and handle these during a museum visit.) They could be asked to guess which was the earliest, and to give reasons for their choice. They could discuss which would get cold most quickly, which would stay hottest longest and why. They could compare the weight of the irons and investigate what they were made of, or look at the energy source they needed and the implications of this – the electric iron is not much use without an electricity supply! They would begin to appreciate the problems of daily life in the past without modern labour-saving equipment, and appreciate just how long it took to do even simple tasks.

Children will also begin to classify (. . .two of the irons are similar because they both could be heated on a fire. . .), and they can be encouraged to make and test hypotheses (for example, how did they heat the flat iron? In the fire? But would it not get covered in soot and spoil the clean clothes that had just been washed? Perhaps then they heated it in an oven, or on a hot griddle?)

Obviously pupils need to move out from the objects to the people and society to which they belonged. They need to come to appreciate the changes that electricity has made to people's lives. One visiting history adviser looking at a display of old washing equipment got the infants to explain by picking up and examining an old flat iron, looking for the flex and asking 'But how did they plug this in?' By pretending not to understand, he got the group of pupils to explain to him exactly how it worked and why they had to use devices like this in the past.

Links with the past

Artefacts can often awaken a natural curiosity which offers links with people in the past who may have made, owned or used the object. Doing history does require an imaginative leap, and contact with real evidence from the past can often assist in this process. History is after all primarily about people. Pupils can continually be encouraged to ask simple questions to make this link. Who made it? Who owned or used it? Where has the object been? What might the object have 'seen' in its existence? How many people have owned or handled this object? What has happened to it in the course of its life? Every object has its own 'story'.

Sequencing activities

Sequencing two or more objects to decide which came first is a strategy which is often used, although caution is necessary here. Later does not always mean better. And different objects might be owned and used by different groups of people. Pupils should be asked to say why they think one object might be earlier in date than another. They can be encouraged to consider alternative explanations. For instance, pupils might be asked to decide whether an object belonged to a wealthy or a poor person, whether it was an everyday object or kept for special occasions. Again they would be expected to give reasons for their decision. They might be asked to match a series of objects with pictures of different periods or different people (see Figure 2.1)

Pupils can be shown a group of objects and asked to say which came first, and why they think one came before the other.

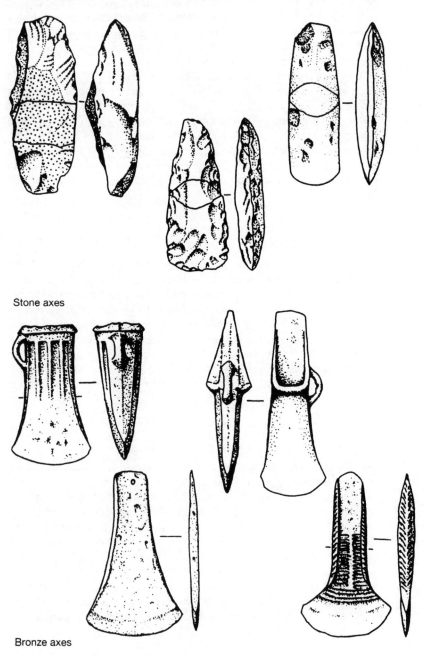

Stone axes

Bronze axes

Figure 2.1 Sequencing objects – Which came first?

Artefacts – If only they could talk!

Infants still occupy a world that is part fantasy and magic, and they readily accept the idea of talking animals and talking objects. This might be successfully exploited by exploring the past from the viewpoint of the object under scrutiny. As well as activities such as observing, measuring, drawing, describing or using the artefact, time needs to be programmed in for creative and imaginative responses – telling the tale of a battered Victorian penny, the hands it has passed through, the articles it has bought, for instance. An artefact can offer a door into another age. Children themselves might be asked to write or tell the tale of a boot, the story of a lost ear-ring, or the possible life-story of a tiny piece of cloth in a patchwork quilt seen at the museum.

Storytime too could capitalise on earlier work done using artefacts. Objects offer a way into the past. The simplest things in the hands of a good storyteller can awaken interest. One student teacher, carrying out a project on food, had done a great deal of oral history work and used pictorial sources. She had also brought to school an old milk-can and other artefacts. Pupils would no doubt be intrigued to learn how the milk-can was used to fetch milk from the farm, or filled up from a churn on the milkman's cart. They could compare that with the way our milk is delivered in bottles today, or sold in cartons or plastic bottles in the supermarket. This milk-can also offered a suitable focus for storytime.

The story was inspired by a small milk-can which was dented and had a bent handle. The retired milkman, from whom I had borrowed the can, told me that the dent was the result of an accident with a bicycle. I therefore told the story of how the milk can got its dent. (Elizabeth Bouchier, PGCE student at Manchester Polytechnic.)[8]

Looking at picture material

Discussing pictures is another valuable exercise that can help to develop skills of observation and inference. At Key Stage 1 pupils are often strongly attracted by pictures of people. Drawing their attention to small details can be important too. Children also need to develop a specialised vocabulary so they are able to describe fully the features they find. To describe a castle they need to learn to use words like moat, turrets, battlements, keep, arrow slits, gatehouse, drawbridge, portcullis, etc.

Output of work at Key Stage 1

Output of work at Key Stage 1 will often be through means other than writing. Some written work will certainly be done, but the 'expected word count' will be small. Infants are still developing their writing skills, and assessment will be through observation and discussion rather than through written exercises. The class teacher will be assessing pupils' achievement across a range of subjects, and will have a very good idea of the child's progress and development. Often an effective assessment activity will involve the synthesis of previous learning and understanding, though history will offer some important cross-curricular opportunities for developing language work and reading and writing.

Oral work

Far more will be done through oral work, describing, explaining, hypothesising, suggesting, imagining, and so on, and also through role-play, model making, drawing and painting, and telling stories. Indeed the value of one-to-one contact or discussion in small groups means that it can be extremely valuable to capitalise, whenever possible, on outside sources of help – classroom assistants, visiting parents, other adults and visitors, as well as visiting groups of teacher training students, who can make an especially valuable contribution. Young children need contact with adults, and need frequent opportunities for oral work.

It is possible, too, to capitalise on topical events, like holidays, Christmas etc. One group at Christmas time invited some elderly people into their school to talk about Christmas when they were children.

Artwork and model-making

There will also be output through model-making, and through drawing and painting or craftwork. Learning in the primary school is seamless and activities in history will merge naturally into work in art, technology, drama, and so on. Three-dimensional work can be particularly effective and young children can achieve some remarkable things using simple materials like cardboard, paint and plasticine. One class, after looking at an old muster roll and hearing how men in their county were called up to fight in the militia, made a cut-out army of 150 cardboard soldiers. Another class, after talking to an elderly lady about life before electricity, reconstructed a kitchen range out of cardboard, and found artefacts, such as an old kettle, saucepan, wooden chair, and so on, to add to the realism. Children were then able to sit in front of their range dressed up in old fashioned costume and role-play. It offered a stimulus to further drama work. Many groups will make models of their village or their high street as it was in the past. After listening to an eighteenth-century description of their village and its green, one class made a model of the village green as it was about 1790.

Role-play and drama

Role-play or drama also has an important place in history teaching with young children. The work of Dr Fines and colleagues has been important in this field (see Box 7). Role-play might carry on a topic begun through the use of stories. Role-play can also introduce more than one viewpoint, allowing a start to be made in empathy work and investigating points of view, even at the age of 6 or 7.

Role-play and drama can be important. So too, is re-enactment in a historical setting. The 'living history' sessions offered on site by the Education Officers at many museums and historic buildings can provide particularly rewarding experiences for this age group, stimulating the imagination, through sight, touch, smells, and so on, and helping them to experience 'what it was like to live in the past'. This could form the climax to work done in class. At a small cottage in Wales, for instance, which was once home to the famous Welshman David Lloyd George, pupils as young as 6 come for living history sessions in the simple cottage kitchen. Wearing old-fashioned clothes which help them to imagine what it was like to live in the past, they help with simple tasks like carrying in water or logs for the fire, or helping to measure out and mix the ingredients for oatcakes or Welsh cakes which are then cooked on a griddle on the open fire. The scent of wood smoke or burning peat, the smells of home baking, the sight of a lighted candle, are all things which make a sharp contrast with life in the present day, and which help to bring the historic building to life. It is a simple exercise, but one which offers a tangible link with the past.

Box 7
Role-play

After listening to a story about a slave, a group of 6 year olds carried out role-play with their teacher. First the teacher became a rich slave owner who ill-treated his slaves. The 6 year olds were allowed free rein to express their feelings about this action, from abuse and expressions of disgust ('You can call me any bad names you want!', the teacher had said), to arguing with the slave owner and trying to persuade him that what he had done was wrong, or that slavery was wrong. A more difficult exercise afterwards involved a reversal of roles with the children on trial as slave owners, having to explain why they had ill-treated their slaves.[9]

Concept based teaching in the primary school

In the past one accusation sometimes levelled against much primary school history has been that work is insufficiently 'historical' in approach.

History in the primary school therefore presents the paradox of some fine work, which is set in an uncertain curricular pattern, and is too rarely part of a firm curriculum plan.[10]

One of the benefits that has emerged from the National Curriculum exercise has been to highlight the need for strategic planning of the history curriculum at all Key Stages, to ensure balance, coverage of a range of different periods and topics, and the adoption of a number of different approaches. The second important factor that has been highlighted is the need for progression.

As well as having a structured approach to content, there is also a need for a structured approach to concepts. Much of the thinking about teaching historical concepts has developed from the work of J.S. Bruner in the early 1960s. The influence of Bruner has been to encourage teachers to define certain organising concepts which underpin the methodology of a subject. Bruner also suggested that one or more of these key ideas or concepts should always be present in any learning strategy.[11] Teachers are also indebted to Bruner for the model of the spiral curriculum, in which pupils revisit the key concepts of the subject regularly, though often under the fresh guise of new content. As concepts are revisited, understanding should become gradually less simplistic, acquiring greater sophistication, and ultimately (though not in the primary stage) more abstract. One aspect that has been somewhat modified by further curriculum development projects, has been the implication that pupils were not receptive to certain ways of thinking until certain stages in their development. One of the most exciting suggestions to emerge from the research of the Schools Council History project, and in later research into primary history teaching methods,[12] has been the idea that certain, concept-based methods of History teaching can lead to pupils reaching certain levels of historical understanding at a rather earlier stage than had previously been thought possible.

Since the early 1960s, considerable debate has taken place in educational circles about the nature of history as a discipline. Indeed by the end of the 1980s, a significant degree of consensus had been reached over the organising concepts behind the historical approach. The School's Council Project 'Time, Place and Society, 8–13' had highlighted a concern with change and continuity, similarity and difference, causation, and time, together with a respect for evidence, empathy or understanding, and hypothesis. Brian Scott has also emphasised that concept-based work was quite feasible in the primary school (see Figure 2.2):

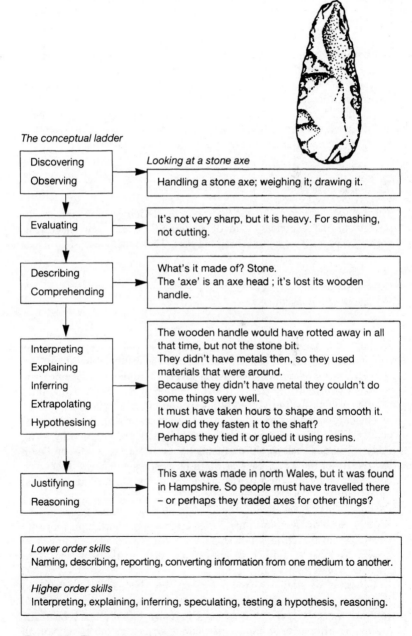

Figure 2.2   The conceptual ladder

We are ... at a point where we can work on the basis that many of our pupils in primary education are capable of undertaking high level thinking skills, progressive, incremental concept formation and rule learning. All this will be possible so long as the materials...possess the qualities of being first hand, sensory, within the pupil's experience, limited in quantity, and making human sense.[13]

Scott also suggested that in addition to carrying out some exercise or activity focused around one of the essential concepts, pupils should be given the opportunity for reflecting on the thinking processes they have gone through. There needs to be a concern with process as well as product. Pupils need to consider the way they approach the past, and to tease out key factors such as evidence, reasons, hypotheses, facts, opinions, criteria for reaching judgements, and so on.[14]

Teaching concepts

The Schools Council History Project in defining an approach for history in the secondary school identified certain key 'historical' concepts, or ways of approaching the past. These included:

(1) change and continuity;
(2) similarity and difference;
(3) cause and consequence.

It was found that these organising 'historical' concepts could be applied just as usefully in the primary school (albeit in a less sophisticated form).[15] Now they are in fact encapsulated in Attainment Target 1 in the National Curriculum levels of attainment scheme. The first two will probably receive most attention at Key Stage 1, the third should certainly be introduced by the beginning of Key Stage 2.

Concept-based history may start at infant level with the concept of change. Through oral history (questioning older people), and by using other resources such as old photographs, or artefacts, pupils can begin to investigate life as far back as 50 to 80 years ago. They will become aware that they live in a world that is changing all the time, and that older people in their lifetimes have often lived through some major changes. This can be demonstrated by exploring suitable topics at Key Stage 1, such as changes in the home, clothes, transport, things that are very close to the child's own experience. At Key Stage 2 pupils will go on to look at further examples, such as work or leisure, and changes over a longer timespan.

Concepts of similarity and difference can be naturally developed from this starting point. Pupils will at first no doubt compare and contrast the past and the present. Gradually too they can be made aware of differences within a particular society in the past. Not all people had exactly the same experiences or the same viewpoint. Slowly pupils will begin to distinguish different periods in the past, (though this may be difficult at first), learning to ask 'when' and 'for how long', and so on. At Key Stage 2 this process will be developed further, for example by looking far more closely at aspects of change, and tracing out the way that some things changed.

Finally, pupils can be encouraged to ask 'why' and 'how'. Why were things so different then? How did things get to be the way they are today? What motives did people have for their actions? What was the effect of certain decisions? An awareness of cause and consequence can begin to develop. This type of enquiry will particularly benefit pupils from age 7 onwards.

Developing children's historical thinking: the questioning approach

It is often stated that young children are in the concrete operational stage of development and that their experience of the adult world and their ability to understand are restricted. Recent research such as that by Peter Knight of St Martin's College, Lancaster, however, has suggested that the technique of bombarding pupils with 'Why?' questions, as well as feeding them historical information, might actually stimulate the earlier development of their historical thinking. In an experiment he taught the same period to two groups. With one group (the control group) he adopted a basically factual approach.

The other group (the 'Explanation' group) took the same time to cover the same materials. However I badgered them with the question 'Why?' They still had to grasp the facts but they were also prompted to explain them: Why revolt? Why be a monk? Why build (and then replace) earth and wood castles?[16]

His research suggested that while the 'Explanation approach' had little impact on infants, the technique did yield measurable benefits with 7 to 9 year olds. The questioning technique can be used at primary level, at first in quite a simple way, but one which can be developed, through worrying at a topic, hypothesising, attacking it from different angles, throwing in a bit of extra information or another piece of evidence, and seeing the effect they had, asking further questions.

Badgering the pupils with questions

This approach could be adopted in introducing aspects of the unit 'Invaders and Settlers'. For example, when dealing with the Vikings, a teacher might start with an account of the first Viking raid on Britain:

Never before has such a terror been known in Britain. Nor did anyone ever imagine that such an attack could be made from the sea. Look at the church of Saint Cuthbert, spattered with the blood of the priests of God; all its treasures stolen. This holy place is plundered by pagans.[17]

or he or she could start with a Viking place name or a reference to a Viking raid in their own area.

- How did the people here feel when they heard of the raid? What did they think of the Vikings? What effect did the Viking raids have?
- Alcuin, the man who described the first attack, thought they were terrifying and wicked. But then he was a monk, and it was the monasteries that were attacked most. (Why was that?)
- But what about the Vikings themselves? Why did they come on raids and why did they burn and steal?
- Did they need the plunder? What sort of countries did they come from and what sort of life did they lead? Did Britain have things that their own countries didn't? Perhaps if we could find out more about where they came from, we might be able to say why they came.
- Why else might they have gone raiding? For excitement? Or as a way of getting rich quickly? It was the young people often who travelled abroad. Was it a way of showing they were grown up?
- And what did Vikings back home think about the raiding? Did they think it was wrong to kill and steal, or did they think it showed what good fighters they were?'

'Badgering' the pupils with questions is a good description. But the class needs to be allowed plenty of time to formulate a reply. Alternative explanations need to be canvassed, and then explored and discussed. Suggestions and hypotheses will need to be tested against the evidence Strategies need to be worked out to try to find the answers. At times the class will be sent away to get information or look for more evidence. 'How do we know' will be at the heart of any enquiry. The teacher must also be prepared to follow up lines of enquiry started by the pupils.

Sometimes a teacher may play devil's advocate, or give the class some dilemma that they have to solve or explain:

Why did the Romans decide to invade the island of Britain? It's much harder conquering an island. (They'd have to get all their armies and horses across.) Why didn't they just stop at the sea? But they didn't, so why did they want to come to Britain?

Questions like these dealing with real people with real motives and posing problems, can slowly help to develop understanding.

Asking questions, and prompting with further questions, can actually push the process of enquiry forward in a way that can provide strong motivation, and which puts the pupils in the driving seat (see Box 8).

Box 8
Key questions in primary history

When did it happen?
What changes did it bring?
Why did it happen?
What effect did it have?
What was it like then?
How do we know?
Is there more than one account?

Teaching the evaluation of evidence

There seems to be a fair consensus that from 8 years onwards the teacher can begin to develop historical enquiry and the effective use of evidence in a meaningful way. Hilary Cooper,[18] teaching 8 year olds how to interpret evidence using historical concepts, made significant progress with one group. 'Key thinking processes in history revolve around the interpretation of different kinds of evidence, often using specialised concepts'. The class in question carried out a project on the Celts and the Iron Age, using a range of evidence both from archaeology and from written accounts of the Romans.

One key feature of her method was to differentiate between

(1) what we know;
(2) what we can guess or infer;
(3) what we do not know;
(4) what we would like to know in order to carry the enquiry further.

Figure 2.3 A scheme for work for Key Stage 2

YEAR 3

Writing and Printing (introduction to written records) Early writing and writing materials in Ancient Egypt Illuminated medieval manuscripts; the printing press	Ancient Egypt introducing archaeological evidence

---

continued

Figure 2.3 continued

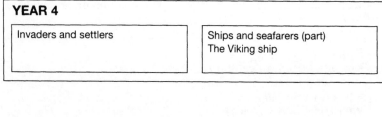

YEAR 4

| Invaders and settlers | Ships and seafarers (part)
The Viking ship |

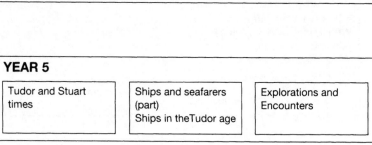

YEAR 5

| Tudor and Stuart times | Ships and seafarers (part)
Ships in theTudor age | Explorations and Encounters |

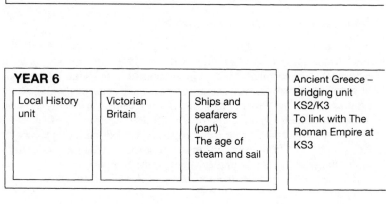

YEAR 6

| Local History unit | Victorian Britain | Ships and seafarers (part)
The age of steam and sail | Ancient Greece –
Bridging unit
KS2/K3
To link with The
Roman Empire at
KS3 |

National Curriculum history at Key Stage 2

National Curriculum history is being introduced in stages in all state schools in England and Wales. When fully implemented, all pupils during particular stages of their school career will have to cover certain prescribed historical periods and topics, with due regard being given to the achievement of the three history attainment targets. Unlike some other National Curriculum subjects, the attainment targets are skills-based, rather than content based, and could be delivered through any theme or programme of study. Content is covered separately in the programmes of study for the various Key Stages.

Planning[19]

All primary teachers need to familiarise themselves with the requirements for history at Key Stage 2 (see Boxes 9 and 10). Whole school planning will be needed to decide when particular core units will be covered, and how the optional units and school designed units will be slotted in. All teachers could usefully participate in an initial brainstorming exercise, sharing ideas and strategies, and perhaps suggesting some local sites or resources. All teachers can contribute even though they may not themselves be teaching the course. Ideas about cross-curricular links and the possibilities for topic work can also be shared. Some of the prescribed topics may not at first seem particularly appealing, especially if they have not been covered in school before, but avenues can be explored for presenting them in an interesting way. Once suitable site visits or useful resources have been identified, the topic will usually begin to appear more interesting, and preparation of strategies and schemes of work can begin.

Box 9
The National Curriculum requirements for history

Teachers planning schemes of work for Key Stage 2 have to consider a range of factors:

(1) *Prescribed content* – the programmes of study must be followed. There are compulsory history units and school designed units.
(2) *Attainment targets* – these cover the historical skills and understanding to be developed.
(3) *Attention to chronology*, developing a sense of time.
(4) *The PESC requirements* – political, economic, social and cultural/religious aspects all have to be covered.
(5) *Diversity* – pupils must look at the experience of men, women and children, and at different social, cultural, religious, and ethnic experiences.
(6) *Resources* – pupils must be introduced to a varied range of resources.
(7) *The past at different levels* – pupils must do some local, regional, British and world history.
(8) *Certain cross-curricular themes* must be covered, and certain common competencies must be developed through all subjects.
(9) *When deciding the order* in which units will be taught, links between units need to be considered.
(10) *Cross-curricular links* must be considered.
(11) *Skills of enquiry and communication* must be developed.
(12) *Certain concepts*, or specialist language, must be learned.

Box 10
Some guidelines for implementing Key Stage 2 history –
A summary

(1) Ensure whole school planning to decide how and when units will be covered and draw up schemes of work.
(2) Target essential historical skills and concepts.
(3) Ensure a wide range of resources is used.
(4) Employ an active, investigative learning approach.
(5) Introduce pupils to primary sources of evidence.
(6) Employ a varied range of learning and teaching strategies.
(7) Whenever possible relate what is studied to the child's own locality or experience.
(8) Relate the history of the local area to the wider context.
(9) Include field visits and work outside the classroom, and integrate this with work done in class.
(10) Take full advantage of whatever support for history is available, and where possible have one teacher in the school with special responsibility for history.
(11) Work towards some climax or memorable end.
(12) Have high expectations and ensure that there is progression.

The National Curriculum orders for each study unit need to be turned into meaningful and workable schemes of work and class activities. The history requirements could be delivered in a number of ways, as the topics or prescribed elements within a unit of study could be introduced in any order and not all topics need be covered in the same depth. It is probably best to begin with the focus statement in the introduction to each history unit, and ensure that the work done takes account of this. Planning need not necessarily start with detailed consideration of the content of a history study unit. It could well start with a close look at the available resources for the period or topic, and these may determine the course of work, the order in which topics are introduced and the learning activities carried out. The list of prescribed topics may look formidable, but not all need to be covered in depth. Primary pupils often work best on the in-depth study, so some selected topics for which resources are plentiful can be given exhaustive coverage. Other topics may be covered perhaps by stories, or by a video, or possibly through work with a time-line, or an outline session. Exemplary material suggested in the interim history reports can be examined, and similar examples may be found that relate to the local area.

At the initial planning stage there is probably no need to worry too much about the three attainment targets. Good historical practice will usually ensure that the attainment targets are covered many times over in the course of the work. Once a plan of action has been worked out, then an audit can be made to ensure all requirements will be covered.

If something does not appear to have been covered, for instance work on interpretations of history (Attainment Target 2), then some extra activity to cover this can be included in the scheme of work. It may need no more than a discussion session, or a change of emphasis introduced at an appropriate point to allow this to be covered.

In a study of the local area, for instance, it is Attainment Target 2 that often poses the most problems. Comparing two different accounts of the place, for instance, or an adverse traveller's account and a hotel advertisement persuading people to stay there might lead to a discussion on interpretations in history.

A check should also be run to ensure that political, economic, social and cultural aspects (the PESC elements) have been covered. Some topics will inevitably lean more towards some of these elements than others, but a balance should be achieved over the whole of Key Stage 2 (hence the need for whole school planning for history). Each core unit should also aim to cover all four PESC elements and all three attainment targets. A site visit is often a valuable device to ensure all the required aspects are covered (see Chapter 4 for more on this).

Resources: the economic use of limited teacher time

Resources may offer the key to planning of the scheme of work. Resources already within the school should be identified. Resources in the locality (sites, museums, specialists), etc. should also be listed.

Further resources may need to be accumulated, and this should be regarded as an on-going process, with useful material being added whenever opportunities arise. A resource box can be built up for each history unit. Books, copies of documents, maps, diagrams, pictorial material, slides, and, where relevant, video, tapes and software can all go into the box. Teacher's notes on the strategies and scheme of work followed can be added once the course is running, together with ideas for activities and exercises, checklists of historical questions, and any assessment material.

The local area will be a most important resource and notes can be included about possible sites, buildings, museums, and so on. Literature about other possible site visits elsewhere, and notes on useful material in museums or museum loan collections, etc., can also be accumulated. Your local archives office or local studies centre may have useful material, and may offer workshops, inset courses or other opportunities to create teacher produced resources. The schools library service may provide a bibliography on the topic, while library loan services for schools can deliver collections of books on the topic under investigation. The teacher may not instantly use all of this material, but the aim should be to build up a growing collection of useful

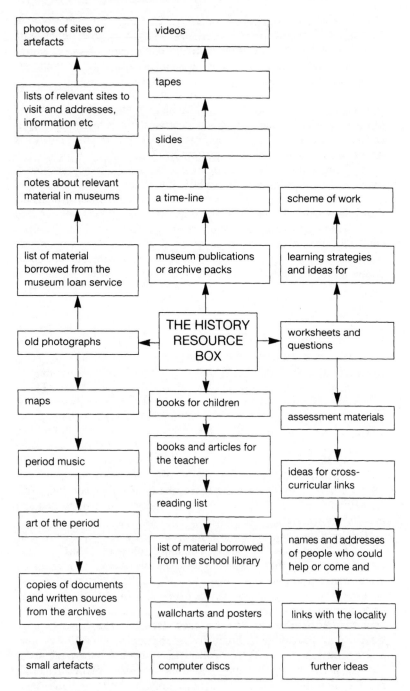

Figure 2.4 The history resource book

resources which will remain the property of the school and which can be handed on to any teacher, or supply teacher who has to teach the course. Old textbooks should not be thrown away, since they may have material (sources, illustrations, diagrams) that at least can be used in a 'cut and paste' session to produce new teaching material. The local secondary school may also have some resources, for courses and topics no longer studied at Key Stages 3 and 4. As well as material to be directly used by pupils, the box could include books and articles that may be helpful to the non-specialist teacher of history.

Teachers from different schools may be able to share ideas and develop joint stategies or joint resources, working through cluster groups or during in-service courses. Teachers in a cluster group might share the work of producing teaching materials or assessment materials. A group of small schools in one rural area, studying the topic 'Ships and Seamen', not only pooled their efforts in collecting resources, and contacting various agencies, but also shared the costs of coach hire for a site visit to a maritime museum some distance away. Groups of teachers in a cluster group or consortium may be able to arrange joint in-service courses at museums or archive offices, or historical sites. One teacher in a cluster group could take special responsibility for history and might carry out liaison, sharing the fruits with other teachers. The history specialists in the secondary school for the area may also be able to offer advice, especially as pupils from the catchment area will ultimately be going on to the secondary school. Schools should also capitalise on any specialist help that is available. Specialists and 'experts' can be invited into the school to contribute on a range of subjects. At Key Stages 1 and 2, these might include someone from the local archaeological unit, the museum or archives or a local historian, especially someone used to speaking to young children.

Reviewing a Key Stage 2 unit

After teaching a unit an assessment should take place. Where strategies were successful this should be noted. Weaker parts of the course may need to be improved, or alternative strategies or materials trialled (see Box 11). Further resources may need to be developed, perhaps by a team of local teachers. The interests of the pupils themselves may also lead up different avenues from year to year, and a wide range of resources will help the teacher to respond effectively. Cluster groups of schools could conduct a joint review, sharing their experiences.

Box 11
The review

CHECK

History requirements
(1) Have all attainment targets been covered and at what levels?
(2) Has attention been given to the focus statement?
(3) Has a balance of PESC elements been achieved:
   • political/military
   • economic
   • social
   • cultural/religious?
(4) What elements in the programme of study have been covered
   • in depth
   • overview/'broad brush' treatment?
(5) How does this unit link with other units?

Other requirements
(1) Has due attention been given to:
   • equal opportunities
   • avoiding bias/coverage of women's history, etc.
   • use of information technology
   • use of a varied range of resources
   • use of primary evidence?
(2) Have all the possible cross-curricular links been exploited?
(3) Does the course contribute to general personal and social development?

continued

Box 11 continued

MONITOR

Methods of work
Has the unit provided opportunities for:

- whole class work
- work in groups or pairs
- individual work
- discussion
- activities
- investigation
- questioning
- listening and observing
- hypothesising
- examining and evaluating evidence
- a site visit or work outside the classroom?

Output of work
Has the course allowed output in a variety of ways:

- written output
- oral work
- creative/artistic response
- drama/role-play
- practical activities
- problem solving
- sharing results of learning with others?

continued

Box 11 continued

EVALUATE

Achievements
(1) What has been learned:
- about the topic
- about the sources
- about working together?
(2) Has the course contributed to:
- understanding chronology
- understanding historical concepts
- understanding interpretations of history
- using evidence?
(3) Has there been progression and development of skills?

Course evaluation
(1) How successful were the chosen methods of learning?
(2) What improvements might be made next time?
(3) Any weak areas needing further attention?
(4) Do I need to seek further resources?
(5) Have the children been involved in the evaluation process?
(6) Has the class been made aware of the links between this unit and other units?

The history curriculum for Key Stage 2: core and optional units

At Key Stage 2 although there are chronological periods of study which must be covered, and a choice of thematic units, there is a wide degree of flexibility. Core and optional units do not have to be studied as discrete units or in a set order. Thematic optional units which span several historical periods can be 'deconstructed', broken down into different periods to form special studies which might be followed alongside the appropriate core unit, or used as bridging units to link one core unit with the next. Detailed guidance has been given by the Curriculum Councils for history which will not be repeated here.

Schools could work forwards or backwards in time (though it is expected that at all times there will be reference to time-lines, and time-charts, and that attention will be given to the question 'when did this happen in the past?'). Arguments can be put forward for either approach. Working backwards in time from the present day offers a natural development of the approach used at Key Stage 1. On the other hand, since the early periods of history involve greater use of material evidence (artefacts, archaeology, and so on), rather than written evidence, there is a lot to be said for tackling this in year 3, when the child's reading abilities are limited. Older pupils with a more developed reading level will be able to make far better use of the wealth of documentary sources for the Victorian or twentieth-century periods.

A bridging unit for Key Stage 1 and Key Stage 2 : 'Writing and printing'

Links between the units need careful consideration. If a chronological approach is adopted, there will almost certainly be a need for a bridging unit between Key Stage 1 and Key Stage 2. Schools have the freedom to do two school designed history units on topics of their own choice, and some schools may decide to use one of the school designed local history units to form an introductory bridging unit between Key Stages 1 and 2. Alternatively, one of the thematic optional units could be selected for the same purpose. There may be a similar need for some bridging unit to link Key Stage 2 and Key Stage 3, and discussions between secondary schools and the primary schools within a particular catchment area may prove useful. A thematic optional unit which spans two different periods might offer a valuable bridge between two core units.

An example – 'Writing and printing'
The optional unit 'Writing and printing' could form a useful bridging unit. In addition this unit could offer an excellent introduction to the use of evidence and to the key question 'How do we know?'

Lead in: Pupils could look back on their own experience of learning to read and write, and discuss why literacy is so important in our society.

Learning activities: Work could include some of the following activities, not necessarily in this order. The limiting factor will be the time available. The topic could easily fill an entire term.

(1) *Investigation of the beginning of writing in different societies:* e.g. the ancient Egyptians and hieroglyphics, or sign language used in some early Scandinavian rock carvings. Pupils could convey messages to each other by inventing their own sign language.

(2) *Looking at different sorts of writing materials:* papyrus, parchment, paper, inscriptions on stone, Roman inscriptions.

(3) *Visit to a graveyard, parish church, memorial or to the local museum* to investigate and record inscriptions on stone. Pupils might make stone rubbings to take back to school.

(4) *A visit to the local record office.* This visit will also serve as an introduction to written records and their importance for history. Here pupils may be able to look behind the scenes at how documents are stored. They can see and handle parchment and paper. The visit will also generate a bank of copies of handwritten and printed material which will form the basis for many hours work in class later on.

(5) *Illuminated manuscripts.* An in-depth study of the production of hand-written illuminated manuscripts by medieval monks.
  • Pupils find out about the life and work of the monks.
  • They look at examples of illuminated manuscripts, and investigate how they can be used as evidence for life in the Middle Ages.
  • The classroom becomes a Scriptorium for the day. Children, dressed as white monks in improvised sheets, work (in total silence!) on the production of illuminated manuscripts. They pause at intervals for prayers, and so on. A messenger arrives and announces a Viking attack on a nearby monastery! The 'monks' record this in their chronicle. Another messenger tells of the death of a lord who gave a lot of money to the church. The monks record this. (This will later form a starting point for a discussion on interpretations of history.)

(6) *Printed records.*
  • Pupils listen to a story about Caxton and the printing press
  • Pupils compare and contrast an illuminated manuscript and an early printed page and list the advantages and disadvantages of each.
  • Pupils learn about how a printing press works.
  • A retired printer is invited into school to talk to the children.

- Pupils work on the examples of printed material, posters, newspapers, books, and so on they collected from their visit to the archives, and look at design and style.
- Pupils spend an afternoon cutting potato prints or lino prints and printing from these.

(7) *New production methods today.* Pupils look at modern computerised methods of printing and prepare their own news-sheet on computer using a simple newspaper software package.

This unit on writing and printing could form a very useful bridging unit either between Key Stages 1 and 2 or between two core units. It should be introduced as a discrete unit, as it would tend to lose its focus if broken up into sections and 'nested' within core units. However there are many links with core units. Inscriptions on stone could link with the core unit on Roman Britain. There are also links with later units, with the early church in the unit on invaders and settlers, and with the dissolution of the monasteries in the unit on the Tudors and Stuarts. There would also be many useful links with printed evidence for later periods. There is even a link with the optional non-British unit on Ancient Egypt.

Cross-curricular approaches

There is no doubt that the Key Stage 2 history proposals represent the greatest challenge, and the greatest break with past practice in many primary schools. Previously the majority of schools adopted topic work and a cross-curricular and thematic approach. Many teachers may be reluctant to abandon this method of working. Indeed, in order to squeeze all the required National Curriculum subjects into the available time, a cross-curricular approach may be essential. Different schools will adopt different solutions. A variety of teaching approaches may offer the best solution. Some at least of the History requirements may be delivered through cross-curricular topic work.

Links between subjects may be sought for to enable a thematic approach or topic work to continue. In this case, schools must ensure that the history requirements are properly covered and that the history attainment targets are addressed. One of the chief criticisms of much topic work done in the past was that insufficient consideration was given to historical objectives, and that the needs of history were sometimes submerged. In other cases, a history-driven approach may be pursued, occupying perhaps half a term's work, during which other prescribed National Curriculum subject requirements could also be covered.

It is important too that the National Curriculum does not become a strait-jacket. Tried and tested methods should not be abandoned.

Motivation is all important to produce the high quality work of which primary pupils are capable. Children need time to experiment, to learn, to discover for themselves, to talk about what they have found and share experiences. In the learning process, they need time too to follow enquiries of their own choice even if at times this may involve exploring avenues not directly relevant. It is also vital to allow time for full creative responses (see Box 12).

Box 12

The school needs to have quiet corners where children can sometimes work at what they want to do. For instance, after one out-of-school visit to a historical site which had been situated by a lake, in very impressive natural surroundings, one child on return to school asked if she could write a poem. The class arrangements were flexible enough to allow the girl to go off to a study corner and to produce a creative response to the experiences of that morning.

Schools will still want to capitalise on topical events, and special celebrations. For example the opening of a new road, bridge or tunnel might be the spur for an investigation of older forms of communication in the area. Even if this does not strictly fit into the history framework, teachers will want to build on such events, or, alternatively, they might perhaps form the basis of a 'once only' local unit.

Remember, too, that some of the general topic work or work done in other subject areas may well offer a historical component. A class doing a study on 'water', for instance, might need to give some attention to the history of water supplies in their area, or to look at past epidemics of cholera and typhoid, to prove that clean water is vital for good health. They might look at how people managed before having piped water and at how piped water and sanitation have led to changes in the home. (Houses now have bathrooms and inside toilets, instead of a garden privy or a toilet at the bottom of the yard.) History work is wider than National Curriculum History, and in many respects learning at primary level is seamless, rather than compartmentalised.

Four approaches to National Curriculum history at Key Stage 2[20]

1. The time-line

A time-line could offer an organising structure for the whole history course at Key Stage 2. A three- or four-dimensional time-line may be used, covering local, regional (English, Welsh, Scottish, Irish), British and International events. Prescribed themes can be introduced in any order but whatever is studied in history is constantly related to the time-line (see Figure 2.5 for one example).

Figure 2.5 A timeline for writing and printing

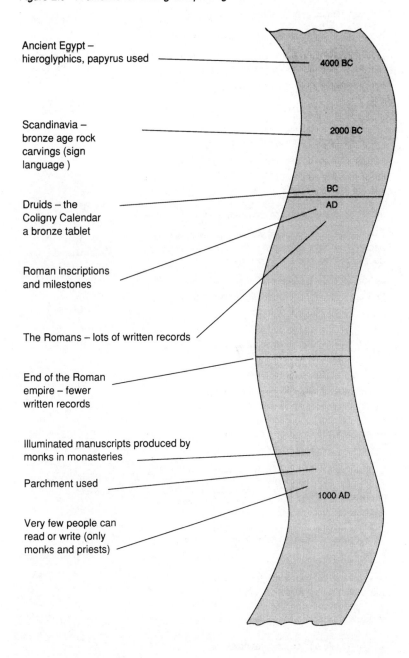

Ancient Egypt –
hieroglyphics, papyrus used

4000 BC

Scandinavia –
bronze age rock
carvings (sign
language)

2000 BC

BC
AD

Druids – the
Coligny Calendar
a bronze tablet

Roman inscriptions
and milestones

The Romans – lots of written records

End of the Roman
empire – fewer
written records

Illuminated manuscripts produced by
monks in monasteries

Parchment used

1000 AD

Very few people can
read or write (only
monks and priests)

continued

Figure 2.5 continued

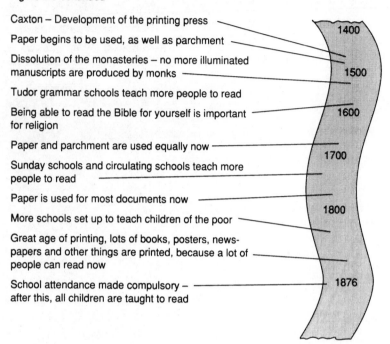

Caxton – Development of the printing press

Paper begins to be used, as well as parchment

Dissolution of the monasteries – no more illuminated manuscripts are produced by monks

Tudor grammar schools teach more people to read

Being able to read the Bible for yourself is important for religion

Paper and parchment are used equally now

Sunday schools and circulating schools teach more people to read

Paper is used for most documents now

More schools set up to teach children of the poor

Great age of printing, lots of books, posters, newspapers and other things are printed, because a lot of people can read now

School attendance made compulsory – after this, all children are taught to read

1400
1500
1600
1700
1800
1876

THE TWENTIETH CENTURY

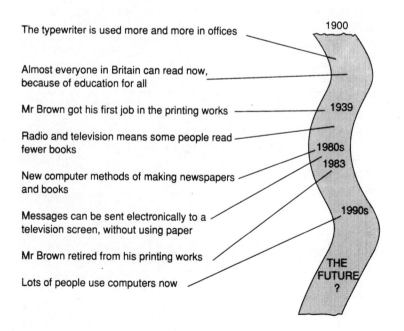

The typewriter is used more and more in offices

Almost everyone in Britain can read now, because of education for all

Mr Brown got his first job in the printing works

Radio and television means some people read fewer books

New computer methods of making newspapers and books

Messages can be sent electronically to a television screen, without using paper

Mr Brown retired from his printing works

Lots of people use computers now

1900
1939
1980s
1983
1990s
THE FUTURE ?

The time-line also offers useful cross-curricular links. Scientific discoveries and inventions, art and music, and so on can also be 'nested' on the time-line. Pupils using early photographs as one of their sources for instance, may want to put the invention of photography onto their time-line, and this could be linked with experiments and science work on the behaviour of light. Tudor composers or Elizabethan playwrights can be added to the time-line for the unit on life in Tudor and Stuart times.

2. Topic work

Certain common linking topics or themes may be chosen for humanities-driven work. In one school a number of 'themes' were identified: homes, school, religion and the Church, trade, and communications (roads, seafaring). These were general 'humanities-driven' themes offering useful cross-curricular links. Some of the

Figure 2.6   A topic-based plan

(Note that the example given is for the National Curriculum in Wales. The programmes of study are different for England.)

TOPIC	c.SU2	c.SU3	c SU4
Homes	Celtic huts Roman Villas monasteries Viking houses	Tudor manor houses	Victorian terraced house Houses of the gentry
Religion and the Church	Celtic and Roman gods Early Church	Religious change Dissolution of monasteries	Church and chapel
Communications Roads ships trade	Roman roads and ships Trade in Roman times Viking ships Exploring Viking traders	Tudor ships and voyages Drover's roads Trade and piracy Exploration	Sail and steam World trade roads, canals and and railways Empire and exploring Africa
Education	Literacy in Roman times Church keeps literacy alive	Grammar schools	Victorian schools

themes (the home, school) also offer useful links with common themes at Key Stage 1 (see Figure 2.6 for further details).

These themes also formed a linking mechanism between the history core and optional units (as well as providing cross-curricular opportunities). Two or three of these general themes offered a focus for work on each of the units. For instance, in SU3 (Study Unit (History Curriculum, Wales)) homes, communications, religion and trade offered a focus for in-depth work. History elements were introduced under this organising thematic structure, and checks were made to see that all the requirements for history (the focus statements, the prescribed content, the attainment targets, and so on) were being fully met. If anything could not easily be covered through this thematic approach, it was covered discretely, through a story, or watching a video, or in a separate activity.

Many other humanities elements and some maths, science, technology and language requirements, and some art and music, were also covered through the same thematic approach. It was initially envisaged that the work would last for about half a term, but provided that most other subject requirements, were also being met, the 'thematic-driven' approach could have encompassed a full term's work.

3. The investigative approach: asking historical questions

If the questions that are asked are of the right kind, then an investigative approach to a topic will automatically ensure that the history attainment targets are met.

A number of questions which focus on 'historical concern' can be identified. These key questions offer a lead in to the investigation of a topic (see Figure 2.7).[21]

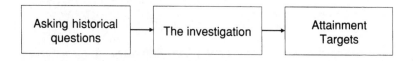

4. The history-driven approach

In a unit on the Romans and the Roman empire, for instance, many of the language attainment targets might be covered (describing an attack on a hill fort; writing a letter home from a Roman soldier at the front on life in Britain, discussion work involving speaking and listening, and so on). Language work can also be covered through drama or role-play (a speech by a Roman general encouraging the troops, an argument between a Celt and a Roman over whether the conquest of Britain was a good or a bad thing). Maths work arising naturally from

Questions about:	For example:
Time	When did it happen? How long did it last? Where does this fit on the time-line? How does it relate to other events? →	When did the Romans first invade Britain? How long was Britain part of the Roman Empire? Where does Columbus's discovery of America fit on this time-line, and how long was this after the Vikings had discovered Vinland?
Change	How did things change? Was everyone affected by the change? →	How have people's houses changed in this century? Did the invention of motor cars affect everyone? Which affected most people, the invention of the bicycle or the invention of the car?
Cause and Consequence	What was the effect? Why did it happen? Why did they do it? →	What effect did the invention of printing have? Why did people decide to enclose the commons and open fields? Why did William think his claim to the throne of England was stronger than Harold's.
Similarity and Difference	How different were things then? Was it the same for all people? →	Did children lead very different lives in the Victorian age compared to children today? What was life like for women workers in the Victorian age?
Evidence	How do we know this? What does the evidence tell us? Is the evidence reliable? →	How could I find out what sort of clothes people wore in the Middle Ages? What does this old photograph tell us about how people dressed in the 1930s?
Interpreting History	Are there different versions of this? How does this account show ....? Is his account affected by what he knew of ...? →	Are there any other versions of the story of King Arthur and Excalibur? Were the Vikings really so savage and cruel? We only have Roman writings about the Celts; does this make a difference?

Figure 2.7 The investigative approach at Key Stage 2: asking questions

the unit might involve simple computation using Roman numbers, and calculations related to the topic – e.g. how much labour and materials would be needed to complete a Roman road or fort, how long the work would take, and so on. Science (force) and technology might be introduced by, for instance, getting pupils to design and build a machine to hurl stones to attack a hill-fort, or cooking Roman recipes (effects of heat on different substances). Indeed a site visit to a Roman fort could be given spice by letting the pupils try out their machines on site. Some geographical targets might be covered, locating historical sites on a map using a grid, and planning marches for the Roman army on a topographical map, which would involve understanding of landforms and contour lines.

Whatever organising method is adopted, there should be an audit, both during and after the course, to ensure that all the requirements have been met. If it is found that certain elements have not been covered, then activities can be devised to ensure that they receive attention, or, if necessary, certain elements can be taught discretely. If certain prescribed content is found to have been omitted, this could be covered, perhaps by a 'broad-brush'/'outline treatment' through a story, video or outline session.

History teaching at Key Stage 2. Methods and resources

The basis of good primary practice

A number of factors are integral to good primary practice. Fundamental is the need to relate whatever is studied to the child's own experience, and also to awaken motivation and stimulate enquiry. This can be achieved by a variety of teaching strategies, which could include:

(1) starting from the local area;
(2) using resources related to the locality;
(3) finding a local example of the general theme;
(4) use of a 'topical peg', some current event of interest from which work can proceed, or with which analogies can be drawn;
(5) the enquiry-based approach;
(6) encouraging 'learning through doing';
(7) capitalising on something a pupil has brought into school;
(8) capitalising on an out-of-school visit;
(9) inviting a visitor into the classroom.

The need for local resources

Pupils at Key Stage 2 will be introduced to a wider range of sources and resources than at Key Stage 1. With improvements in reading skills, written documents and books will become far more important, though artefacts, pictures, stories, and oral history remain central. All teachers of history at Key Stage 2 need to develop links with their local archives service, which offers a storehouse of local material.

To the primary teacher 'teaching resources' mean far more than the school textbook. Resources for learning also include the local area, the environment, the countryside and the townscape, museums and historic buildings and their collections, the extensive range of local material offered by local record offices, or the local study centre, or reference library, as well as pictures and artefacts brought in from home, reminiscences of family members or the elderly, interesting visitors to the school and many other things (see Box 13).

Box 13
From monastic site to country house to golf course and country club

For a class studying the dissolution of the monasteries reference could be made to a local monastery or abbey. A site visit may be possible. Often monastery lands passed into the hands of the gentry, and a country house is quite often to be found at or near the ruins of the monastery. Houses of the gentry have themselves often undergone further change in the twentieth century. Many are now hotels, or country clubs and their grounds have often been appropriated for golf courses. This sort of local example can help pupils to appreciate change over long periods of time, and give them an understanding of some of the phases through which the landscape has gone.

The primary teacher can draw upon many of these to provide a lead in to a topic, or to develop a theme or push forward an enquiry. Often the teacher will search for analogies or local examples, to introduce a general history topic. Even a reference to some current event close to hand can offer a lead in to a topic. The building of a new stretch of dual carriageway nearby might offer a lead into the building of the Roman road network across Britain.

Building on Key Stage 1

In many cases pupils at Key Stage 2 will use the same kinds of resources as were used at Key Stage 1, though they will be using them in a more sophisticated way. Use of oral history, for instance, should not be restricted to Key Stage 1. All age groups will benefit from using oral evidence. But at Key Stage 2, oral evidence could be complementary to written forms of evidence, and the two could be compared. Oral evidence, it will be found, is a useful counterbalance to more 'official' sources. An elderly person's reminiscences about his or her schooldays might be contrasted with reports in an official log book, or an education report. It also provides a more personal viewpoint.

Artefacts too are equally useful at Key Stage 2, but skills can be developed further. Pupils could investigate change by examining a series of articles of different dates, and discussing why changes occurred. In Wales for example where HSU 3 (History Study Unit (History Curriculum, England)) consists of the core unit 'Early peoples, Celts and Romans', on a museum visit or using material from a museum loan collection, the class might compare a flint scraper and the remnants of an iron knife blade, and look at the importance of the discovery of metals, and the differences it has made to people's lives. They could discuss the problems of skinning an animal, or scraping skins to make leather using only stone tools. They could be asked about the improvements that metal tools could bring, Through discussions like these, pupils should be brought to realise that what people could do in the past was often limited by their technology.

At Key Stage 2 it is important to begin to relate artefacts studied to a wider social context. Attention will move from the object to the people who made and used it. After examining an iron age metal object, pupils could investigate and discuss the great social and economic changes that the discovery of metal must have entailed.

Anyone, almost, could pick up a stone or work a piece of flint to use as a tool, but making metals was a far more skilled job. It needed cooperation. They had to find and dig or mine the iron ore. Then they had to smelt the ore. To do this they would need lots of wood or charcoal. (Perhaps they despatched certain people to chop down the trees and make the charcoal? And what effect would cutting down all these tree have on the environment? There would be less forest and more open land that could be grazed or farmed.) After the rough ingots of metal had solidified, a smith would need to work the metal and hammer it out, or perhaps he would make moulds and pour the molten metal into the shaped mould. Certain people with special skills (metal workers) would be very important. And of course people who had metals would have an advantage over groups who did not know how to produce metal. Perhaps they would trade metal for other things, like food, furs, horses, cattle, or slaves? The people who possessed the skills to make metal might not need to work at producing their own food – someone else could grow food for them. And of course metal could also be used to make weapons. Metal weapons might have been better than earlier weapons. So the groups that owned metal might perhaps conquer and enslave other groups.

These sorts of points could be brought out by oral work, or through role-play. Pupils at Key Stage 2 will also benefit from listening to stories. In the above example a useful way of introducing the theme might be through a story about the (accidental) discovery of how to make metal.

Turning the 'heap of evidence' into a meaningful account

Much primary school investigation begins with the local area. Published histories of every town or village or suburb are in many cases non-existent, so frequently primary pupils are by necessity plunged into the world of do-it-yourself local history. Often instead of reading about their local history from the printed page, they are required to piece together from an assortment of contemporary evidence (old maps, photographs, log books, census returns, directories, evidence from local buildings, and so on) a coherent picture of what their settlement was like in the past. Far from being a restriction this is a positive advantage. It can help to develop historical enquiry skills and can accustom pupils from an early age to handling and evaluating and synthesising historical evidence.

Beginning local studies – the school designed unit

Every school at Key Stage 2 is expected to do some local history. Schools must design their own local units to take account of local circumstances and special interests. The following suggestions are exemplary only, and they are based upon a concentric approach starting with the school.

The school

Many local studies begin with the history of the school. County archives can often supply copies of material such as school log books and other education records, old school textbooks and copy books, photographs, plans, newspaper accounts, and so on. This material can often be supplemented by school photographs, school reports and other material from local residents who were former pupils. Their reminiscences about their early school days can be recorded, or they can be invited into school to talk to the pupils. An event such as a school centenary can often produce a wealth of material from the local community.

Some museums offer Victorian classrooms where pupils can dress up and experience Victorian schooling methods. Some museum loan services may offer examples of such things as writing slates and slate pencils or steel-nibbed pens and old inkwells and sample pages from old copybooks, to allow pupils to try using these old writing materials.

The High Street

A project on the high street of a town or village might be the basis of one of the school-designed history units. This is a topic with great potential for cross-curricular work. (Linking with geography, to give just one example, could involve using maps, making plans, studying the functions of different buildings and uses of land, looking at the different jobs done by people today, and perhaps even carrying out a traffic census or statistical survey.) For history work it involves pupils instantly in using evidence (Attainment Target 3) as they search for clues about the high street in former times, – looking at building frontages (especially the part above the shiny modern shopfront), hunting for coal-holes, lamp brackets, investigating letter boxes and many other things, measuring the width of the street in different places. Further pictorial and documentary evidence will help to fill in the picture later. Understanding of change (Attainment Target 1) will grow as the enquiry progresses. Nor need this remain a purely local study. Goods sold in the shops can lead out from the immediate locality to the mills, workshops and factories of the industrial revolution, and indeed Empire produced goods will introduce a world horizon. The wider world will also demand attention as pupils are encouraged to find out why the changes took place (cause and consequence Attainment Target 1).

Starting with fieldwork

Another strategy is to begin with fieldwork. At a school in Kent pupils beginning Key Stage 2 were taken on an exploratory tour of a certain street. The task they were set was to decide which were the oldest buildings in the street. This apparently simple exercise raised all sort of issues and problems. 'How do you know how old it is?' Pupils had to construct criteria for 'oldness', and create hypotheses. The exercise required the class to observe the building very closely, and to examine such things as building materials and styles very carefully. Of course such an exercise generated a great deal of discussion, and heated argument. It also threw up confusions. Houses with black oak timbers were old, they decided, but they were confused by mock-Tudor black and white timbered buildings of the interwar period.

One result of the exercise was that pupils urgently needed further evidence. Only early photographs and documentary and other materials could begin to resolve some of the arguments and questions and it was at this point that material from the archives, old maps, early photographs, traveller's descriptions, census records, trade directories, window tax or hearth tax assessments, and so on could be meaningfully introduced to children hungry for further knowledge.

The history of the town or village: turning history on its head

The history of the pupil's own town or village is also a highly popular topic in the primary school. Rather than trying to start in the depths of prehistory, when local material may be scarce, or difficult to interpret, a better approach may well be to begin in the present and work backwards. In this way cross-reference can be made to work already done at Key Stage 1. Pupils might begin by examining their area about 50 years ago. This has the advantage of involving pupils in oral history work, which may lead to the loan of photographs, documents or artefacts. Further documentary material can be sought from the county archives service, and museums also may offer relevant material. At Key Stage 2, with older pupils, the enquiry can easily be pushed back to the Victorian Age, when pupils are now faced with the 'problem' that all the people who lived at that time are now dead. To resolve the dilemma they must piece together the sort of documentary and pictorial evidence that is usually plentifully available for the nineteenth century. Fieldwork in the town or village or the high street can also yield good results. This topic also offers useful links with geography and other subjects.

Going back in time

With earlier periods evidence will inevitably become more scanty and more difficult in nature, but pupils will be better equipped to handle it with their experience of using evidence. What can be found will inevitably vary according to the area under study and the survival of evidence, but it may be wise to capitalise on whatever special feature the particular settlement has to offer, perhaps an old building, church or archaeological site.

Pupils may well need to look beyond the immediate local area, the further back they go, though starting with an example not too far away can still be useful, and allows for field visits. The teacher may wish to introduce pupils to evidence from archaeology, and perhaps from aerial photography. The local area, of course should be a springboard not a straitjacket, and pupils need to be encouraged to move out from their locality to see it in a wider context, to compare it with other places, and above all, whatever period is under study, to begin to understand why the changes they have documented took place.

Moving out from the local area

Although the local area will often be the natural starting point for many topics, even for the core history topics, it is very important that primary pupils be encouraged to look beyond the local area at the wider scene. A number of approaches can be employed to assist this process.

Some topics may offer their own inbuilt links. Often focus on a theme such as transport, or trade and communication may well provide the link to the wider context that is needed. With the Roman Empire, for instance, Roman roads could offer a valuable link between Roman features in their own locality and the experiences of Roman rule elsewhere. In a study of the Vikings, pupils might begin with the Vikings in their own area, but could go on to use the computer simulation 'Raiders', putting them in the role of Vikings deciding where and how to attack the British Isles. Indeed the Vikings, Viking ships and Viking trade routes are topics that can widen horizons to encompass the whole of Europe, the Middle East, Iceland, Greenland and north America.

Pupils could be asked to compare and contrast their own area with another different area. This will encourage focus on similarity and difference, as they look at population, industries, the patterns of settlement, different types of buildings, and so on. An urban area could be compared with a rural area. An area in England could be contrasted with the experience in Wales or Scotland. Many pupils go on field courses, and the area they visit could form a focus for contrast with their own home area. Getting the pupils to tackle a completely unfamiliar area, after they have sharpened their skills nearer to home can offer a valuable means of assessing how well they have mastered various skills of historical enquiry. Pupils often respond positively to a challenge, and there is the advantage of something completely new.

There could also be possibilities for fruitful links between primary schools in different areas of the country. The process of sharing information about their own area with another school will also encourage valuable skills of communication, presentation and cooperation. Information technology could play a useful part here. Not only are there the possibilities offered by electronic mail in communicating with the other school, but classes might put their information onto the computer and exchange data disks.

Schools can make use of video or educational broadcasts, to extend study to the wider world. Schools broadcasts have an important role to play here. Computer software packages and simulations offer another possible approach. These media are also useful for introducing pupils to sites that are some of the best of their kind. Not every school will be able to travel down to Portsmouth to see the wreck of the *Mary Rose* for themselves, but they could watch a video about the discovery and raising of the wreck, and carry out a computer simulation to search for the wreck.

Developing historical skills

While it has been demonstrated by the work of Piaget and others that, at primary school age, children's understanding functions at the concrete operational stage, more recent research in primary history has tended to suggest that children's 'historical' thinking can be developed and encouraged by certain teaching techniques. In particular, it has been suggested, it is important to bombard pupils with questions, particularly with questions of the 'why' and 'how' type, in addition to the 'what' type and comprehension type of question. Even at the primary level, key historical concepts such as cause and effect, similarity and difference can be developed by intensive questioning.

Young children have great difficulty in handling more than one set of variables at a time, so there is a need for a fair degree of simplification. Often concepts of similarity and difference can be best encouraged by starting with a simple 'now' and 'then' comparison. Pupils begin by contrasting the period in the past with their own experience today, using familiar topics like homes or the family. However by Key Stage 2 pupils should be encouraged to compare different elements in the past – the differences between the Celtic and the Roman armies, for instance, or the lifestyle of the Celts and the changes that the Romans introduced to Britain.

Pupils also need to recognise that the past was often very different from the present, and avoid the error of a 'Flintstones' approach to history (cavemen watching television, and so on). Indeed 'spot the deliberate mistake' is one technique that might be used on occasions – a plastic object might be included in a collection of Victorian bric-à-brac, for instance, and the pupils would be required to explain that plastic had not been invented then.

Skills of handling and evaluating evidence can develop over time. At first it may be sufficient simply to ask 'How do we know?' Whatever topic or period is under study, pupils can be introduced to many of the varied sources of evidence. Much of this evidential material will have an emotive quality which can help to increase motivation and interest. (A yellowed parchment document with its faded handwriting, for instance, really can convey a sense of age! The

---

Box 14

Pupils often respond positively to sessions which involve trying out equipment or wearing uniforms or old-fashioned clothes. Even where they may not actually *enjoy* them, such sessions can fire the imagination or increase understanding of people's experiences in the past:

'Because somebody had worn it in the seventeenth century in a battle and I felt as if I was going back in time.' (*One pupil's response to wearing a Civil War uniform*);

'Heavy and prickly.' (*Another ten year old's response*);

'I thought it was easy to write with and it was not. It kept dripping all over the paper.' (*A 10 year old girl's attempt to write with a quill pen*);

'It really made me feel like a Victorian girl in a Victorian street, which was great because I haven't been one before.' (*A 10 year old's response to a dramatic session*).

past becomes suddenly real.) The thrill of seeing or touching something really old on a museum visit can be extremely important (see Box 14). Learning to substantiate statements about the past by reference to evidence is of great importance. – 'We know that the first bicycles looked like that because they've got one in the museum.' More sophisticated evaluation of evidence will certainly be developed in the secondary school, but a start can be made. The upper classes at Key Stage 2 when asked how they know can begin to make reference to census records, or old maps or photographs to 'prove' the truth of what they claim. Top juniors are capable of beginning to detect differences between two pieces of evidence, if it is presented at a simple language level, and even bias and attitudes to events. This is especially true if a piece of evidence with a very strong and obvious bias is used, or if two contrasting views of the same event are chosen and the pupils encouraged to compare the two. For the unit on Victorian Britain, for instance, they might compare the evidence of an employer or factory owner to a Royal Commission with the testimony of one of the workers. Discussion to emphasise key concepts has a very important role to play.

Drama and re-enactment at Key Stage 2

Living history approaches, allowing children to dress up and experience activities carried on in the past can be extremely successful in the primary school. Many museums and historic sites now arrange these sort of sessions. English Heritage, for instance, can offer a range of activities at different sites.

Using information technology at Key Stage 1 and 2

Even at Key Stage 1, it is possible to make use of information technology for history. The use of concept keyboard touch screens, or use of a 'mouse' rather than the computer keyboard, has opened up many exciting possibilities. Using a simple authoring programme like Touch Explorer Plus, a teacher might employ information technology to prepare a class for a site visit. They might even use the computer to print out some simple questions to use on site.

Pupils at Key Stage 2 will be extending their computer skills, and it is important that part of the history course is delivered through computers. At Key Stage 2 pupils will make far greater use of databases. Indeed, they will often create their own databases to record information collected on museum visits or site visits or through fieldwork. Collecting information to input onto a database could offer a very valuable means of 'taking something back to the classroom' from a field visit or museum visit for this age group (see Figure 2.8).

OBJECTS SEEN OR HANDLED IN A MUSEUM
EVIDENCE RECORD SHEET
The object – what is it?
What is it made of?
Is it plain or decorated?
How big/heavy is it?
How was it made?
Where was it made?
Where was it found?
How was it used?
Is it special or an everyday object?
What date is it/ what period does it belong to?
What does it tell us?

Figure 2.8 Collecting structured information from a museum visit to input into a database

Many of the simpler commercial software simulations will be usable with this age group. Simple simulations of archaeological excavations like Dig are particularly useful.

At Key Stage 2 pupils can also begin to make use of viewdata compilations of simple written sources, provided that the material is presented at an appropriate language level. Often use of the computer source-base can generate activities. Pupils could interrogate a data disk holding a collection of source material on the Vikings, for instance, to find out where the Vikings travelled on their voyages and why. From this they could create a map of the Viking world, using different symbols for settlement, raiding, trading activities, exploration, etc. This exercise would also offer valuable cross-curricular links.

Working towards a goal or climax

Children's motivation can be maintained during a project if they are working towards some culmination of the activity. This might be a display for others to see, a school open day when work is displayed to outside visitors, going on a site visit, bringing in a special visitor to view what has been produced, taking part in a play or pageant, or recreating something like a Victorian school day, or some other event, or compiling a class book to hold the results of their work.

It is important for a project to have a definite goal and for the pupils to feel something has been achieved. Often this will also encourage important skills of presentation and communication (see Box 15).

Box 15
WORKING TOWARDS A GOAL OR CLIMAX

A case study (for HSU4)

Pupils did a lot of work on the history of their school to celebrate the school centenary. As well as working on copies of old photos and school records from the county archives, former pupils at the school were interviewed, an activity which generated the loan of further photographs and memorabilia. An exhibition of the material collected or borrowed was staged for parents and visitors. But the culmination to their work was holding a Victorian school day in school. Parents responded by making caps and pinafores for some of the girls and providing waistcoats or breeches for the boys; others borrowed braces and caps or long skirts. The teachers too entered into the spirit of the occasion and put on 'Victorian' clothes. Drawing on the information they had gathered previously a series of old-fashioned lessons were carried out.

Varied learning strategies? – a final check

Are you giving your pupils varied experiences, teaching strategies and activities?

Activities and methods

(1) Fieldwork
  • in the locality of the school;
  • a visit to a historical site or historic building;
  • a visit to a museum.
(2) Whole class teaching sessions.
(3) Contact with the teacher or other adults
  • individually;
  • in a small group.
(4) Carrying out individual work.
(5) Working in pairs.
(6) Working in a group.

(7) Classwork using primary sources
  - written documents of various kinds;
  - old photographs or engravings;
  - other sources.
(8) Handling or analysing statistical data.
(9) Looking at art, architecture, inscriptions or statues, etc.
(10) Working with a map or atlas.
(11) Reading a book.
(12) Doing reference work, e.g. work in a library or an archive or local history centre.
(13) Writing
  - creating;
  - descriptive;
  - narrative.
(14) Telling or retelling a story.
(15) Making a presentation to the class or to a group.
(16) Discussion
  - in a group;
  - in pairs;
  - with the whole class.
(17) Using a computer
  - interrogating a database;
  - consulting a viewdata programme;
  - carrying out a simulation of some kind;
  - inputting data onto a database;
  - using word processing packages to produce written work for history;
  - using a computer to generate barcharts, graphs, etc.
(18) Watching video or film.
(19) Listening to a tape recording.
(20) Listening or talking to a visitor or outside 'expert'.
(21) Performing or listening to period music.
(22) Taking part in historical reconstructions or re-enactments.
(23) Interviewing and tape recording people, e.g. elderly people.
(24) Surveying and measuring.
(25) Examining an artefact or object.
(26) Drama work, role-play.
(27) Problem solving activities.
(28) Sketching, or painting, or making annotated drawings.
(29) Using a camera, video or tape recorder to record something.
(30) Reading historical fiction, or poems or literature.
(31) Debate.
(32) Conducting a 'trial' of some historical character.

For further discussion: history at Key Stage 1

A starting point in history at Key Stage 1 could be the child's own life history. What alternative ways can you suggest for introducing the concept of time?

How can you ensure that oral history exercises contribute to one or more of the history attainment targets at level 1, 2, or 3? What contribution can they offer also towards general personal and social education?

Devise a history project for Key Stage 1 that would allow output in the form of role-play or model-making.

Tell half a story. Tell a story set in the past and decide where you will stop to let the class take over. What further activities could arise from this exercise?

For further consideration: history at Key Stage 2

One example of a possible bridging unit between Key Stages 1 and 2 has been given. Suggest another one and devise a scheme of work to implement it.

Devise two alternative four-year plans for delivering the history programmes of study at Key Stage 2, paying particular attention to links between the units.

Look at one of the suggested organising approaches for delivering the Key Stage 2 history curriculum, and devise a detailed scheme of work to implement one of the core units.

Devise some questions covering elements of the unit on the Tudors and Stuarts that will help to develop historical reasoning and understanding of key historical concepts.

Choose one of the history units and carry out a detailed audit of the possibilities for cross-curricular links.

Notes and references

1.   Department of Education and Science, *Primary Education in England*, HMSO, 1978.
2.   *Aspects of Primary Education – The Teaching and Learning of History and Geography*, HMSO, 1989.
3.   Arthur Marwick, *The Nature of History*, Macmillan, 1970.
4.   D. Fontana, *The Education of the Young Child,* Blackwell, 1984.
5.   Joan Blyth (ed.) *History 5–9*, Hodder and Stoughton, 1988.
6.   Joan Blyth, op. cit.
7.   Sallie Purkiss, 'Oral History in Schools', Oral History Society, n.d.
8.   Joan Blyth, op. cit.
9.   Work with 6 year olds described by John Fines in a speech to the Association of History Teachers in Wales, June 1989.

10. *History Curriculum Matters*, 13, HMSO.
11. J.S. Bruner, *The Process of Education*, Harvard University Press, 1960.
12. For instance, see the introduction to the *Schools Council History Project*, 1978, and Joan Blyth, op. cit.
13. Brian Scott 'The place of concepts in historical education in the primary school', Association of History Teachers in Wales, Discussion paper no. 7.
14. Brian Scott, op. cit.
15. Introduction to the Schools Council History Project, 1978. Schools Council Publications.
16. Quoted in Joan Blyth, op. cit.
17. Letter of the English scholar Alcuin to the King of Northumberland, describing the sacking of Lindisfarne, 793.
18. Hilary Cooper, 'Teaching 8 year olds how to interpret evidence using historical concepts', *Journal of Education in Museums*, Vol. II p. 2, 1990.
19. I am indebted for many of the ideas in this section to suggestions from Richard Waller, a member of the History Committee for Wales, and to Gary Brace, of the Curriculum Council for Wales.
20. Some of these approaches are based on work currently being carried out in Gwynedd primary schools, and on the suggestions of Robert Wyn Roberts, primary advisory teacher.
21. With acknowledgement to Gary Brace 'Non-statutory Guidance for History', Curriculum Council for Wales, 1991.

CHAPTER 3

Effective teaching: Key Stage 3

Irene S. Perry

Transition from primary

In recent years many secondary schools have sought to improve their pastoral links with their associated primary schools. This may or may not have involved departmental heads in planning induction sessions with year or house heads for in-coming pupils. Too rarely has it involved the specialist in the secondary school in regular discussion with primary colleagues.

The advent of the National Curriculum makes it imperative that much closer curricular links are developed between secondary schools and their feeder primaries in order that continuity and progression can be ensured.

Knowledge of the organisation and content of the teaching of History on either side of the infant/junior and junior/secondary transfer points should be a factor in helping teachers to plan for continuity. Each phase should share their knowledge and experience of the following:

– approaches and methods used with pupils;
– the range and nature of materials used;
– the subject content covered;
– the outcome of pupils' work (e.g. particular levels of attainment that could be expected or anticipated).

The programmes of study for each key stage provide opportunities to use units as links between key stages.

Good liaison should also ensure that duplication of content does not occur or that where repetition of a topic does take place, there is a significant variation in the depth, focus and treatment of such a topic.[1]

While parental choice embodied in the Educational Reform Act has broken down the traditional secondary-feeder primary school catchment areas, for the vast number of secondary schools their associated primaries are unchanged. Indeed the 'clustering' of primary schools for curriculum development has and will continue to benefit the continuity and coherent planning for secondary schools. Although pupils will transfer with a variety of experiences they should have learned a core of prescribed knowledge. In addition, they should have been introduced to communication skills involving questioning, simulation and judgement and opportunities should have been given to prepare the pupils to cope with conflicting evidence in actual historical issues. This must be fully acknowledged by the secondary school history department when planning its work. Unplanned duplication can no longer be excused. Repetitive exercises to introduce the concept of evidence without consultation with primary colleagues is at the least unimaginative. One measure of a successful department will be its primary/secondary links in terms of the frequency of consultation between phases, the level of joint planning between them and where possible the coherent management of a cross-phase unit of study.

Pupils transferring at the end of Key Stage 2 will bring with them a statement of attainment. While the actual form of SATs is liable to change, the process of testing pupils at the age of 11 is unlikely to do so. The results of these tests will be matched to the teacher assessments and used to determine the level of attainment reached by each pupil in each attainment target. It is vital that secondary schools participate in the design of exchange records and understand the content of transfer documents. Primary colleagues will have spent many hours compiling this information and it is incumbent on secondary teachers to use these to inform pupil progression. In the past there has been an assumption that pupils' attainment will dip as a result of transfer and a settling period will be needed. While this remains true perhaps in the physical and emotional sense, it need not be true of the learning situation if sufficient curriculum liaison has taken place.

Planning history for the lower school curriculum

The whole school approach

Planners of the History curriculum will need to take account of contributions that History will be able to make to a whole range of aspects of learning, as well as recognise the possibilities for the delivery of elements of the History curriculum in other ways and through other subjects.[2]

It is essential that the members of a history department do not see the introduction of National Curriculum history as their entire curriculum. Rather the programme of study for Key Stage 3 while being set in its subject context of a 5–16 continuum, should also be set in the context of the whole school curriculum framework. This means that planners should be fully acquainted with and supportive of the school aims and be able to identify the special contributions which history can make to their achievement. There should be a curriculum map available which shows how each of the subject areas in the school deliver their specific remits and where there are areas of possible overlap. The history department can then draw on the skills and processes being developed by other departments and extend them.

Similarly, with a clearly enunciated history curriculum other departments in the school can see how they can be served on occasion or a basis can be laid in history which they can reinforce.

A concrete example could be in the use of computer databases. Census materials are an invaluable resource for the historian but the technical manipulation of figures may be thought of as being the remit of the mathematics department or even the geographers. In a school with clear lines of communication between departments it can be agreed which department will actually teach the way to manipulate data and analyse results and which will use this skill elsewhere for extension work. There is no need for the history department to teach the skill before using census materials if the mathematics department has already done so but even more importantly if the historians need to know how to do this at an earlier stage than the mathematics department would teach this skill in their programme of study then the historians must negotiate this with their colleagues in the best interests of the children. It is only through a combined approach that school will be enabled to deliver all their programmes of study and make enough time to do more.

The history department should also share in the drawing up and implementation of school policy statements. These will cover areas such as equal opportunities, multi-cultural education, cross-curricular themes, competences and dimensions and special needs. Where a new member of the department is appointed time should be taken to induct this person into the overall role of history within the school and its curriculum mission.

Devising a programme of study

The history department has to set about devising a programme of study for Key Stage 3 which embodies all the National Curriculum requirements, plus any local or county initiatives and any school based requirements. This appears to assume that most secondary school departments have scrapped all their previous work and started again, which of course is not the case. Most departments will select their supplementary study units with due regard to their existing resources and from their experience of what motivates their pupils. Similarly, this choice will be influenced and informed by the school's locality. Some areas may provide a rich vein of local history which is also well related to a supplementary unit.

For example:
(1) a school in Liverpool may feel their local history to be linked to part of the world of work on American cotton plantations;
(2) a school in rural Wales may wish to exploit connections of Welsh emigrants to Patagonia;

(3) a school in Lancashire may feel it essential to include a study of textiles in the nineteenth century as an in-depth study in a Victorian core unit.

Teachers should try to identify criteria such as those mentioned above to guide their selection of content. Simultaneously, a programme of study must be planned for the whole key stage bearing in mind what comes before and after. Consideration needs to be given to the balance of time and coverage devoted to core units as against supplementary or school designed units. Historians have always complained of content overloads in syllabuses and National Curriculum orders are no different. The whole of year 7 could be devoted to the medieval world but cannot be. There could be and possibly will be a wide range of views as to what features of the medieval world are most deserving of study but again teachers will have to make judgements about which elements are more significant and which could be given a 'broad brush' treatment. This means that the organisation of the units will have to be established in order to gauge the available time.

Several planning models can be adopted.

(1) *Delivery of discrete units.* Here each unit would be taught separately from the others although links could be made at the end of the unit.
(2) *'Nesting'.* This refers to the placing of a section of a supplementary unit within a core unit, e.g. the World of Work (nineteenth century factories) could be nested inside the core unit on Industrial Britain.
(3) *Integrating units.* In this example the core unit would draw on both parts of the supplementary units and parts of the local study or school designed unit.

In examples 2 and 3 teachers will have to ensure that the focus of the parts making up the units is not lost within the organisational strategy. This means that clear linkage must be made between contributing parts in order that the pupils can see the overall theme.

The *Non-Statutory Guidance* available from the National Curriculum Council in England and the Curriculum Council for Wales in Wales offers useful models for teachers planning a study unit (appendix 1). There has to be a selection of content and teachers have to identify the key elements which they will focus upon and those which will receive the 'broad brush' treatment. Since everything cannot be covered in equal depth teachers need to develop the knowledge, skills and understanding required to progress through each attainment target. It is helpful to specify concepts which underpin the content, e.g. kingship, migration, war and conflict and from these to highlight aspects which enable pupils to meet statements of achievement. This means that teachers must try to think simultaneously about the attainment targets and the statements of attainment within the levels.

In constructing a scheme of work then the selection of content must be closely related to a judgement on the depth of coverage to be attempted. Further refinement can be achieved by trying to pose questions or hypotheses relevant to the content. This will show what is significant and appropriate teaching activities can then be designed for pupils. Since at Key Stage 3 the core units have to be taught in a chronological order that does give an initial structure to the overall plan of the three-year period.

Many teachers will wish to make use of a planning grid such as that suggested in the aforementioned *Non-Statutory Guidance*. The following stages in the process may be helpful:

(1) Having identified the unit ensure that the statutory content is clear.
(2) Pose the key questions or ideas which you perceive to underpin this topic of study. This may also involve specifying the important concepts to be developed.
(3) Design activities which relate to the attainment targets and enable the pupils to ask questions and communicate their understanding in a variety of ways.
(4) Ensure the activities provide learning experiences for pupils through which you can assess their attainment of each attainment target or one in particular.
(5) Identify links with other areas of the curriculum and cross-curricular elements and seek to negotiate these links as and when appropriate.
(6) Evaluate the available resources. This can involve materials already in school, some supplementary materials or the careful planning of a visit or trip.

At this stage the planning grid gives the teacher an overall direction for the work of a class or a group but further refinement will be necessary. At the wider level each of the units h
as to be sequenced to achieve a balance through the entire key stage. At the classroom level, the teaching and learning methods have to be organised to allow for much more than simple coverage of the topic. Specific tasks have to be designed which allow evidence of attainment to be gathered and retained. Continuity and progression have to be built in to the programme and there has to be scope for differentiation and extension. However at least the teacher with a series of grids will have a programme of study which serves as the foundation for the scheme of work.

Classroom methodology – teaching and learning strategies

Good practice in the classroom can only be achieved where the teacher has evolved a clear framework wherein pupils can become secure, confident and interested. At a basic level it is necessary to foster an approach which emphasises responsibility, good manners and good working habits. The teacher must stress the need to bring equipment and text materials to every lesson. The children must have impressed upon them the need for personal cooperation within the classroom as essential to the variety of learning situations with which they will be faced. Moreover pupils need to learn appropriate modes of behaviour for a range of off-site learning activities, e.g. a visit to a cathedral, a climb up to a hill fort, following a town heritage trail or exploring a castle.

Having established such behavioural parameters the teacher needs to consider also the classroom environment. It is always easier if a teacher has major ownership of her/his room. Where a teacher is peripatetic in a school building it is much more difficult to display materials and motivate pupil contributions. Given room ownership, the effective teacher will establish areas of display. Some will be to provoke interest and curiosity, others will be to reinforce learning, still others will be for extension work and most importantly some areas will be for the pupils' own work which will serve as a major focus of attention. Some displays may remain in place for lengthy periods. The obvious example would be a time-line with a movable reference point throughout the term or session. Other displays, however, should be changed regularly in order to maintain enthusiasm.

In addition to wall displays thought needs to be given to the equipment which can be used in the room, e.g. does the teacher always have to use the overhead projector or slide projector with the whole class or can groups of pupils go and view a selection of slides independently as needed? The teacher might think of extra resources: a box of artefacts (some of which may be replicas) which the pupils can handle; a bookcase with additional reference materials including dictionaries and atlases as well as appropriate texts of higher and lower levels or a selection of visual materials for study. Where paper based source materials are being used, the teacher must give thought to ease of access for retrieval as well as the effectiveness of storage.

Worksheets which are in good condition are treated with more respect than those which too quickly are crumpled, torn or part company with the staples or covering. This is equally true of texts and even more expensive. Therefore some early thought should be given to protective covers and storage.

The teacher should also make certain decisions about the arrangement of furniture in the room. The layout can give as many messages to the pupils as it does to colleagues and senior management. A room laid out in rows with the teacher's desk centre front suggests a more didactic approach than one designed in groups with the teacher's desk less prominent. It is up to the individual to decide the most appropriate arrangement and this should be informed by the range of strategies which he or she intends to use in the classroom. It may be that at various stages the teacher will rearrange the room. Having established a good working relationship with classes the new teacher may well be able to adopt a freer design with confidence.

Historical methodology

Before considering the strategies to be used in teaching history the teacher should be clear about the objectives he or she has in mind. While its main purpose is not to produce professional historians, the teaching of history in school should enable pupils to gain some understanding of what history is and what historians do. This means developing the pupils' ability to ask historical questions and interpret their answers. As shown in the National Curriculum Council *Non-Statutory Guidance* the process of enquiry might involve pupils in:

(1) posing questions and formulating hypotheses;
(2) planning investigations;
(3) finding, collecting and recording information;
(4) assessing and organising information;
(5) interpreting;
(6) analysing the information as evidence for the enquiry.

These skills are further illuminated by the general requirements stated at the beginning of the Key Stage orders in the National Curriculum folder.

Pupils should be helped to investigate topics on their own. They should have opportunities to:

– use a range of approaches for investigating the past, including outline, in-depth, thematic and comparative.
– ask questions, identify sources for an investigation, and collect and record information.[3]

Pupils should already have been encouraged to ask historical questions in the primary school but this should be reemphasised throughout Key Stage 3. The following chart is a useful *aide-mémoire*:
Adapted from CCW *Non-Statutory Guidance* for history, 1991.

Questions about chronology, such as:	• When did the Battle of Hastings take place?
	• How long did the Peasants' Revolt last?
	• How does the effect of the Black Death relate to the Revolt?
Questions about change, such as:	• In what ways have coal mining methods changed?
	• How much have they changed?
	• Why did mining change before transport changes?
	• Which industries changed more quickly than others?
Questions about the different features of historical situations, such as:	• In what ways was government the same at the end of Victoria's reign as at the beginning?
	• What was it like in Victorian Britain?
	• Why did some people see this as a time of greatness and wealth while others emphasise the poverty of many?
Questions about evidence, such as:	• How do we know about Henry VIII?
	• What evidence is there about his personality?
	• What is the truth about his marriages?
	• Does the evidence help us understand him?
Questions about interpretations of history, such as:	• Why are there different analyses of the causes of the Second World War?
	• How do you evaluate the similarities and differences?
	• Are some forms of evidence less reliable and/or incomplete?

To encourage the asking of such questions is central to the study of history. While the questions asked by the teacher are vital and shall be referred to later it is the development of this skill in pupils which is crucial to their progression. If they are to study evidence they must know the right questions to ask.

Every step in the argument depends on asking a question. The question is the charge of gas, exploded in the cylinder head, which is the motive force of every piston-stroke. But the metaphor is not adequate, because each new piston-stroke is produced not by exploding another charge of the old mixture but by exploding a charge of a new kind.[4]

The materials which the historian questions are evidence. Pupils need to realise the wide range this encompasses: written and printed material, evidence in the local environment, oral accounts, artefacts and visual records such as pictures, maps, posters, photographs and film. The teacher must provide opportunities for pupils to examine the widest range of evidence, to question it and come to conclusions. As they become more familiar with using evidence pupils should extract as much information as possible and by asking increasingly complex questions become more able at evaluating its usefulness and its reliability. As an example pupils at the beginning of Key Stage 3 studying the Norman Conquest could be given this exercise on 'Who should inherit the throne?'.

Figure 3.1 Who should inherit the throne?

Viewpoints[5]

SOURCE 20

Edward, king of the English, being without an heir, sent Robert, Archbishop of Canterbury, to the duke with a message appointing the duke as heir to the kingdom which God had entrusted to him.

William of Jumieges, *Deeds of the Norman Dukes*, 1070

activity

1 Look at sources 20 and 21 which show what the Normans said happened before King Edward died. How do they support William's claim that Edward promised he would become the next king of England?

SOURCE 21

The Bayeux Tapestry shows Harold making an oath to William.

SOURCE 22

Edward, in bed, speaks to his most trusted followers. Harold is shown at the front. From the Bayeux Tapestry.

William of Poitiers was a Norman. He studied in the French town of Poitiers and then served as a soldier in Normandy. Later he became a priest and was made chaplain to Duke William. He did not go with the duke on his expedition to England; but he was in a good position to find out what happened from those who did.

Figure 3.1 continued

SOURCE 23

A messenger from Harold is speaking to William just before the battle of Hastings:

'He certainly remembers that King Edward long ago decided that you would be his heir, and that he himself in Normandy gave surety to you concerning that succession. Nevertheless, he knows that this kingdom is his by right, as granted to him by gift of that same king his lord on his deathbed.'

William of Poitiers, *The Deeds of William, Duke of the Normans and King of the English,* written about 1071

---

activity

2 Look at sources 22 and 23.
a How do they support Harold's claim that Edward made him his successor at the last moment?
b Are they Norman or English sources?
c Does that make Harold's argument stronger or weaker? Why?
3 Look at sources 24 and 25. One was written by a Norman and one by an Englishman.
a Which is which? How can you tell?
b Why do you think the two sources report the same events in such different ways?
4 Sources 20, 21 and 24 all support William's claim to the throne of England. What difference would it make if sources 22, 23 and 25 did not exist?

SOURCE 24

There came the unwelcome report that the land of England had lost its king, and that Harold had been crowned in his stead. This unfeeling Englishman did not wait for the public choice, but breaking his oath, nd with the support of a few discontented friends, he seized the throne of the best of kings on the very day of his funeral, and when all the people were bewailing their loss.

SOURCE 25

The next day Edward was buried in kingly style amid the bitter lamentations of all present. After his burial the under-king Harold, son of Godwine, whom the king had nominated as his successor, was chosen king by the chief magnates of all England; and on the same day Harold was crowned with great ceremony.

SOURCE 34

William Guildeborn:	hanged, 5th July; his goods seized, among them 75 sheep
Thomas Guildeborn:	a fugitive.
Richard Francueys:	hanged, his goods seized, among them a cottage
John Wolk:	hanged, his goods seized.
John Devin:	his goods seized
Ralph White:	his goods seized
Ralph Tripat:	a fugitive
Robert Knight:	a fugitive; his goods seized, among them a boat with all its gear (oars, sails etc.)

activity

1 Look at source 34.
What do you think these punishments meant to the families of each of these men?

The record of punishments given to the men of Fobbing.

In addition to asking questions pupils have to develop the ability to analyse historical evidence, make judgements about it and in doing so develop a sense of perspective about the people of the past. With clearer understanding they will be able to use concepts such as change and continuity, cause and consequence and similarity and difference.It takes time for pupils to appreciate the complexity of these concepts but this is what distinguishes history from other disciplines. As the pupil progresses so the demands increase. For example in studying the Peasants' Revolt of 1381 the analysis of the causes is further refined by their division into long-term causes and short-term causes:

assignments

It is often useful to divide the causes of an event into two kinds. The 'long-term' causes are the ones that have been going on for a long time and make the event possible. The 'short-term', or 'immediate' causes, are the ones that come just before the event and set it off. For example, when a tree comes down in a storm, the short-term cause is the storm. The long-term cause is whatever makes it likely that the tree will fall in a high wind. Perhaps it has rotted inside, or its roots are weak, or it has grown too tall.

a Here are two long-term and and two short-term causes of the Peasants' Revolt. Add as many others as you can to each list.

Long-term causes
• Peasants lived hard lives a very bad conditions.
• The Black Death killed many peasants so there was a shortage of labour.

Short-term causes
• The king needed money to fight the French Wars.
• Wat Tyler was a strong leader.

b Decide which you think are the two most important of (i) the long-term and (ii) the short-term causes and give the reasons for your choice.

To encourage the analysis of evidence pupils must be asked to weigh up the sources which may contradict one another. Similarly gaps in evidence need to be acknowledged not ignored. Responses have to be expressed in appropriate terminology and be based on historical insight not simply on emotion. The effective teacher needs to give thought to the abilities pupils will require in order to be successful historians themselves. A useful model was presented in the *Schools Council Project 13–16: A New Look at History* (1976) as a way of considering analysis, judgement and empathy where associated skills were tabulated in ascending order:[6]

(1) Finding information – ability to use:
       • an index, library catalogue, table of contents, glossary.

(2) Recalling information – ability to recall and use:
- standard abbreviations such as, e.g., i.e., sic., viz.,
- general historical vocabulary, e.g. statute, act, treaty;
- chronological conventions, e.g. century, decade;
- particular terminology, e.g. middle ages, chivalry, domestic system, *laissez faire.*

(3) Understanding evidence – ability to:
- state information in other words;
- summarise, interpret graphs, charts, cartoons and maps;
- give examples of general points.

(4) Evaluating evidence – ability to:
- distinguish between facts, assumptions, inferences and hypotheses and value judgements;
- distinguish between valid and invalid conclusions, verifiable and non-verifiable information, relevant and irrelevant material, compare information and recognise contradictions.
- recognise the kind of information necessary to support a judgement, argument or an hypothesis;
- detect logical fallacies;
- recognise an author's attitude or bias;
- recognise propaganda and its purpose;
- recognise lack of connection or gaps in evidence.

(5) Making inferences and hypotheses – ability to:
- suggest sources of relevant information where there are gaps;
- make inferences either logical or intuitive from evidence, draw and state conclusions;
- suggest causes and consequences of actions and events from hypotheses as starting points for further investigations.

(6) Synthesis – ability to use:
- organising themes or ideas (temporal, behavioural, causal) to make a credible narrative[6]

This list can serve as a useful check for teachers. The development of these skills has implications for teaching and learning strategies because only with a wide range of evidence can pupils gain adequate experience. Furthermore, the situations which enable understanding of past events and people's responses to them must be such as to spark the imagination. If a pupil is to enter the mind and feelings of more than one person in the past then classroom activities must be designed to facilitate and promote this.

Teaching and learning strategies

There are many ways in which history can be presented to pupils and the effective teacher will select the most appropriate vehicle to achieve each identified learning outcome. Only a few are suggested here.

The well told story

While great emphasis has rightly been placed on the active involvement of the pupils in their learning, it should always be remembered that there is still a place for the teacher to convey a feel for an event or person by presenting the story. Its accuracy, bias, and so on can be judged later but the dramatic effectiveness of this approach can often serve as an excellent starting point for further study, e.g. the murder of Beckett.

Role/play and drama

In a similar vein pupils themselves can be asked to act out various parts in order to explore contemporary feelings. Dramatised television and radio productions can be included in this category. A lesson on the Roman invasion of Britain can be enlivened by a radio re-enactment where the sound effects of galley oars and blood curling yells create scenes of notable impact. Likewise a television dramatisation of British social history can often bring home to pupils the harsh realities of the workhouse and desperation of unemployed and impoverished labourers in the early nineteenth century.

Simulations and games

With pupils in lower secondary years their enjoyment of pretence is not yet impaired by age. They can enter into a simulated situation with gusto. Hence the challenge of building a Norman motte and bailey castle on behalf of a conquering lord (Fletcher's Castle, a computer programme from Fernleaf Productions) can become a real one in which the balances between defence and construction and survival have to be struck. On an even broader front the use of an integrated package on computer such as Wagons West from Tressell Publications not only develops empathetic understanding of the dilemmas facing early American pioneers but allows cross-curricular links with geography, religious education and English.

Board games can enable pupils to interact and consider different viewpoints and motives at times in the past. Into the Unknown, another Tressell Publication, played on board or computer can allow pupils to examine different attitudes towards exploration in the sixteenth century. Similarly, a nineteenth century trade game can explore the motives and consequences in the development of the British empire and its diverse nature.

Diagrams, cartoons and pictures

The visual impact of materials never fails to illicit a response if it is well chosen. The teacher can often save lengthy explanation by carefully constructing a diagram or chart which encapsulates the main points of a lesson. Similarly pupils will often remember a pictorial representation which sums up an event or development. Cartoons are sometimes criticised as an invitation to anachronistic interpretation but provided they are used selectively they too can enable a wider range of pupils to access information.

Model-making and posters

This approach is perhaps more common in the primary schools but pupils at Key Stage 3 can still derive great pleasure from working with papier mâché and glue to construct their design of an Edwardian castle or an Inca palace. Also as has been suggested in the *Non-Statutory Guidance* for history from the National Curriculum Council pupils could be given a selection of materials in a scissor and paste exercise to design a poster explaining why French people wanted a revolution in 1789. Such activities need to be researched for accuracy but by focusing on a different type of outcome greater enthusiasm can be engendered.

Question and answer sessions in group or whole class situations

This is good traditional practice but the teacher should consider carefully the type of question to be asked. Pupils can be helped to come to a deeper understanding of other peoples and/or events with the questioner's guidance. Therefore a study of the types of question is a useful preparation point:

Types of Question

Question type	Explanation
(1) A data recall question	requires the pupil to remember facts without putting them to any use, e.g. 'When was the Battle of Hastings?'
(2) A naming question	asks the pupil to name something without showing how it relates to the historical situation, e.g. 'What are the men in the picture wearing?'
(3) An observation question	asks pupils to describe something without relating it to their knowledge of the situation, e.g. 'Describe what is happening in the picture?'
(4) A reasoning question	asks the pupils to explain something, e.g. 'What does the picture tell us about how the Normans and Saxons fought?'
(5) A speculative question	the pupil is asked to consider how the situation might have developed or what led up to it, e.g. 'What do you think happened next?'
(6) An empathetic question	asks the pupil to become involved personally with the evidence, e.g. 'If you had been the soldier standing behind Harold, say what you might have thought, felt and done at the moment the arrow hit him in the eye.'

(7) A hypothesis generating question	asks the pupils to speculate about possible causes and consequences, e.g. 'What factors led Harold to fight the battle at that place and time?'
(8) A problem solving question	one which asks the pupils to weigh up the evidence. 'What evidence does the picture contain that Harold was shot in the eye?'
(9) An evidence questioning question	questions that look at the veracity of the evidence, e.g. 'On what do you think the weavers of the tapestry based their picture?' 'How reliable is the tapestry as evidence about the battle?'
(10) A synthesising question	a question that pulls the questioning process together, and allows for a resolution of the problem, e.g. 'Write an account of the Battle of Hastings from the viewpoint of either Bishop Odo or Harold's standard bearer.'[7]

As can be seen from the above it is possible to give questions a greater focus of purpose by considering what process it is that you wish the pupils to go through.

Differentiation

The preceding approaches are means by which the techniques applied in the classroom can be varied but effective teaching must go beyond this.

The introduction of National Curriculum History will have an impact on teachers' methodologies and on classroom management techniques. Teachers will be in a position to form more accurate judgements about strengths and weaknesses of individual pupils in relation to attainment targets for history and will need to develop approaches which allow for a larger range of learning activities to be occurring than has, hitherto, been the case.[8]

While the variety of approaches can be extended this must be planned in relation to the outcomes which the teacher has identified through the programme of study and attainment targets.

Whatever the nature of class organisation there must be greater focus on the pupils as individuals. Whether they be in mixed ability, banded, streamed or set groups, the teacher must cater for each pupil's progress by providing tasks at the appropriate levels. Several issues arise from this premise:

(1) Teachers must use diagnostic records as pupils come to them, be it across a phase or year on year.
(2) The credence of such records must be ensured.
(3) Teachers must set appropriate learning activities for each pupil, i.e. differentiated.

(4) Teachers must provide opportunities for pupils to progress to higher levels.
(5) Teachers must track the progress of pupils and collect evidence of their attainments.

The question of records and record-keeping will be addressed in a later section. Here it is the strategies of differentiation which must be considered. Teachers have two main forms of differentiation at their disposal – differentiation by outcome and differentiation by task. Historians are by and large more familiar with the former. The traditional essay-type question can be set for the whole class and pupils can respond at their own level. There is still a valid place for this type of extended prose. Indeed it has been a skill whose weakness has been at the root of many criticisms of GCSE papers where short answers are not deemed to be adequate foundation for A level. Of course there can be differentiation by outcome within subsections of structured questions without those subsections themselves being differentiated. Teachers may well find that particular statements of attainment can be achieved and confirmed through such exercises.

Differentiation by task is a more complex and demanding strategy which does not take one simple form:

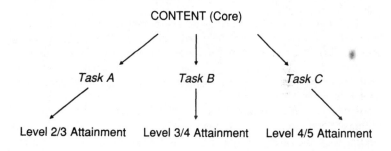

In this example the teacher identifies the topic content which pupils should learn (the core), then sets different tasks for different ability levels within the class and these tasks are directed to achieving particular levels of achievement. It requires great skill on the part of the teacher to match tasks to attainment levels and in reality it will prove unusual starting from a core to have a task which only addresses one level within one target. However it is achievable. There is one major drawback to this approach. It does not allow for the pupil who is able to achieve in this example level 6. In other words it places a ceiling above which such a pupil is prevented from rising. This can have a demotivating effect on more able pupils and can lead to under-achievement. This can be avoided in the second model:

Structured tasks

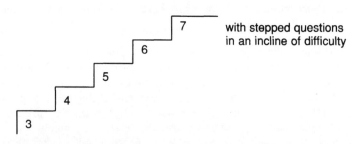

Here pupils would begin at an agreed level and be guided through tasks with demands at each step increasing so that every child can positively achieve, i.e. reach their place on the ladder while the most able can continue to show their abilities beyond a fixed range. Obviously such structured tasks are more difficult to set. It does require very careful planning and use of resources. Some guidance can be derived from a study of flexible learning methods where whole courses have been designed for students in this staged progressive fashion. The quality and accessibility of materials have to be high if this approach is to succeed and no organisational barriers are placed in the way of learning.

This means for example that an assessment exercise could be set around two sources which have contradictions. The language of the sources could be simplified for those who had difficulty reading the sources or they could be copied on to tape for listening. While the pupils are evaluating the sources prompts could be given to encourage positive achievement. As the pupils continue through the tasks a wider range of source materials could be added which also included more sophisticated language. Higher level tasks could involve using extraneous knowledge to reach conclusions. It can be seen that a high degree of organisation and ample provision of resources would be essential for such an exercise to work.

It is important that teachers see differentiation not only as a strategy to ensure progression but also as a vital tool in countering under-achievement. Where the work is clearly defined and structured the effective teacher can dictate to a greater extent the pace of the work and this will pay dividends across the whole ability range. Hand in hand with the planning for differentiation goes assessment and record-keeping which must be linked to the programme of study.

Assessment, record-keeping and reporting

Assessment

Statements of Attainment are targets or objectives related to the overall attainment target to which they belong ... Statements of Attainment are also guides which enable teachers to see how far pupils have progressed in each Attainment Target. They form the basis for assessment but are not in themselves assessment objectives ... Assessment based on Statements of Attainment will need to take into account the whole range of abilities to be found in any Statement of Attainment and the context – task and type of historical content – in which attainment of these abilities is being shown. It will be the teacher's judgement, made over time and through observing performance in different tasks, whether pupils can be said to have attained the abilities identified in a Statement of Attainment.[9]

This extract contains important messages for teachers. The Statements of Attainment need to be in some ways 'unpacked' in relation to the chosen programme of study and reordered not in sequence of difficulty but in terms of their place in the programme to ensure that opportunities for assessment are capitalised upon. Secondly, despite the impression of the diagrams accompanying the TGAT report pupils do not always progress in a linear fashion but often reach plateaux and can even regress! Any assessment scheme should take account of this. Thirdly progression may not be identical across the attainment targets. A pupil may reach level 6 in Attainment Target 1 but only be partially achieving at level 5 in Attainment Targets 2 and 3. Finally and most significantly the closing sentence of the extract is well worth repeating : 'It will be the teacher's judgement, *made over time and through observing performance in different tasks*, whether pupils can be said to have attained.' This is the crux of teacher assessments. Over the whole of a key stage a teacher or group of teachers will assess a pupil's progress through a variety of methods and reach a judgement.

A recent publication from the Schools Examination and Assessment Council on advice for assessment at Key Stage 3 in mathematics and science holds useful information for the forward thinking history teacher. It suggests that teachers gather formal evidence which can be written work by the pupil but also encourage the collection of 'ephemeral' evidence, i.e. evidence gained through observation, discussion or interaction. Where a teacher is confident that in his or her professional judgement attainment has taken place but there is not a piece of concrete supportive evidence as outcome they are asked to annotate the context and their view of the achievement.

This whole area is one in which many of the practices of the 'new History' can be safeguarded. Role-play situations can be set up, annotated and pupils' demonstrated understanding evaluated by the teacher *in situ*. Group work can continue and through on-going observation and judicious questioning the teacher can establish the contribution and attainment of the individual members of the group. Indeed it may be that this is also a direct aid in setting tasks which have stepped differentiation within them.

Another implication of this advice is that teachers need not begin keeping cupboards full of evidence from every pupil over three year periods in case they are selected for a random sample check on teacher assessments. Those schools selected for the first quality audit in mathematics or science have recently been asked to supply 12 pieces of work from across the entire year group reflecting the spread of the ability range. This does not suggest that schools would need to amass great quantities of pupils' work for an audit. Therefore it would be more effective to select a cross section of the tasks set within a programme of study from which evidence will be retained. This should be done at the planning stage. While experience may show that certain tasks were not as good discriminators as others there is likely to be an abundance of evidence over the three-year period for teachers to use. It should also be remembered that teachers are always assessing their pupils' performance on a daily basis and will know their pupils well over the period of time. Provided such views are informed by good practice teachers should remain confident of their own expertise.

At this moment the actual tests which pupils will sit at the end of the key stage are in the process of design. It would seem that differentiated papers will be set in history as in other subjects. We must await more information as to the elements of content which they will focus upon. It may be that only core units are tested and perhaps only one or two of those. The danger of course will be that once the form and nature of the tests are known some teachers may be tempted – some even told in schools where league tables will be revered – to teach to the test. It is hoped that the effective teacher will not need to do so.

Record-keeping

There has been increasing confusion over the terms 'assessment' and 'record-keeping'. As already stated assessment is a daily practice of a good teacher who uses every opportunity to become better informed of the developing abilities of the pupils. Record-keeping is the charting of the progress which need not be a daily procedure. Again valuable lessons can be learned from those subjects which have been under National Curriculum orders longer than history. There is and has been a great temptation to design many types of record sheets which involve complex systems of ticks, crosses and shadings to represent attainment. While these may look impressive the experience within other subjects seems to indicate that the most common outcome of such systems is the over-assessment of pupils and an unacceptable burden on the teacher. Record systems should be designed to meet the needs of teachers, parents and pupils, not to get in the way of effective teaching.

Therefore the record-keeping system should be easily used and understood. It should only aim to record that which is necessary for accurate reporting of a pupil's progress according to the agreed reporting format of the school as a whole. It will incorporate National Curriculum attainment but there must also be a place for the wider skills of the subject which the teacher will wish to develop. Furthermore, to avoid the necessity of duplication of records, there should be a place for recording the profiling categories common to most record of achievement schemes.

No-one in authority has yet ventured to say how often a level should be attained before it is confirmed or what allowance should be made, if any, for the pupil who will unlearn. These are questions which history departments must pose for themselves but it should be borne in mind that it is at the end of the key stage that a final assessment will be required. Teachers are not required to give a confirmed level for a pupil at any one moment during the key stage. The best indication which can be given to pupils, parents or others concerned would be the level or levels at which the pupils are working. It will be rare to find a pupil working at one level only; they are more likely to be working over two or three levels. Record-keeping systems will therefore have to allow for this.

Reporting

At the end of the key stage, the teacher assessment will be matched to the test results and the pupils awarded a level of attainment. It is not yet known what form this report will take but one can presume that a national format will be designed eventually. Since school reports can stand separately from this it is possible to revise present reporting systems in preparation for the whole National Curriculum to come on stream. The history department would be expected to participate in this process and then match up their own practice to that agreed. The timing of the end of Key Stage 3 assessment does have some knock-on effects. If a school intends to operate a form of option system allowing pupils to drop history at Key Stage 4 or to opt for the short course or continue with the full course, pupils and parents will presumably wish to base their decision on performance to date. If tests are in June of year 9 followed by marking, standardisation and quality audit the results are not going to be available before July. However, schools plan their staffing levels at least three months earlier and the timetable is usually worked on throughout the summer term. Any major changes in the size of groupings in the last few weeks of term could create significant problems. Does this then mean that pupils will choose their options from some estimated grade or does this mean that schools will begin to set 'mock' tests around option time? These are the current questions being asked but no simple answers have yet been given.

Conclusion

History teaching has undergone many developments in the last three decades and no doubt change will continue although it is to be hoped that the pace of that change may diminish. Key Stage 3 is a vital bridge between the primary school and the upper stages of the secondary sector. To ensure the continuing popularity and growth of the subject at Key Stage 4 and beyond, teachers must not simply teach the programme they must aim to instil an interest in and enjoyment of the subject. A blend of methodologies and careful selection of stimulus materials is valuable but above all a clearly enunciated plan of what is to be taught and assessed is the necessary prerequisite. The National Curriculum has given the basis, it is up to effective teachers to use their professional skills to translate this into a worthwhile and meaningful experience for each of their pupils.

Further questions to consider

(1) What is your function within the history department?

(2) How are the delegated responsibilities allocated?

(3) On what criteria are resources selected?

(4) Are resources easily retrieved? Are they differentiated?

(5) How are classes organised? Mixed ability? Setted? Banded?

(6) Do you have a departmental scheme of work which is realistic and usable?

(7) Have you contributed to it?

(8) How would you deliver the Key Stage 3 programme of study? Nesting of units or discretely?

(9) Have you established the time allocation over the three-year period?

(10) How would you manage a group work situation to ensure that all pupils are actively involved?

(11) Do you have a clear assessment policy which conforms to the whole school policy?

(12) Is your record-keeping system efficient?

(13) What type of ephemeral evidence are you aiming to collect?

(14) Are there any strategies you can use to help pupils prepare for the tests without teaching to the test?

Notes

1. *Non-Statutory Guidance for History,* CCW, June 1991, p. 21.
2. Ibid. p. 12.
3. *History in the National Curriculum, Final Orders,* National Curriculum Council, 1990.
4. R. G. Collingwood, *The Idea of History,* Oxford University Press, 1946, p. 273.
5. J. Mason, *Medieval Realms,* Longmans, 1991, p. 15 and p. 116.
6. *Schools Council 13–16, A New Look at History,* Holmes McDougall, 1976.
7. *Non-Statutory Guidance for History,* CCW, June 1991, p. 23.
8. *Non-Statutory Guidance for History,* National Curriculum Council, May 1991.
9. Ibid.

CHAPTER 4

Resources for teacher-designed units: some general guidelines

Mary Aris

The programmes of study prescribed for National Curriculum history are merely outlines. Before they can be implemented, they need to be turned into meaningful schemes of work. There will be many ways of delivering the topics and requirements. Individual teachers, or in some cases groups of teachers in cooperation, will need to plan their own school units. In the process of delivering National Curriculum history it is most important that pupils are introduced to a wide and varied range of historical resources, and it may be useful to offer some general advice on the resourcing of such units.

The prime consideration should be the evaluation and use of evidence, which lies at the very heart of the historical method. Effective history teaching at all levels must bring pupils into contact with primary evidence, and it is important therefore that, from the outset, the teacher of history forms a clear idea of the important distinction between primary and secondary sources.

Primary and secondary sources: 'evidence' and 'interpretation'

Primary sources are more 'first-hand' than secondary sources. They are sources that are contemporary or near contemporary with the period being studied, documents that were written by the participants, or by people at or near the time. Often they are what we would call eye-witness accounts. Primary sources also include the material evidence, the artefacts, buildings and structures that were created, modified and used by those people in the past. Old photographs, and some archive film footage or earlier radio broadcasts would also be included, depending on the period being studied. All our interpretations about what happened in the past must ultimately rest upon this evidence surviving from the past.

Secondary sources, in contrast, are interpretations of the past produced at a later date. They are also written with hindsight. They include the writings of historians, and textbooks, stories about the past, and historical fiction. Secondary sources also include dramatisations and reconstructions by theatre in education groups, actors, or museum staff acting 'in role', and many film or video or radio and television productions. Secondary sources also include artists' illustrations and interpretations of historical events, archaeologists' reconstruction drawings, and models or pictures purporting to show how things used to be.

Of course, when the topic is examined in detail all kinds of problems of definition and qualifications arise. There are a number of problems in defining 'first-hand accounts'. How close to the event does a writer have to be? The account of the Roman conquest of Britain by the Roman writer Tacitus, is certainly more 'primary' than Collingwood's *Roman Britain* written in the twentieth century, yet Tacitus was describing events in which he himself had not participated, though his father-in-law, and one of his key 'sources', was the General, Agricola, who had played a leading role in the campaigns. Memoirs and autobiographies may be written some considerable time after a key event, and usually enjoy the benefit of hindsight. Some sources are both primary and secondary sources, in relation to different periods in the past.

Despite the difficulties, the teacher needs a rough working definition. If the teacher is not clear in his or her mind about what is 'evidence' and what is 'interpretation', there will be confusions and it will prove impossible to do full justice to Attainment Targets 2 and 3. Attainment Target 2 is concerned with studying interpretations of the past. Attainment Target 3 is about using historical evidence.

Books written in the present day by historians are undoubtedly secondary sources, each representing one person's view of what happened in the past. But other interpretations may not be so obvious at first sight. Simulations and reconstructions found in some theme parks and interpretation centres are also useful secondary sources. Indeed, one approach can be to investigate whether they offer a 'sanitised' or nostalgic view of the past. But the situation can be very confusing, as many museums and archaeological sites now also employ models and simulations in attempts to interpret their holdings and make their displays more attractive.

Some things are more genuine than others, or rather more firmly rooted in evidence. The straw-covered Viking houses at the Yorvik Viking Centre hide steel frames beneath their wattled walls; the figures and displays of goods are reconstructions, though the interpretation is rooted in evidence which is carefully displayed alongside the reconstruction. In fact the most recent reconstructions of Viking figures are very carefully based on evidence and are the result of a great deal of lengthy scientific research. The newest models at Yorvik are based on a computer reconstruction, which can take a skull and remodel the flesh on the human face; building up from the skeleton is the nearest we can get to what individual Vikings actually looked like.

Period rooms in a museum are usually reconstructions and interpretations of the past, though they may well contain primary source material, the furniture and genuine artefacts from the past, and an assortment of objects which may well belong to the same period but which come from many different sources. On the other hand, a room in a country house with its original furniture is genuine evidence, though even this will bear the marks of later alterations and additions and later use. Even at the primary stage, it has been shown that children can often grasp that a country house contains material that has accumulated over a long period. 'Is this genuine?' and 'When was it produced?' are vital questions when dealing with material evidence.

Primary sources are not necessarily more accurate than secondary sources. An account written by someone participating in some event or controversy may give a far more partial view than the carefully researched, balanced interpretation of a later historian who has sifted and weighed up all available evidence. Indeed a primary source, a written document or a newsreel film, may be biased, mistaken, or occasionally totally inaccurate (some wartime propaganda for instance). What is important for its value as evidence is that it is contemporary with the period under study.

In teaching history, pupils need to be encouraged to treat evidence from the past in a rather different way, from a secondary source. It is not simply information to be taken at face value. It is material that needs to be questioned, and evaluated. Pupils should be encouraged to cross-check one source against another. Nor is the fact that a document is biased a reason for dismissing the document as worthless or unreliable. Pupils need to learn that a biased document can be very useful indeed to the historian, because it may offer us insights into motives and attitudes of people in the past.

The distinction between primary and secondary sources will not always be immediately obvious to the pupil. Discussion and questioning will be needed to establish if it is evidence from the past, or if it is a later interpretation. With video, for instance, some children can be genuinely confused by dramatisations, though others can use the visual clues to categorise black and white archive film as coming from 'the past'. Dramatisations and reconstructions can be of great value in trying to convey to pupils an idea of the past, but they are none the less interpretations. They will be useful for Attainment Target 2 (Interpretations of History) though not Attainment Target 3 (Using Evidence).

The effective teacher of history will need to use both primary and secondary sources. The attainment targets in National Curriculum history require the use of both, but it is important to be aware of the distinction between them to avoid great confusion. Secondary sources and interpretations depend upon and must be tested against surviving primary evidence. 'When was it written?' and 'Is it real?' must be key questions to ask about any historical source or resource (see Figures 4.1 and 4.2).

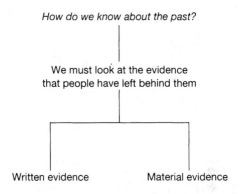

How do we know about the past?

We must look at the evidence
that people have left behind them

Written evidence   Material evidence

Figure 4.1   How do we know the past?

Documents

Written sources have become almost indispensable for today's history teaching. There are three prime reasons why they are so important.

First, no other type of historical evidence offers the historian such depths of insight into human conduct. Without devaluing the important contribution made by archaeology or place names or other kinds of evidence, written documents offer us so much more insight into the past. Often documents illuminate people's thought processes. They hint at how people thought and felt, at why they acted as they did. Even where things are not made explicit, we can sometimes infer information or attitudes. By definition 'history' begins when written records begin. Archive sources have very special qualities, and should therefore lie at the heart of any attempt to use primary evidence in the history classroom.

A second factor is the versatility of archive sources as a teaching resource. Documents (whether in facsimile, as transcripts, or in the form of short selected extracts) are particularly suitable for use in the classroom. There are many different ways in which history lessons can be 'document led'. Archive sources can be used for a wide variety of purposes, not just as illustrative material, and not only for their informational content, but also because of their potential for the development of historical skills and historical questioning.

Thirdly, it has long been recognised that written documents produced in the past often have a special quality, which is not

Visual evidence

Decorations
Statues, carvings, ornaments
Paintings and drawings
Tapestries and textiles
Seals
Coins
Engravings
Photographs
Cartoons
Film, television and video
Maps and plans
Air photographs, satellite
   photography

Other evidence

Children's games
Old customs
Ceremonies

Written records

Letters
Documents
Accounts
Bills and invoices, etc,
Minute books
Other financial records
Deeds
Registers
Acts and laws
Posters
Catalogues
Log books and diaries
Writs and orders
Census records
Maps and plans
Reports
Pamphlets, broadsheets
Newspapers and magazines
Posters and adverts
Books
Statistics
Inventories
Mathematical notations
Notes, memoranda
Other papers

Records of local government
Records of Parliament and
Central government
Business and industrial records
Estate records
Personal papers
Religious and philosophical writings
Literary writings
Scientific writings
Histories and chronicles
Biographies and autobiographies
Reminiscences written down
Memorials, gravestones
Coins
Inscriptions
Other records

(Written evidence includes material written or inscribed on paper, card, parchment, papyrus, stone, wood, metal, etc. or magnetic tape or disk.)

Oral evidence

Place names
Myths and legends
Sagas and Chronicles, etc,
   which may originally have
   been passed down orally
Reminiscences and interviews
Rhymes and poems, songs
Stories
Gramophone records and
   tape recordings

Figure 4.2   Types of evidence

THE EVIDENCE OF THE HISTORIAN

Landscape evidence

Field pattern and farm distribution
Settlements
Roads and tracks and paths
Buildings and monuments
The plan of settlements
Hedgerows and woodlands
Bridges, railways, harbours, etc.
Effects of man on the environment
Aerial photographs (these are useful
for showing historical features
surviving in today's landscape)

Physical evidence

Objects which have survived from
the past such as statues, carvings,
everyday objects, furniture,
clothing and jewellery, tools,
vehicles, etc.
Objects which may be collected in a
museum
Monuments and historic buildings

Archaeological evidence

Ruined or buried sites and buildings
Artefacts (things found on these
sites, for instance pottery, bone,
coins, charcoal, tools, weapons).

possessed by school textbooks or the writings of later historians. They were produced by people in the past. They offer a direct link with the past. Their physical appearance, as well as any informational content, is often important. More than twenty years ago, the archivist Emmison tried to convey to teachers what he felt to be the special qualities of an original document:

> The original document is in a sense more real than any text book can hope to be; for the writer, though he may have been misguided, biased or mistaken, at least lived through the events of which he speaks; and whatever his shortcomings, he was in certain respects better informed about the times and conditions in which he lived than is the interpreter writing two or three hundred years afterwards.
>
> There is too the fact that the original letter or document is charged with an emotion, an urgency, and an immediacy, to which the later printed record can never pretend ... At least for some – and probably for more than is generally imagined – the original document, letter or journal is the best door into the past.[1]

The local example of the national theme

When documents first began to be widely used in history teaching, local documents were often cited as a local illustration of the national theme. Using local sources in this way the history teacher was able to relate the particular history topic to the pupils' own locality and so to their own experience. In 1969, a number of contributors to 'history' had proposed the use of local documentary sources as a remedy for the perceived 'crisis' in history teaching at this time.[2] Local records offered one of the key ways of making history more 'relevant'. Often too a local document might be used as a springboard, as starter material allowing the teacher to work from the known and familiar locality to the wider historical context.

Use of local examples can often motivate, and hold attention. With primary school pupils and with lower ability pupils in particular, the local connection can be important, but all pupils can benefit from such material.

Sources for local history

Document sources are indispensible for most local history studies. Using the local area is particularly important at primary level, for instance. The square mile around the school can be the starting point for many enquiries, including investigations of a historical nature. Many primary teachers start investigations of the past by working out from the history of the school, village or local area.

The history of many localities and of most schools has still to be written, however, and a search in the library may often prove disappointing. Fortunately, most local record offices contain an abundance of sources for local history, going back at least two hundred years. Standard sources such as census, tithe maps and schedules, trade directories, school log books and school records, parish records, maps, government reports, newspapers, old photographs, and oral history sources offer a quarry of evidence which can be used in an active learning and enquiry process from Key Stage 2 onwards. This raw material, the 'building bricks' of local history, offers evidence which pupils can sift and use to piece together the history of their locality. Turning this 'heap of evidence' into a coherent and meaningful account of the past is a process which can directly foster historical skills.

National Curriculum history now requires all schools to produce their own school-designed units on local history, and in most cases teachers will need to make use of material from their county archives or local study centre.

Document-led exercises in history

Documents can form the basis of many exercises or activities in class.

Using single documents

An entire lesson's work can be generated by even a single document. Exercises, worksheets, and questions can centre on it. Ideas, hypotheses and historical concepts can be developed from it. It can form a focus for comprehension and discussion.

In approaching any historical document there should be a progression from lower order to higher order thinking. Pupils should be encouraged to move on from simple comprehension and factual questions to questions of a more historical nature. Comprehension questions are intended initially, to familiarise pupils with the document, and, in addition, to establish a certain body of knowledge about the document and especially about the process of its creation, that will form the foundation for enquiries directed at more 'historical' preoccupations.

Single sources can be used in a variety of ways and at various levels of sophistication (see Box 1). Younger pupils may be encouraged to compare the past with the present, developing concepts of similarity and difference. Pupils may be required to present information from the document in a different form. Some documents may offer evidence about attitudes. Others may deal with motivation, causation or the consequences of human actions. Some may be used to develop skills of inference, seeing meanings that are not explicitly stated. Documents can often be interpreted at several 'levels of meaning'. Some documents offer superb examples of bias. Different documents have different qualities and offer different avenues for discussion and investigation. An effective history teacher needs to be able to spot the potential of particular pieces of evidence and select carefully for a particular task.

Box 1

The following basic questions can be adapted and developed to suit virtually any written source. They are so simple that they can be used with pupils of any age group. They offer a graded level of difficulty, and they help to achieve progression towards higher order thinking.

- What is it?
- Who wrote it?
- When was it written?
- Why was it written?
- What does it say?
- How can I use it?
- How far can I trust it?
- What else can I compare this with?

Very often questions and tasks can lead on from work on the document to more open-ended enquiry or discussion, and to further research and investigation.

Groups of sources

Groups of documents offer even more versatile and creative teaching strategies. The teacher of history needs to learn how to put together a group of sources to target particular historical skills or concepts. One approach could be to select a number of different types of evidence on a related theme. A written source, a visual source and a statistical source is one fruitful combination. Pupils can be asked to assess the value of different types of sources and to compare the evidence they offer.

Two sources offering different accounts of the same issue or event, provide the history teacher with another very useful device. Sometimes this approach will be useful to highlight different viewpoints and attitudes to a particular event. Often this can lead on to valuable work on the subject of bias in documents. At other times the evidential value of two sources can be assessed. Pupils can be encouraged to compare and contrast different accounts, and to cross-check particular points, highlighting discrepancies, and correlations between the sources. Follow-up work could involve discussion of possible reasons for the discrepancies. Another technique might be to put a primary source alongside a later secondary account, inviting pupils to explore the differences between primary and secondary sources.

Documents have an important role in child-centred learning methods. Since pupils often learn far better by doing than by listening or looking, documents can be useful for a variety of active learning situations.

The evaluation of evidence and the study of bias

The evaluation of primary source material has been given increasing emphasis in recent years, most notably with changes such as GCSE or National Curriculum history. Pupils are often invited to ask questions about the completeness or the reliability of a source. To explore these avenues we usually need to know something about how or why the document was created, and what the writer could reasonably have been expected to know. Pupils will need to distinguish between fact and opinion, and to explore underlying motives or attitudes.

Documents offer many possibilities for the study of bias. Careful selection of the document is crucial. Often it can be useful to select a source with a strong and very obvious bias, at least initially. Even a single biased source can be useful. There is great scope for the study of 'value-laden' words and terms. Pupils could be asked to pick out or underline all the things which suggest bias or which are opinion rather than fact. A useful follow-up activity which can counter-balance the particular bias of the chosen document is to ask pupils to rewrite the document from an opposite point of view.

Some sources have a subtle rather than a very strong and obvious bias. These can be used to sharpen skills of inference and to focus on underlying attitudes, prejudices and entrenched beliefs, about which even the subject himself may not have been fully conscious.

This kind of exercise can build up a certain caution in approaching a document, and a realisation that not everything is to be taken at face value. The degree of sophistication will vary according to the age and abilities of the pupil. Pupils will also become aware of the need to check one source against another whenever possible. It is important, however, to ensure that a positive attitude is maintained towards the sources. There may be problems with using some sources, and documents may sometimes need to be treated with a degree of caution. A source might not tell us all we would like to know; a document may sometimes be biased – but these sources are still the only direct evidence we have, and the historian has to learn to use them effectively. Indeed, pupils should come to realise that biased sources are often very valuable to the historian in revealing the attitudes and values of people in the past.

Understanding viewpoints/empathy

The School's Council History project defined empathy as 'understanding without approbation'.[3] Although empathy has attracted considerable criticisms (and perhaps a degree of misunderstanding) a key objective in history teaching involves appreciation of how people in the past thought and felt. There is a need for pupils to appreciate a range of viewpoints. (This can be especially useful for coverage of Attainment Target 2.) The Schools Council history team rightly foresaw many difficulties and problems which could arise from empathy work. Many of these surfaced with the introduction of GCSE, in a heated debate over empathy, in the press and among parents, as well as among the teaching profession. Yet empathy is essential for historical understanding. It helps us to understand motivation. It underlines the fact that history is about real people. Very often it helps pupils to make the imaginative leap that is required of a historian.

One of the solutions adopted by teachers has been the use of specific documentary extracts to introduce and focus an empathy exercise. This has tended to replace previous strategies such as 'Imagine you were ...' Documents can offer stimulus and provide the sort of concrete detail and differentiation which are necessary for a successful exercise on empathy. One very fruitful device adopted at GCSE has been to select a certain kind of document, or group of documents, that carries an apparent contradiction. Getting the pupil to resolve the apparent 'dilemma' forms the basis of the exercise. It is the documentary sources that provide the heart of the exercise.

Using documents as a basis for class activities

Many class activities can arise from work focused around original written sources. This may include written work, answering questions or completing worksheets on a source, and whole class or group discussion. Activities can also take the form of drama, role-play or debate. Certain controversial issues may even be suitable for a trial.

Group presentations offer another approach for active learning using documentary sources. Groups can work on different sources or cover different topics, and the result of their investigations and conclusions can be shared with the rest of the class in a group activity or presentation.

Follow up work to the study of original sources might include elements of reconstruction or re-creation, often drawing on and synthesising information from a range of sources. Re-creating a typical Victorian school day is a highly successful follow-up at Key Stage 2 to work on school log books, school photographs, and inspector's reports, and so on. Re-creating an old-fashioned Christmas, cooking and trying out old recipes, modelling or trying different solutions to a problem such as bridge building – these are a few of the numerous possibilities for follow-up work. Often these activities may offer highly desirable cross-curricular links.

Successful work using primary evidence may lead on to creative expression, which may come from a synthesis of the information gathered from the documentary evidence.

Ways of presenting documentary sources

Ever since the spread of offset-litho printing and the photocopier, documents have been used extensively in facsimile to give some of the flavour and feel of the original document. Published compilations of documents have become readily available. Teachers can also visit their own local record office and obtain copies of local records of their own choice. Very localised examples from a particular town or village are often obtainable, and these can give history an added immediacy. Extracts from documents are increasingly being used in a range of textbooks. At first these tended to be employed mainly as illustrative material, but they are now increasingly being used as a means of developing certain historical skills or concepts.

Written sources can be used in transcript. This is a useful method, which shortcuts any possible problems of palaeography. It allows short extracts to be presented. The language of the original, or oddities of spelling or punctuation, can be amended to some degree – an important consideration when using such material with primary school pupils or pupils with learning difficulties. In editing a transcript some of the wordiness or digressions and sub-clauses, which are often found in official documents, may be omitted. While purists may question the editing of documents, with younger age groups or lower ability, some simplification is justifiable; pupils must be able to understand a source before they can make use of it. Young children, too are incapable of grasping many variables at the same time, and a source that is too complicated can confuse or distract. Any simplification can also be justified by the fact that there will be progression in the National Curriculum course. Skills can be refined at a later date. Topics can be revisited, when pupils are capable of greater understanding and a more sophisticated approach.

More recently, archive sources have also been used in newer computer formats, in databases, viewdata programmes or telex simulations for instance. Often the computer can be connected to a printer to provide an instant printout.

Presentation of documents by oral means offers another avenue. In its most sophisticated form radio has produced some memorable compilations, dramatising the texts of documents and adding in a variety of sound effects. Taped sources can be effective, especially for pupils with reading difficulties or visual handicap. Certain sources, such as letters or diary extracts lend themselves particularly well to this form of presentation.

Although these methods offer an effective means of using documentary source material in the classroom, there are strong arguments for bringing pupils into contact with original documents at some stage in their school career. The original documents are themselves artefacts, and there can be great value for pupils in seeing and even handling parchment and yellowed paper. It can bring them literally in touch with the past. Most local record offices encourage educational group visits. Often groups can be given a 'familiarisation visit', going behind the scenes in the archives to learn about the range of documents and the methods of preserving and caring for them. Such visits can form a very useful introduction to a history course.

Much of the time pupils will work on sources that have been carefully selected by the teacher. At some stage a visit to the archives can also be useful to introduce a wider range of sources. Coursework at Key Stage 4, for instance, can have a valuable function of requiring the pupil to select material that is relevant for a particular enquiry.

Box 2
Instructions for your coursework

(1) Select at least three pieces of evidence that relate to your chosen topic.
(2) Say why they are relevant and explain how they are useful as evidence.
(3) Remember to keep a record of where you got your material.

Coursework is making increasing use of primary sources.

How to use your local record office

The county record office or other local archives should be a focal point for all teachers of history. Some have an education officer and can offer schools special help, but even offices with less developed services offer an important bank of local primary source material. Any history teacher moving into a new area should make contact with their local archives. The following points should be noted:

(1) It is important to get to know how the finding aids work, so that history teachers can locate relevant documents.
(2) Teachers should appreciate that the staff cannot do their research for them, and should be prepared to help themselves, though they will usually find the staff to be extremely helpful.
(3) Many archives have compiled reference 'packs' for popular topics which can be extremely useful, even if they do not cover every need. Many archives also publish a variety of document packs, source books, posters, postcards, and so on.

(4) Most local record offices allow group visits to the office. As well as offering tours of the record office and general introductions to archive sources, some have a group room/classroom where groups can work on particular topics.

(5) Some record offices offer in-service courses, or workshops to allow teachers to prepare their own teaching materials, or will cooperate with teachers' groups producing resource materials.

(6) Pupils may need to visit individually for coursework or project work. The teacher should always notify the record office in advance and check that there is suitable material for a particular topic. Pupils should be well prepared, and it is advisable to issue them with a guidance sheet that can be shown to the staff.

(7) Archive material is unique and irreplacable, and history teachers should handle original material carefully and encourage their pupils to do the same. On occasions offices may require pupils to use copies, especially of popular or fragile material.

(8) Staff in record offices will appreciate occasional feedback about how their material has been used.

(9) Many offices produce teacher's handbooks or information sheets, offering further guidance.

Pictorial sources

Visual sources, pictures, sketches and paintings, photographs and engravings are usually eagerly sought after for use in teaching history. Old photographs can be located in the collections of archives, museums, or local studies centres and in some libraries. Friends, families and members of the community may be another source for photographs of the last 50 years or so.

Photographs

Photography was invented in 1827 by Niépce. The earliest photographs (available from the 1840s generally) tend to be formal posed portraits. Not all old photographs are dated, but internal evidence may help to establish an approximate date. The original source print, (whether daguerrotype, albumen print, gelatine print, and so on) can offer valuable dating evidence. The back-drops to portrait photos in the photographer's studio can also offer important dating clues. Particular backdrops were fashionable at different times (and the furniture or background in an old photograph may tell us more about tastes and fashions in photographers' studios than it does about furniture in homes). By about 1880 street photos and action photos had become more common. Some photographs offer internal evidence (fashions, transport, and so on) that can help to date them.

Although it is often claimed that the camera does not lie, when using old photographs for historical purposes pupils need to give attention to the processes involved in choosing a subject and taking a photograph. They need to realise that a photograph can be just as carefully 'composed' as any painting. The intention of the photographer is something that needs consideration. 'Why was this photograph taken?' is one of the most important questions pupils can ask (see Box 3).

Box 3

This official war photograph and its caption were used in an exercise to investigate bias. There is a tendency to assume that 'the camera does not lie' and that photographs are bias-free, but in fact this exercise offers a useful corrective.

First, the photograph was introduced to the class without its caption. Pupils were encouraged to discuss the evidence in the photograph, to suggest who the people were and when it was taken. Suggestions and hypotheses had to be backed up wherever possible by evidence in the photograph. Pupils were also asked about the impact the photograph had upon them. Then they were asked to write their own caption for it.

Next, the pupils opened sealed envelopes containing the original caption. Presenting the caption sealed in an envelope (strictly not to be opened until the word was given!) offered a simple device which had the effect of heightening curiosity and motivation. After some initial discussion of the caption, pupils compared it with the captions they themselves had written.

Next, they were asked to underline all words (value words) that carried any suggestion of bias or attitude. This led on to a great deal of further discussion, about bias and the role of propaganda in war-time.

The pupils then reconsidered the photograph in the light of their new knowledge. They were asked to consider the process of taking the photograph and why the photographer had selected these particular soldiers. Pupils were now alerted to the 'messages' the photograph was carrying. Gradually they came to realise that even a photograph can be biased, that certain aims of the photographer can influence the choice of what is photographed.

Finally the source was related to the wider context, the course of the Second World War, and the audience for whom this photograph was intended. They went on to consider in more general terms the important role played by propaganda in the Second World War.

As well as offering useful material for the evaluation of evidence (How far can I trust it?) and for Attainment Target 3, this photograph and caption could also offer some useful material for Attainment Target 2 on interpretations in history. Differences between the pupils' own captions and the 'official' caption might be examined. Pupils might also be asked to consider how the German side might have captioned the photograph, or reacted to it.

The Master Race! Wearing a ground sheet to protect his oversized great coat from the rain, a German prisoner who surrendered after heavy fighting in the Hurtgen Forest area stands dejected and war weary. On the left a young Nazi soldier still wears a look of sullen German arrogance, as they await disposition to a prison camp.
Source: US Official Photo No. EA 47224 (WA)
Distributed through the OWI (Office of War Information)

roduced by artists – engravings, wood-cuts, portraits
aintings

efore the age of photography, engravings and wood-cuts are available
from the fifteenth century to the nineteenth century. These originate
from artists' sketches that were engraved onto copper or steel plates, or
wooden blocks in earlier times, and reproduced by a printing process.
Paintings, drawings, and portraits are other useful pictorial sources,
and for the Middle Ages the decorations and embellishments in
medieval manuscripts, books of hours and church panels form another
excellent pictorial source.

While all primary sources need to be assessed and handled with a
degree of caution, with artist's material there are additional
considerations. As well as allowing for the 'artist's licence' we need to
remember that artists often had to satisfy patrons, or produce work that
would sell. There were also different conventions surrounding painting
at different periods. Picture appreciation may involve reading clues or
decoding messages which give information about the subject's social
status, tastes and fashions at that time. There is sometimes a hidden
symbolism that would have been apparent to people at that time. We
should also try to gauge the attitude of the artist to his subject; here
again there may be coded 'messages'. Some pictures, Victorian
engravings for instance, may be more useful for telling us about
Victorian tastes, fashions, and expectations than for the scenes they
portray.

Artists do not only record the world about them. They often choose
to depict historical scenes. These should be treated as secondary
sources, 'interpretations' of the past. Such things are extremely useful
for that purpose, and for Attainment Target 2 in National Curriculum
history.

Symbolism can be another complicating factor because art operates
on many levels of understanding. Quite soon after the execution of
Charles I, for example, many artists rendering his final moments, show
Charles almost as a 'Christ figure', a martyr. This may not be very
accurate as a depiction of what actually happened, but it is extremely
valuable in showing the myths and popular interpretations that have
grown up afterwards.

Learning to 'read' pictures

There seems to be a general assumption that picture sources are
particularly suitable for use at Key Stage 1 and Key Stage 2.
Doubtless this view is influenced by the fact that children's reading
ability is more limited at this time. However, studies by Gill Aslett and
Joan Blyth[4] and several more recent investigations have stressed that
young children need to be trained to 'read' pictures. Indeed on being

presented with a picture, pupils may look at it for only a very short time and give only the most cursory replies when questioned about various features. Training is needed to enable them to derive greater value and information from the source. One of the tests of the success of this training in 'picture reading' will be that pupils will gradually spend more and more time looking at the picture, and 'reading' it at various levels (see Box 4).

Box 4
Some ways of using pictures in the primary school

(1) looking for the story in the picture;
(2) looking for clues;
(3) reading the picture at different scales;
(4) looking at the picture at different levels;
(5) using the picture as evidence;
(6) comparing things in the the picture with things today;
(7) comparing an old picture with a modern picture;
(8) comparing two pictures with similar subjects from different periods;
(9) sequencing two or more pictures;
(10) on-going research into some topic covered in the picture.

Methods and techniques for using pictorial sources

Various techniques can be employed in this process:

(1) *How do we look at pictures?* One teacher started by asking her class what caught their attention first. Pupils then drew the path that their eyes travelled round the picture. Leading on from this, the class discussed how they looked at pictures, and how the picture was composed.
(2) *Is there a story in the picture?* The importance of story at Key Stage 1 and 2 is highlighted by this approach. Pupils could be encouraged to ascertain what is going on in the picture, what has happened or is about to happen, why are people doing certain things.
(3) *Pictures can be read at various levels.* There is the overall impression of a picture, and focus on sections of the action, and finally on small details.
(4) *Looking for clues.* It is important to encourage children to look for clues, and to realise that some small detail (a crest on the side of a coach, for instance, or a sign above a shop) may have an important bearing on the story or meaning of the picture.

(5) *What does this tell us about the people in the picture?* Enquiry can be fostered by asking 'Who is the most important person in the picture?', looking at gestures and expressions, or asking 'What clues can we get about a person's wealth or social status?'

(6) *Use of symbols.* Sometimes pupils can appreciate that certain things are used as symbols.

(7) *Is there a sub-plot?* Artists' pictures in particular often contain several storylines within them. Sometimes there are 'sub-plots' taking place in the picture as well as the main story.

(8) *Skills of inference.* Pupils can be encouraged to use a picture as evidence and to deduce and infer further things from what they see. Often the topics explored may be quite different from the ostensible main subject or happening in the picture. A picture of a street scene, for instance, can give rise to many avenues of investigation. What does this tell us about people's clothes at that time? How did people travel then; and does this suggest anything about the state of the roads? What were houses made of at this time? Were the streets paved? How are things different today?

(9) *Generating activities.* Use of a picture will often lead on to further activity. A class might be asked to tell a story to explain the picture, or they might be provided with more information to help them understand it. There could be drama or role-play. They may go on to use further sources to discover more about a particular topic.

(10) *Comparing pictures.* Very often more than one picture can be used in an exercise. Initially pupils often find it far easier to compare a past picture and a present picture than to compare two pictures from different periods of the past. Pupils could be asked to sequence two or more pictures, to say which came first. The exercise should be followed by discussion with pupils being asked for their reasons.

(11) *Learning specialist language.* Often children's response to a picture is limited by their vocabulary and their ability to describe features. It is important that they slowly build up a historical vocabulary, and learn some of the technical terms that will allow them to talk about what they can see.

(12) *Using pictures of people.* A group photograph can be the starting point for further investigative work with pupils at Key Stage 1 or 2. A family picture or a photo of a group of workmen, servants, and so on could be used. Children can be asked to 'be' one of the characters and describe their clothes, tools, work, or lifestyle, doing further research to fill in the details.

> **Box 5**
> **Using the Bayeux tapestry at Key Stages 1 and 2**
>
> Picture sources used can include very old sources. Some excellent historical work has been done at Key Stages 1 and 2 using carefully selected frames from the Bayeux tapestry. John West, for instance,[5] successfully used the following exercise with infants and with a remedial group of 10 year olds. He selected eight frames from the tapestry which related to key points in the 'story' behind the tapestry – William's claim to the throne of England and Harold's denial of that claim. After a whole class introductory session, he gave groups one of the frames together with an outline of the story and asked them to decide which event their frame showed. The class later put the frames in the correct sequence on the wall to tell the story. Further work and questions focused particularly on the concept of cause and consequence (now part of Attainment Target 1) discussing reasons for various actions; who had the best claim to the throne of England, William or Harold?, etc., etc.
>
> In a similar exercise another student teacher on her teaching practice encouraged pupils to use the tapestry as a fountain of information and evidence on medieval life. Groups were allocated a topic such as clothes, houses, buildings and castles, fighting techniques, and so on. Each group was asked to find evidence in the tapestry about their topic, then share their findings with the rest of the class in a display. This time it was Attainment Target 3 on the use of historical evidence that lay at the heart of the exercise. The same material can be exploited in very different ways to develop different skills.

Artefacts

Artefacts, that is objects that were produced in the past, have great value for the teaching of history. In a very real way they put us in touch with people in the past, especially ordinary people. Objects are often excellent material to use with very young children, who have not yet developed reading and writing skills. They are also for the same reason very suitable for lower ability pupils or for multicultural groups, and can be a useful leveller. But all pupils will benefit from contact with genuine artefacts from the past. Use of artefacts also offers many important cross-curricular links. Even damaged or broken objects can be useful. It is not always necessary to have the entire object – a broken piece of the rim of a plate can give us nearly as much information as the entire plate could have done.

The previous experience of many teachers of history may have been largely book-based or document-based, and teachers may need to acquire skills in using and questioning historical objects. The support of museum education services and the in-service course offered by many museums will be important in equipping the history teacher with the skills for utilising artefacts and other museum resources.

Museum objects are versatile and can be used to develop historical understanding in a number of ways.[6]

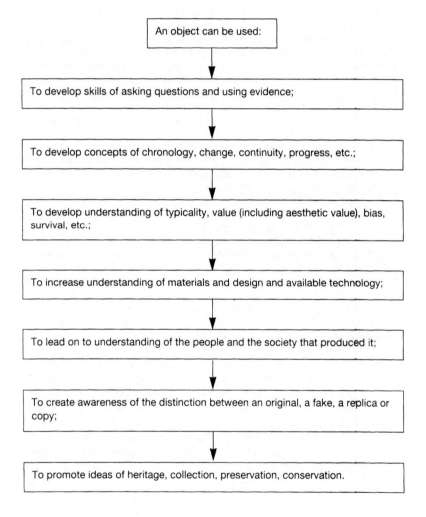

Figure 4.4   Using museum objects to develop historical understanding

Questioning objects

Asking questions about objects, classifying
information from close observation can sign..
understanding. 'What is it?' or 'What date is it?' are no.
the best questions to ask first (see Box 6). These two question..
paradoxically, may actually stop further historical enquiry in its trac.
as pupils may feel that once an object has been labelled and identified,
there is little more to be said about it. 'What is it made of?' and 'How
was it made?' are far better starting points and can lead on to the
extraction of a great deal of information about the people and the
society that produced it.

Box 6
Looking at an old object

(1) What is it like?	What does it look like, feel like, smell like? What is it made of? Is it made of one substance or several substances? Is it complete or broken, or a fragment? Why did they use these materials?
(2) How was it made?	Do we know who made it or how or where it was made? Is it made in one piece or several pieces? How has it been fixed together? Is it handmade or machine made? How many people helped to produce it? Are there any clues that tell us about the process of its manufacture?
(3) What was it for?	Why was it made? What is it? How was it used or how did it work? Is it well designed? Has it ever been used for a different purpose?
(4) How old is it?	Do we know when it was made or used? Do we know where it has come from or where it was found? Does it look old, and if so why? Is it real or a replica? Is it worn or damaged? What is it made of – does that give us clues? Does the way it is made give us any clues? Has it been altered or mended?
(5) What does it tell me about the people in the past?	Was it a special or valuable object or was it something common? Is it decorated or carefully designed? Was it valuable? Would we use something like this today? Is it valuable today? What sort of people owned or used it – were they rich and important or ordinary people?
(6) What else can I compare it with?	Can I compare this object with any others? Have they used the best materials? Have objects like this changed very much? Can I find any pictures of people using it?

any objects offer clues that tell us how they were made – an air ble in a piece of mouth-blown glass, or the tell-tale edge that the n in the mould has left all around a cast-iron object, or the mpression of a paw print left by a stray cat on a Roman clay roof tile. Items such as these indicate just how much information objects can carry about the processes of their creation. Some questions may be answered from the object itself. Other questions may lead on to further enquiry and research.

Using objects calls for close observation, and allows pupils to develop hypotheses 'What could it have been for?' 'How did they use it?' 'Is it genuine or a replica?' 'Which of two objects is earlier?' It calls on pupils to test their ideas against the evidence, and to give reasons. It forces them to tease out information from inanimate objects.

Comparing two objects, or sequencing a number of objects is an activity that can help to deepen understanding of change and continuity. Historical objects provide links with the people who made and used them. Actually handling an old object can provide a tangible link with the past. Objects ought to lead to investigations about the society that produced them and the people who used them. Objects frequently provide a link with very ordinary people in the past, the sort of people who may have left few other records of themselves (see Box 7).

Box 7
The quarryman's boot – a pupil's response

Mr Williams found this old boot in the attic. It is very heavy. There is so much grey dust that you can't see the colour it was once. He must have worked in the quarry. It is a size 8. Inside it says T. Ingham, Manchester. There is metal round the toe to protect his foot if he dropped a big stone on it. I wonder who it was that wore this boot and what he was like.[7]

An artefact should lead on to the people who made or used it.

Where are historical objects to be found?

Some common, fairly recent objects may be brought into school by pupils, or may be fairly easily acquired from junk shops, or as loans from parents or the elderly, although prices are rising even for twentieth-century objects. It is not necessary for every school to have its own collection, however, especially as old objects require care and conservation. Certainly for earlier periods the rarity and high monetary value of items will place them beyond the reach of schools. Replicas offer one possible channel, and many museum shops and heritage shops sell these. Replicas are very useful for reconstruction activities. A class can fill and light a replica pottery Roman oil lamp, whereas a 2000-year-old original would need to be handled with great care. But schools should not rely continually on replicas, and when they are used the fact that they are copies should be acknowledged. As was emphasised earlier 'Is it genuine?' is an important question, but there is a real need for pupils to come into contact with genuine, quality artefacts, that are some of the best examples of their kind, and this involves regular visits to the nearest general museum, to do work in depth on particular groups of genuine old objects.

Museum education services

Many museums offer schools on-site object handling sessions, organised by a professional museum education officer. Teachers should certainly take advantage of these services where available. Close first-hand contact with a small number of genuine artefacts is of tremendous value, allowing pupils to see and touch, and to develop techniques of questioning. Introductory handling sessions followed by work in the galleries generally allow pupils to get far more benefit from a museum visit than use of the exhibition galleries alone, where objects may be displayed behind glass.

Museum loan services to schools are another useful resource for history teaching. Boxes of objects and associated material can be borrowed for use in the classroom. A class doing the Home Front, for example, could borrow a box containing gas masks, ARP (Air Raid Protection) equipment, a ration book and other associated period objects. When using museum loan services, history teachers should also take advantage of any support offered by a museum's education staff. In-service courses, for instance, are offered by many museum education services, and can show teachers how to get the full potential from an item. Some museum education officers will also travel out to a school with a handling collection and conduct sessions in school. This could be especially useful as preparation before a museum visit.

Using groups of objects

Just as small groups of documents are often far more useful to the history teacher than the single source, so artefacts often yield their greatest potential when grouped together.

Sequencing
Sequencing objects can help to develop ideas of chronology, and concepts of change and continuity. Groupings of objects can highlight similarity and difference between different periods and cultures.

Grouping objects of the same period
Examining a number of artefacts of the same period can help to build up a composite picture of a society and culture. This calls for skills of synthesis. Objects can also be used most successfully alongside documents and other sources.

Using objects in problem solving exercises
Small groups of objects can sometimes be most effectively used in problem solving activities. These activities are sometimes offered by museum education services. They can develop skills of deduction and evaluating evidence. Pupils may be invited to play at being a detective to resolve some mystery, or they might investigate the contents of a seaman's chest, a collection of craftsman's tools, or a doctor's bag, or a lady's valise, for example to help pupils to build up a picture of the people who used them.

Using artefacts in living history and recreations
At museums or historic buildings children, often dressed in costume, may be able to use and handle old equipment – old washing equipment, for instance, or Victorian schoolroom equipment.

Museums and historic buildings
It is important that field trips and museum and site visits form an integral part of the school curriculum for history (Report National Curriculum History working group)

Ideally an out-of-school visit of some kind is desirable in nearly every history study. This could involve use of the local environment, making use of a relevant local site or sites in the locality, or it could involve a visit to a major historic site, building or museum which offers an example of the best of its kind.

Site visits and museum visits should be a regular feature in the schemes of work for history. It is important, too, that a particular class group or year group should enjoy varied experiences on different visits. They must be allowed to benefit fully from the rich experiences that museum and site visits can offer.

Museums, historic buildings and historical sites and places of historic interest are key resources for history teaching. There is a vast range, and the facilities and opportunities offered by these vary considerably. Ideally, if finance permitted, there would be a site visit, or perhaps several visits for every history topic. Teachers will wish to use local examples near at hand, in order to relate the themes and issues of history directly to the pupil's own area, and also because encouraging appreciation of the built heritage is a key objective of history teaching (appreciating history all around us). At some stage teachers will also wish to take groups further afield to see examples that are some of the best of their kind. If there is a good general historical museum within the region, offering wide ranging collections, then this is a resource that pupils should return to many times over the years, to pursue different enquiries.

Whatever the topic covered, museums and historic sites offer pupils the genuine article, whether it is a Roman sandal or a nineteenth-century crinolene, an English country house or a medieval castle. Going on a site visit widens pupils' horizons and offers stimulation and 'hands-on' experiences that the classroom cannot provide. Reports of the National Curriculum History Committees in both England and Wales have stressed the importance of museum visits and site visits for the teaching of National Curriculum history. Objects and buildings made by people in the past offer a direct link with the past.

Site visits also generally offer teachers an excellent mechanism for covering all of the required key elements in the 'PESC' formula (the political/military, social, economic, and religious/cultural aspects of a topic or period). A visit to a country house for instance will probably include reference to some of the social groups and classes of the period under study (upstairs/downstairs, the estate workers, the craft or factory workers who produced many of the goods seen in the house); the role of the gentry as leaders and rulers of their society can be covered; there will be ample scope for looking at the economic and technological aspects of life in the period, especially if the house is related to its setting and the surrounding estate and countryside that supported it; finally there will be objects or rooms in the house which relate to cultural or religious life in the period.

Active learning through site visits

A visit to a museum, historical building or site of historical importance should involve far more than passive looking and listening or sightseeing. In the 1980s there has been a general move in museum education circles towards active learning experiences on site. This move towards child-centred experiences has been further encouraged by initiatives such as GCSE (General Certificate of Secondary Education), TVEI (Technical and Vocational Educational Initiative), CPVE (Certificate of Prevocational Education) and so on. Increasingly the guided tour or the teacher-dominated exposition is being replaced or supplemented by activities, experiences and exercises demanding greater participation or thought from the pupil.

Activities on the site visit

A range of on-site activities can be carried out during a visit. These may include information gathering, problem solving, participation in workshops, completing a task sheet, taking part in practical activities, creative work, handling and touching museum objects, looking at related documents or pictures, listening to music or participating in a tape recorded tour, or listening to a talk from an education officer. Some sites offer the potential for role-play, drama or an empathetic exercise, or even a full 'living history' experience, where pupils wear historic costume and carry out historical activities. Other activities may include following a trail. Educational visits involve doing and experiencing, as well as looking and listening.

Information collecting

Using a site visit as an information collecting exercise is one strategy adopted by many groups. This will be most successful if advance preparation has been carried out. Tasks should be clearly defined and every pupil must be clear about what is expected of him. On a large site pupils will not be able to cover everything in the time available, so pupils can be divided into groups and instructed to investigate different topics or features. Motivation is often increased if it is made clear to a group that they are covering a topic on behalf of the whole class and that their results will be shared by the rest of the class.

After the visit the information recorded by the groups needs to be pooled. The process of sharing 'their' information with others has a constructive role to play. It involves further active learning, calling for skills of presentation and communication, and also of listening, and questioning on the part of other groups. Above all it takes seriously the work done by the pupils on site, and incorporates it into further classwork. The exercise is not simply completed and then forgotten. The process as well as the final product is important. Working as a team, and working in unfamiliar surroundings are important.

Preparation for an information collecting exercise

(1) *How will information be gathered?*
Discuss with the pupils ways of gathering information:

listening;
looking;
handling and touching, feeling;
perhaps tasting or smelling;
seeing how things work;
seeing how things are constructed;
measuring and surveying;

asking questions and discussing;
reading;
looking at associated documents, or museum publications;
re-enactment and recreation;
using the imagination.

(2) *How will the information be recorded?*
Discuss with pupils various techniques of recording information during a visit:

making notes;
making sketches;
making a plan;
noting down measurements, etc.;
taking photographs;
using a video camera;
speaking into a cassette recorder;
recording various sounds on the site;
brass rubbings or stone rubbings;
artwork of various kinds;
collecting vocabulary to describe the place;
completing questions on a worksheet;
taking compass bearings.

(3) *What equipment do we need to take?*
Following on from these discussions, prepare a checklist of the equipment the group will need to take:

pencils and field notebooks;
clipboards;
graph paper for plans;
paper and crayons/charcoal for sketching;
tape measure;
compass;
other art materials;
camera;
video camera;
tape recorder.

Problem-solving activities

Problem solving is a strategy that has proved useful, especially with older pupils at Key Stages 3 and 4. In essence problem solving presents a new and challenging angle on a site or feature. It may involve role-play, or skills of presentation. It will certainly involve close observation and careful thought (see Boxes 8 and 9).

Box 8
What can problem-solving activities offer

(1) Problem solving offers a novel angle.
(2) Problem solving can motivate.
(3) Problem solving demands close observation, careful thought and skills of presentation.
(4) Most people respond to a challenge.

Box 9
Problem solving – some examples

At a castle site
The castle is not a ruin. It is the year 1284 and the new castle is just half completed. You are the King's officer sent to report progress on the castle. Write your report on the work that has been done so far, and what further work must be done to make the building secure against an attack.

At any site
There are proposals for a new motorway through here, and the building/site will be demolished/destroyed. Prepare a petition arguing that the site should be preserved.

At a prison building
You work for an organisation concerned with the welfare of prisoners. Write a report about the conditions and the treatment of prisoners at this building.

At a country house
You are a designer working for the BBC and want information about seventeenth-century costume and house interiors. Is there anything in this building that can help you?

Every site is different and the possibilities offered will vary, but problem solving offers teachers a transferable method that can be adapted to most sites. On most sites there will be dozens of possibilities. Some of these may offer opportunities which lean more towards science, technology or maths work – drawing up and costing a cleaning contract for a historic building (How exactly does one clean that crystal chandelier? What sort of cleaning method will avoid damaging those fragile old fabrics? How did people in the past clean this room, and are old-fashioned methods or modern methods better? How long does a job take? How many hours of labour will be needed?). These may be very useful where it is hoped to build in cross-curricular links. However, often the history teacher will look for problem-solving exercises which involve historical objectives – historical understanding, empathy, synthesis, use of evidence, and so on.

On-site interpretation – talks, guided tours, audio-visual presentations, etc.

Some establishments offer talks, or guided tours (with a guide or with audio equipment) or audio visual presentations. The teacher should always preview these to determine if they are suitable, and assess if the language level, content, and so on is suitable. Often most benefit is gained if the teacher goes over key points with the group afterwards to check on understanding. If there is a museum classroom the group can gather there to recap on what they have learned, towards the end of the visit.

It is important that the teacher should find out exactly what the museum, site or building offers. Certain museums offer a set 'visitor experience', at others there is flexibility or choice over what is offered (see Box 10).

Box 10
Museum education services

These are some things a museum education service may offer schools:

- advice on planning visits;
- introductory talks, guided tours;
- handling sessions using real museum objects;
- workshops, on-site activities;
- demonstrations;
- 'taught sessions';
- activity packs, worksheets;
- teacher's notes;
- in-service courses for teachers;
- sessions for trainee teachers;
- living history activities, re-enactments;
- sixth form courses;
- loan of resources to use on site;
- possible loan of material to use in school;
- possible visits by education officers to schools.

At some museums interpretation is offered, in whole or in part, through people in role carrying out craft work or demonstrations, or talking to visitors. The Museum of the North at Beamish, for instance, is one where people provide the main interpretation on the site. In these cases it can be useful to know whether the interpreters are instructed to stay in role at all times or whether they may step out of role. This might be relevant for National Curriculum history Attainment Target 2 on interpretations of history, for instance.

Wherever there is a museum education officer, it is well worth requesting advice or on-site help for an educational visit. Museum education officers are professionals with considerable experience of the educational use of museums. If he or she is apprised in advance of your particular aims and objectives, and work the pupils have already done on the topic, and so on, the session can often be very carefully tailored to get maximum value from the visit. The education officer will also pitch his or her talk at a suitable level for the age group concerned, something that is not always achieved by an ordinary guide. Education officers are aware of many possibilities for using and interpreting the site, and can often pass on methods or good ideas that have proved successful with other groups.

Worksheets

The use of worksheets on a site or museum visit evokes varied responses among teachers and museum education officers. Some oppose the use of worksheets, others make regular use of them. Others make occasional use of them to structure observation and enquiry (see Box 11).

Box 11
Worksheets for use on site

(1) They should encourage pupils to look carefully at the site or objects.
(2) They should encourage higher order thinking.
(3) There should be an element of progression.
(4) They should demand a varied range of activities.
(5) They may include a creative, empathetic, or problem solving exercise.
(6) They could encourage comparison of two things that are not adjacent.

There is no doubt that some worksheets are simply banal, and it may be these that have given them a bad name – especially the quiz type that simply ask 'How many?' or 'What?' Pupils can become bored if asked to complete a lengthy worksheet at every site. However, worksheets can be useful. They can structure activity and direct attention to particular topics. They can focus on historical concepts like change over time. They can convey important information as well as ask questions, which can enhance understanding of the site. Many can be extremely imaginative, and attractively illustrated. Some can develop higher order thinking in a highly constructive way – for instance pupils could be asked to compare two features that are not adjacent to each other, but are found in different parts of the building.

Pupils must not become so intent on filling in the answers, that they ignore other important factors such as the 'feel' and atmosphere of the site. Direct experience of 'the real thing' must after all remain the primary purpose of any site visit. Organisation during the visit can play a part. Worksheets could be distributed in the second half of the visit, once the group has had an opportunity to explore and react to the site.

Much will depend on the particular aims and objectives of the teacher. Generally, however, worksheets should ask questions that require direct observation on site. They should not consist purely of lower order questions, 'What?' 'How many?', etc. (e.g. 'How many arrow slits are there in the north wall?'), but should include questions of 'Why?' and 'How?' (e.g. 'Explain why it is so difficult for an attacker to get in through the castle gate').

Worksheets can be especially useful if they encourage the pupil to compare one feature with another, especially features in different places on the site. They can also include questions which ask pupils to put themselves in the place of some person in the past. They may include a problem-solving activity. At the end a creative response may be required. Generally there should be some question which asks pupils to synthesise the data they have gathered at different parts of the site.

Some worksheets may begin with simple lower order questions, leading on to a higher order question. For instance, after completing some lower order questions about individual features in a Victorian gaol, pupils were asked to synthesise this information: 'Explain why it is so difficult to escape from this prison.' On a complex site, rather than try to cover the whole site, it may be far better to structure a worksheet around the investigation of one particular feature, or one particular theme.

Many museums employing specialist education officers offer teachers sample worksheets. Museum professionals know the site and the collections very well, and their productions may often prove helpful (especially to teachers who may be less familiar with the site or museum). They frequently offer useful ideas and strategies, but should usually be considered as examples only. Inevitably they will not suit every need, but in many cases they can be adapted, used as models or as a source of ideas for a teacher-produced worksheet, which can target particular objectives and be tailored for a particular age or ability range.

An alternative to the questionnaire-type of worksheet, is the field booklet or pamphlet with pre-selected headings and blank spaces where the pupils can jot down their own notes on particular features, or make plans and annotated sketches.

Increasingly pupils who have prepared in advance for the visit may arrive armed with their own list of questions and topics that they wish to investigate. The computer or concept keyboard is becoming a useful tool in the preparation work for site visits. Pupils could use the computer to prepare for their visit and arrive provided with printouts of data-sheets or lists of questions. Data collected during the visit could be input onto a database on return to school.

For instance, before a visit to a castle, pupils could draw up a list of features often found in castles and investigate how many of the features their chosen castle possessed. Has it got:

a moat;
a gatehouse;
outer walls;
concentric defences;
projecting towers;
a drawbridge;
portcullis;
draw bars at the gate;
a keep;
towers;
murder holes?

Where is it?

on a hill;
by the sea;
at a river crossing;
on an important route.

Data about different castles could be put into the computer and the different castles compared. This exercise would be especially useful if it was used in work looking at the development of castles, from motte and bailey, to stone keep, to sophisticated fortress.

Using other resources on site

The history teacher adopting an evidence based approach will regularly use document sources in the classroom, but there can be an added advantage in looking at relevant documents or pictures in the historic surroundings themselves. Many historic buildings and museums offer their own resource packs. If there is a museum education officer, he or she may be able to offer help or resources. Period music could be played or performed on site. A poem or a literary extract might be read during the visit. Site visits can offer valuable cross-curricular links. One group of children built working models of medieval seige equipment in their technology class (e.g. a trebuchet and a mangonel). One of the aims in technology was to evaluate different designs by a series of tests. The exercise was given added spice when pupils carried out their tests (to see which machine could hurl a missile the furthest) on a site visit to a real medieval castle where such machines would have been used.

Drama, and role-play on site

On occasions pupils may engage in drama and role-play during a site visit. This is easiest at places which allow schools access at times exclusively for educational visits, or where some special space can be set aside where a group can work undisturbed. Often it is easier to arrange this out of season than at the height of the busy tourist period. The museum staff should always be informed of your intentions in advance. Some museums will offer specialist help for this activity.

Drama work in a historic setting need not involve a polished 'performance' but rather a workshop situation where every pupil is encouraged to enter into the thoughts and the feelings of a historical character, or perhaps several characters in turn. It may involve the use of relevant historic documents. It will certainly involve a lot of discussion and asking questions, and an appreciation of the setting. It is excellent for developing empathy (putting themselves in the shoes of a person from the past), or perhaps exploring an event from different viewpoints (to target interpretations of history). Imagination can be stimulated by the setting itself and also through awakening the senses, touching objects, experiencing sounds, tastes and smells, perhaps even playing a short excerpt of period music.[8]

Organised events, 'living history sessions', activities, theatre in education workshops, etc.

An increasing number of educational days or events are being offered by bodies such as English Heritage at historic sites. These usually involve pupils wearing historical costume and carrying out tasks of a historical nature appropriate to the site. Pupils may become medieval monks (or nuns) in a monastery, listening to an address by the abbot, taking part in worship, acting as medieval scribes, or doing more mundane tasks such as gardening or preparing food and eating a medieval meal.

Many smaller museums offer similar shorter sessions, where pupils can carry out certain activities appropriate to the historical site in question – such as lessons in a Victorian classroom, washday or cookery sessions in a cottage or kitchen, or working as a servant in a large country house. If it fits in with your scheme of work, these may be extremely useful at Key Stages 1 and 2. For older pupils, theatre in education workshops may be more appropriate.

Many historic sites and museums will also be willing to cooperate in events and performances at historic sites devised and organised by the schools themselves.

Handling sessions, workshops, etc.

Where there is a museum education officer, pupils will often be offered sessions handling objects, or participating in other activities. A considerable number of museums have special handling collections, usually drawn from the reserve collection. Very often pupils will benefit from the opportunity to see and handle, and discuss a few selected artefacts at close hand, before going on to work in the display galleries. Sometimes the sessions may take place in the galleries themselves. There are advantages in being able to relate the objects handled to other items on display. In other cases, especially if space is limited, handling sessions will take place in a special classroom, where there may be other related resource material available and where practical follow-up activities can be carried out.

At Warrington museum, for instance, pupils were offered opportunities to handle Roman tiles and pottery. Careful examination of one roof tile revealed the impression of an animal paw-print. This offered clues about the process by which they were made. They may have been left outside to dry before being fired. Because this museum possessed its own pottery kiln, pupils went on to make and decorate their own clay roof tiles, which were then fired in the kiln.

Museums and the lower ability pupil

Site visits are of great value with the so-called 'lower ability' or 'remedial pupil'. They offer valuable sensory experiences, and opportunities. However techniques need to be developed to make best use of the opportunities. The visit may need to be broken down into a series of short and varied experiences. It may be necessary to stop at intervals to go over certain key points in order to check on the degree of understanding, or to reinforce a point while it is fresh in the memory. Full use needs to be made of tactile and sensory experiences. Site visits can awaken motivation, and pupils learn by direct experiences which are not dependent on reading ability.

Cross-curricular possibilities

In museums or on site visits pupils may learn in ways not possible in the classroom. The 'hands-on' experiences and direct sensory experiences are unique strengths of museum education. Museums and site visits also offer oportunities for learning across the curriculum. Nor are the curricular links only with humanities or 'arts' subjects. There are many excellent opportunities for work in science or technology during an out-of-school visit. Very often the experience of a site visit can be enhanced by cross-curricular work. A visit to a historical site may be enhanced by carrying out artwork or creative writing or drama work. Pupils sometimes respond to a site more fully if their senses are heightened.

There is also a strong practical argument for involving teachers of other subjects. Out-of-school visits are expensive and can be disruptive of the curriculum and of school routines. Therefore the more subjects that can benefit, the greater the chance there is of such visits taking place. With the advent of the National Curriculum, many museums will be able to offer advice on what subjects and attainment targets can be covered by a visit, and at what levels. The museum education officer may well be able to suggest combinations of subjects applicable to a particular age group. Primary schools will of course carry out a range of cross-curricular work, but there can be great benefits from this approach at secondary level also.

Preparation and follow-up

To get full value from a visit, adequate preparation and follow-up are vital. This involves preparing the pupils for the visit as well as dealing with all the practicalities of the arrangements for transport, bookings, and so on (see Boxes 12 & 13).

Box 12
How to get the best from a visit to a museum, historic building or site

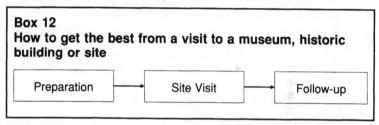

Preparation → Site Visit → Follow-up

Box 13

What the museum needs to know from the school

(1) Name address and phone number of school.
(2) Name of contact teacher.
(3) Date and time of visit.
(4) How many pupils, and teachers/helpers.
(5) Age/ability range of the pupils.
(6) How long class will spend on site.
(7) What the group wishes to see on site and special areas/galleries/facilities the group intends to use.
(8) How the group will be organised on site.
(9) Aims and objectives of the visit.
(10) Whether any assistance is required from the education officer or other museum staff.

Continued

What the teacher needs to know from the museum

(1)   What the site/museum can offer. What is there to do or see?
(2)   When is it open, and what are the arrangements for booking school visits? Is it open by arrangement out of season?
(3)   Are there any times when schools can enjoy exclusive use of the site?
(4)   Where is it? How to get there. Parking, etc.
        Cost. Arrangements for payment, etc.
(5)   Any capacity restrictions on the size of group that can be accommodated at one time?
(6)   Any requirements on teacher/pupil ratios?
(7)   Whether certain facilities need to be pre-booked.
(8)   Is there a classroom or reception area for groups, or a place where packed lunches can be eaten?
(9)   Is there an education officer and can the museum offer any special help, activities or facilities?
(10) Practical details like toilets/refreshments/shop.
(11) How much of the site is under cover?
(12) Will it be cold, or wet or muddy underfoot?
(13) Any guidelines on what to wear, e.g. footwear?
(14) Is there any material to help plan the visit? – sample worksheets, teacher's notes, backgound information?
(15) Are there resources to use in follow-up work – publications, computer software, slides, cassettes, packs?

If it is at all possible a teacher should preview the place to be visited, though this may not always be possible with places at a distance. Most charging sites and museums offer teachers free admission for a preview visit. There should be liaison with the staff of the museum, and especially with the museum education officer if there is one. Most museums offer relevant publications, guide books, document packs, slides, teachers' notes etc. which can be purchased in advance. Some museums provide teachers' information packs, which can contain sample worksheets, a plan or gallery guide, and other background material. Teachers and helpers who are not familiar with the site also need to be briefed.

Pupils need an introduction to the topic, and may need background information to appreciate what they will see on site. It is vital that the teacher make clear what they will do on the visit, and what activities they are expected to carry out. Reminders about safety may be needed on some sites and agreements about appropriate standards of behaviour may need to be negotiated. It is also important that pupils arrive on site appropriately dressed if they are to be comfortable. Appropriate clothing may be determined by how much of the site is under cover, whether there is any walking between places, the nature of the building, or if there is any special experience, like going down a mine.

Many historic sites and buildings can be cold even in summer, and warm clothing and appropriate footwear may be needed.

Follow-up work will ensure that the site visit is integrated with that term's scheme of work. A visit may raise questions and offer topics that will involve further enquiry and the use of further resources. This is the point when museum packs, document packs and other resources will be most useful. Groups may need to present and share their findings with other pupils. Results of investigations and the like will need to be written up. A visit may lead to a display, or an audio-visual presentation or perhaps drama, role-play or empathetic work.

Presentation of work

After the visit there is a strong case for giving such activities a high profile within the school, through written reports, exhibitions and other presentations, for instance at school open days and parents' evenings. A good school is one which provides opportunities for such visits.

On occasions museums will appreciate feedback from teachers about the results of the visit. An invitation to see work resulting from the visit will often be appreciated. Thank you letters from the children themselves, a note from the teacher outlining the benefits of the visit, or even a sample of the work produced as a result of the visit will be extremely welcome.

Video, television broadcasts and film

The visual image has largely replaced the written word as our principal means of communication (R.W. Unwin)[9]

Today's pupils operate in an environment where the visual media are paramount. Television, film and video have the capacity to command attention and often pupils have a positive attitude towards television or video. The moving image has immediacy and can offer vivid detail. It is useful too for pupils with limited reading abilities. Video can enhance the study of history in the classroom, and for many teachers it is perceived as one of the key resources for learning. As primary source material too, for the study of the twentieth century, the moving image is a valid and important form of evidence.

When using video film or broadcasts for history, pupils should be encouraged to make the distinction between primary and secondary sources. It should not be assumed, however, that the distinction will be immediately clear to all pupils. Key skills need to be taught, not assumed. Indeed recent surveys by the National Foundation for Educational Research have revealed that there is often a great deal of confusion in pupils' minds, particularly as so many educational programmes for history now employ dramatic reconstruction.[10] In a recent survey carried out on over 300 pupils aged between 10 and 11 years, when pupils were shown an extract from the Yorkshire television series 'How we used to live', only 40 per cent of pupils identified black and white archive film as representing 'the past'. Ten per cent suggested that the use of black and white film meant the film-maker could not afford colour! (results reported in *The Times*, 14 October 1991). It is the history teacher who will have to bring out the distinction. 'When was this made?' is a crucial question for discussion of follow-up work.

Effective use of video

Box 14

After a preliminary viewing of a video sequence, pupils could be shown a short extract a second time, with one particular focus or question in mind. With a piece of archive film or newsreel film of, for example, one of Hitler's speeches, in a first viewing of the extract, the pupils' attention would probably be focused chiefly on Hitler, his manner of delivering a speech, his gestures, and so on. However, pupils could be asked to look at a second showing of the sequence, but this time to look for evidence showing the effect of Hitler's speech on other people, for instance, by observing onlookers' expressions and reactions.

Film, television output, and educational productions are mainly used in schools in the form of video, as this is cheap, easy to operate, and versatile in the ways in which it can be used (see Box 14). A great deal of video material is now readily available: documentaries, dramatisations and feature films, educational broadcasts, and archive film (which includes official war film, newsreels, amateur film, and more recently old television material). Material is often also available on loan. Where educational broadcasts are used, in the majority of cases it will be better to record a programme, rather than watch it live, not just for the convenience of the school timetable, but because video, as opposed to a live broadcast, is a more versatile educational tool.

Using television and video effectively for teaching history, must involve far more than the passive watching that most pupils engage in when they watch television at home. A number of techniques can be employed to make the experience more valuable.

Alan Farmer[11] suggested that with a vivid feature film, children should be allowed to watch it through without a single interruption. Afterwards he recommended that the class should go over selected extracts, looking at them with a worksheet. At other times a teacher may wish to use only a very short sequence.

Video can be stopped and re-started. This is one of the most effective ways of using video in the classroom. After running a short video sequence, a question and answer session, or analysis of some key point, or a discussion can take place. This procedure also allows the teacher to check on the degree of understanding. It may enable him or her to highlight some salient point, or to focus pupils' attention on a particular question as they view the next sequence.

Modern video recorders with their freeze-frame facility offer further possibilities. The teacher can stop the video, re-run a short sequence, and then freeze on one particular frame. Exploration of body language can be illuminating. With the frame frozen the attention of the class might be drawn to a particular gesture, or to an expression on someone's face. Or they might discuss the juxtaposition of certain symbols, or certain strong visual images. This can be especially useful with archive film.

Another useful device, which offers a check on understanding, is to play the sequence through initially with the sound track running. The video is then played through a second time without the sound. Pupils working in pairs or groups are required to operate the equipment, and to record a commentary on to audio tape. Even pupils as young as 6 have been able to carry out this exercise.

With film or video there are also opportunities for investigating how the media have presented a particular topic, or a particular personality. Video has a useful role to play in 'interpretations of history' (Attainment Target 2 in the National Curriculum for history). One teacher showed a brief extract from a historical film that had proved a great box office • success. 'That wasn't history, that was Hollywood!' he exclaimed as he kicked off an examination of interpretations of history.

All of these 'intensive' methods of using film and video can introduce greater depth of understanding than passive viewing, and help to realise the potential of this extremely powerful medium.

Types of film and video available

Educational broadcasts

Many of today's educational broadcasts for history are extremely professional. Usually the programme is intended for a certain age group. It will generally be carefully structured. Key points can be clearly and carefully made. It may often form part of a series, although history teachers need not be tied to utilising the whole series. In a busy timetable, video may be only one of a number of varied resources that the teacher wants to use. Educational broadcasts are secondary sources (though some programmes may contain extracts from archive film).

Box 15
Key points to look for in an educational video

(1) Does it have a particular age group in mind? Is it suitable for the age and ability range of my class?
(2) Is it brief – no more than 15–20 minutes to fit comfortably in a lesson period and still allow time for introduction and follow up?
(3) Does it include dramatisation, or film shot in the location where the historical events took place? Does it include extracts from archive film?
(4) Does it make some reference to evidence? Does it explain why we think this happened?
(5) Does it offer a balanced viewpoint?
(6) Is it open ended, leaving certain questions for further discussion?
(7) Does it deal with key themes and issues clearly and concisely?
(8) Does it include something which a young person can relate to – focus on the experiences of children in the past, for instance?

General historical documei. aries or historical dramatisations
Often these can provide extremely useful teaching material, despite the fact that they have been produced for the general public, rather than with a school's audience in mind. The length of these broadcasts may be a problem, though perhaps a film could be shown in its entirety through a school history society rather than during a history lesson. Even if the entire programme is too lengthy or unsuitable for classroom use, there may well be short sequences which could prove useful in teaching history. Recent concessions on recording television programmes have made it much easier to use this type of material in education. Schools can now apply for licences to record any television programme, not just educational broadcasts. Many videos can also be hired. As with educational broadcasts these are secondary sources, someone's interpretation of the past.

Archive footage
This is a source that is of course only available for the twentieth century. Archive footage is becoming more widely available. Also television documentaries are making increasing use of archive film from the stores of national and regional film archives.

Much early archive film is silent film. Where there is a commentary this was generally dubbed on. It is important too, to appreciate the limitations of early film, and the technical problems of shooting sequences. Much war footage was filmed far behind the actual front lines. Many sequences were staged. There is a famous sequence of 'Going over the top' in the First World War which has been shown to be a staged sequence. When viewing film it is important to bear in mind how it would have been produced (see Box 16).

Box 16
Key questions to ask about any sequence

(1)   How and where was it produced?
      When and by whom?
      For what purpose was it taken?

(2)   How was it actually filmed?
      Look at the processes that would take place as it was shot.

(3)   What editing processes has it gone through?
      Does it give a particular interpretation?
      What effect was it intended to have?

Creators of film and documentaries sometimes drew upon stock shots, and the actual sequence shown is not always what it purports to be.

Twentieth-century archive film is direct evidence, but it is also a producer's or director's creation, sometimes biased, and often an interpretation of events. All film needs critical evaluation. Film is something that has been edited and this should always be borne in mind when using it. Despite these caveats archive film is extremely useful. Indeed it can be an excellent vehicle for exploring bias or interpretations of history, precisely because of the considerations outlined above. Usually the teacher will use only a short sequence. This is primary evidence (material produced in the past), though it may well also offer a particular interpretation of an event. Film evidence can be extremely useful in investigating how the media both influence and reflect contemporary events and opinion.

Film in a foreign language can be usable, even if the sound track is unintelligible. Focus on visual information may be sharpened, when pupils are not trying to follow a sound commentary at the same time. Sometimes, even speech in an unintelligible foreign language can be illuminating. The rhythms and tones of a public speaker, for instance, can help pupils to appreciate his techniques of rousing an audience, even if we cannot understand the words.

Period amateur film
This is a primary source potentially as useful as archive film, although often of lower technical quality. Sometimes amateur film has a value for local history. Occasionally amateur film is the only visual record of a particular event or topic. Technical deficiencies may irritate, but judicious selection of a short sequence can provide useful evidential material. Extracts can be shown, without the sound commentary if necessary. It may be especially useful, if used alongside other types of evidence.

Computers for history teaching

Computer technology is experiencing rapid change. When computers were first introduced in schools, they were the preserve of the maths or science departments or of special computer studies courses. However, as the use of computers has spread rapidly to large sectors of work and business, there has been a growing trend to encourage the use of computers in schools across the curriculum. Information technology has become one of the cross-curricular requirements of National Curriculum. The teacher of history will need to plan the use of resources so that some parts of the scheme of work are delivered through computers.

Databases

One of the earliest uses of computers in history teaching involved the use of database software. This is a highly structured software where data is divided into fields. The first applications therefore were with archive material, which was itself highly structured and which was available in quantity. Documents like census ennumerator's schedules, parish registers and registers of all kinds, some shipping records, certain kinds of crime and punishment records, and so on, are highly suitable for this sort of software.

Historical data can also be collected from a range of other less structured records and diverse kinds of sources, and input by pupils themselves under agreed headings.

The chief value of the computer in this instance lies in its ability to search a large number of records very quickly. As software has improved computers can also output the results in the form of bar-charts, pie-charts, scattergraphs, and so on. Database programmes make it easier to use 'bulk' material like a census in the classroom, which previously presented considerable handling and organisational problems for the teacher. It is not necessary to use very large databases. A sample of a few hundred census records is often just as useful as a database of several thousands. There are many ways of interrogating the data. Pupils can be given question sheets and required to carry out searches of the database to find the answers.

Databases are only as useful as the questions pupils ask of them. Some use of databases involves mainly lower order questioning ('How many people had work connected with the railway?' 'What was the average number of children per family in 1881?'). One means of engendering higher order questioning of a more 'historical' character has been to encourage pupils to construct hypotheses and then test these against the evidence. This sort of work may involve as much discussion and 'off screen' work as actual use of the computer (see Box 17).

Box 17
Using a database to test hypotheses

A group of third year pupils in a secondary school were investigating education in the nineteenth century. They used a census database of their local area to find out how many pupils went to school in 1861. These were recorded on the census as 'scholars'. They chose a particular age range 5–11, and recorded what proportion did or did not attend school.

They then wanted to find out why some pupils did not attend school. Various possible explanations were suggested – did it perhaps depend on the occupation of the child's father? Perhaps on how much money he earned? This idea was tested against the evidence on the census database. The findings were quantified, examined in detail and discussed. Cases where widows (presumably quite poor) still sent their children to school, while other tradesmen (presumably wealthier) did not, began to cast some doubt on this hypothesis.

The group turned to a second hypothesis – that attendance at school might be affected by the number of children in a family. Were children in large families less likely to go to school? The suggestion was again tested against the evidence, and this time a very high correlation was found. Size of family was one very important factor affecting school attendance.

The investigation continued testing other suggestions for factors that might have affected school attendance. Perhaps children who lived on farms or whose parents ran a shop were more likely to be kept at home to help out? This hypothesis was again tested against the evidence on the database and the findings were quantified, analysed and discussed. Later pupils went on to look at other types of evidence, such as school log books, and school registers.

Some data disks are available in commercial packages, and indeed some record offices offer packages. Teachers' groups or pupils could also create their own databases using local sources obtained from their county archives office, after first seeking permission from the record office whose source material it is.

Computer simulations

An increasing number of history simulations are available. Children can search an area of sea for the wreck of the *Mary Rose*, for instance, decide on a site for a medieval castle, or play the part of archaeologists excavating an archaeological site, deciding where to excavate and evaluating the evidence of the finds. Certainly these can motivate pupils and offer variety and enjoyment. The best are those that do not simply rely on a historical setting, but encourage historical skills, evaluation and understanding. In general they are most useful for Key Stages 2 or 3. Many simulations tend to be rather too simplistic for work at GCSE level, at least among the range currently available. Even a less than ideal package can offer useful insights, however. A group of fifth form pupils when asked for their response after using a simulation on the Arab-Israeli situation, remarked that one thing it had demonstrated was how easy it was for the countries to slide into war!

Telex-type simulations

These are programmes that release screens of information or sources at timed intervals. They are particularly useful for events of a narrative kind, a battle, the course of a war, a plague or cholera epidemic, etc. The screens can consist of either information, or, perhaps more useful still to the history teacher, of actual contemporary sources. The course of a cholera epidemic, for instance, can be reported and its causes investigated by means of excerpts from documents written by people at the time. These are useful programmes also in that they can utilise a wide range of archive source material, (excerpts from letters, diaries, newspaper accounts, official reports etc). They are not restricted, as formal databases are, to record material that is highly structured. Some record offices are producing disks, but disks can also be produced by a teacher or teacher's group.

Using telex programmes

One effective way of using telex-type programmes is to cast pupils in the role of a newspaper editor and his staff. This exercise was carried out by a third year group in a secondary school studying a cholera epidemic.

Reports are coming into the newsroom of a cholera epidemic in a nearby town. As reports flood in [in this case they are drawn from contemporary accounts] groups must produce a front page story about the cholera. Groups will also need to organise themselves and delegate different tasks in order to produce their newspaper by a strict deadline. You must evaluate your evidence, check it against other sources and decide if it is reliable. Your readers will also expect the paper to investigate the causes of the epidemic ...

The process as well as the final product was important in this exercise. It helped to develop skills of cooperation and communication. It also encouraged historical skills, such as handling and evaluation of evidence, investigation of cause and effect and empathy. Working under pressure to meet a deadline had a motivating effect.

Viewdata programmes

Viewdata programmes offer great potential for history teaching. 'Data disks' of original source materials can be compiled for instance, allowing pupils to access pieces of evidence on particular topics. In one data disk on the First World War, for instance, pupils were able to access an official report of an attack, an entry in a private diary and also to see how a newspaper reported the incident. An advantage is that the software (which is usually menu driven) allows pupil choice over what is called up. Multiple screens can offer a range of sources and screens could also include questions and exercises, historical information, or secondary sources as well as primary source material. Careful structuring of the disks can allow key concepts to be targeted.

Unlike structured databases, Viewdata is useful for a great variety of written source materials. More recently software has been produced which combines the characteristics of viewdata screens with the sort of search capability usually found on databases. Appian Way, for instance, offer data disks that can conduct searches and produce material relevant to specific topics.

Teachers can even search on a skills basis, to produce material that would target change and continuity, or cause and consequence.

Authoring programmes, concept keyboard, etc.

Although concept keyboard was initially developed for special education, this is a type of software with a far greater potential, which could be used from Key Stage 1 up to Key Stage 3. Using authoring software such as Touch Explorer Plus, this offers great potential for the teaching of history. Concept keyboards allow areas of an overlay, which could for example be a historical map or a picture, to be touched by the pupil, calling up associated sub-screens of data or questions about the feature in question. Screens can be created at several levels, allowing for rising levels of difficulty in one case or for thematic treatment, or for a mix of information and questions and exercises. Other computer based variations on the basic concept use a mouse-driven pointer to select key areas of an image. Genesis for the Archimedes is one of these. One advantage of this range of programs is that teachers or groups of teachers could produce local teaching materials for themselves.

There are endless possibilities for creating teaching materials. Pupils could select areas of a historical map, for example, and call up further screens of related data or sources – the census records of families who lived in a particular house, perhaps.

Spreadsheets

Speadsheets have not so far figured largely as a resource for history, but they could be used with certain types of documentary sources. Like databases they require source material that is structured in format. One possible further use in history might be in modelling what might have happened. By inputting alternative values, pupils can investigate other possible outcomes.

Wordprocessors, desk-top publishing software, etc.

Although these are general programmes, whose value is not confined to history, the use of wordprocessors for the output of some written work can motivate pupils, and encourage pride in presentation. The use of non-standard typefaces, such as gothic, to produce historical material is a simple device that has proved highly successful at Key Stage 2.

Other computer resources

Interactive video as its name suggests gives pupils control over what is accessed. Although the production of disks is expensive at present, the situation could change very rapidly. Other software uses computers to stop and start ancillaries, such as tape recorders or videos. There is also other equipment which can be used in distance learning situations. No doubt there will be many further developments, but already there is a great range of material available for history teaching.

Classroom management for the use of computers

A new style of classroom management may be required when using computers in history teaching. Arrangements will depend on how many computers are available. A single computer may be constantly available alongside other resources as a reference tool, or for some simulations. Better provided classrooms may have a number of computers, but groups may have to be rotated in turn to use a computer, while other groups carry out other tasks. Generally small groups of children working together stimulate each other. Effective history teaching may also require that pupils spend as much time away from the screen, discussing, hypothesising and analysing their findings, as actually working at the keyboard. Indeed one possible advantage offered by computers is that they free children from lower order tasks and allow far more time for higher order thinking – instead of laboriously drawing a graph, pupils have more time for analysis of a graph produced by the computer. Teaching strategies need to adapt to this new situation, to exploit the potential offered by computers.

Computers should also complement not replace other resources, and where sources are offered on screen, there should also be 'hard copy' examples of what the original documents actually look like. Many packages offer supporting booklets or documents as well as disks.

Teacher produced resources

Computer resources can be created by teachers, or pupils, as well as purchased from commercial sources, using viewdata, telex or database software. This has the great advantage of allowing local history materials to be used. While few individual teachers will have time for extensive projects, there are many possibilities for teachers' groups, or for collaborative projects with local record offices or museums. Permission should always be sought from the institution concerned for the use of its material in this way.

Games

At one time most games relevant to history were board games. Many of these were war games which involved the movement of fighting forces and resources over a map on the board. Some like 'Diplomacy', which is set in pre-First World War Europe, involve pupils in negotiations with other 'countries', setting territorial goals, and forming (and often breaking) alliances. Now computer-based games and simulations have replaced many of these.

Teachers may find history games valuable for occasional use. Certainly too they may be extremely useful for the history club and after-school activities. Perhaps the main value is in illustrating the complexity of cause and effect. History has no inevitable outcomes. Games show the cumulative importance of individual human decisions on events, and demonstrate that different decisions at particular points could have led to very different outcomes. They are most useful if discussion is programmed in afterwards.

Books and printed sources

In the course of school history, pupils will need opportunities to use a wide range of secondary sources and printed material. As well as books written specifically for school use, pupils should at some stage come into contact with biographies and memoirs, published diaries, historical fiction and some writings about local history. They should be encouraged to consult basic reference books, such as the Inventory of Ancient Monuments, the *Dictionary of National Biography* and encyclopaedias. The range of books used will increase over time, but introduction of these resources needs to be planned.

Work in history will also at times involve the use of libraries and reference libraries, record offices or local studies centres. History teachers need to ensure that their pupils have the basic reference skills that will allow them to make effective use of books. These skills should be taught not assumed. They include the use of contents pages, index and glossary. Pupils may need to know about ways of classifying books – the Dewey system in public libraries for instance. In the later stages pupils need to know about the use of references, and in their own work should be encouraged to keep a record of the sources they have consulted. They need practice at making notes when they have found information (see Box 18).

Box 18

Before sending pupils to research a topic for themselves in a library, local studies centre or record office:

(1)   phone or visit to check what is available, and how easy it is to use the material;

(2)   teach any necessary reference skills;

(3)   provide each child with a duplicated guidance sheet;

(4)   warn library, local studies centre and record office in advance about the project being set.

Contact with books and other printed material published in an earlier age is also important. These are primary sources in their own right. Handling and using them may give a sense of the past. They will include government reports, travellers' descriptions and antiquarian books, trade directories, old newspapers, early school textbooks. These will often be found in a local study centre, or the rare books section of a reference library, and local record offices in particular will have a wide range of early printed material as well as manuscript sources. To use these effectively pupils need to be able to work out when a book was published.

Pupils should come to appreciate that all history books are interpretations of the past, that interpretations can vary, and that the best are those strongly rooted in evidence. Twenty years ago history textbooks did consist principally of 'text'. Publishers today have provided teachers of history with a wide and varied range of books for class use. Many of these are attractive, well-illustrated and include primary source material. Books or packs which offer compilations of primary source materials have also become more plentiful, including those produced by local record offices and museums. Peter Roberts writing in 1981[12] put in a plea for more textbooks that deal with the processes of historical enquiry. He pleaded for sources to be used for more than just illustration or comprehension. Roberts stressed that if a textbook is to form the main staple of the course then it should teach historical procedures, as well as offering a historical narrative. Increasingly, books for school use are targeting skills and concepts as well as content, though very few of the first wave of National Curriculum history titles, hurriedly rushed out by publishers, were in fact written after the final reports for history had been issued.

Not all teachers today use a single standard textbook as their staple material and many schools have difficulty affording class sets. Many departments buy a varied selection of relevant books and source material and use these alongside teacher-produced resources. These books need to be readily accessible to pupils, both in the classroom and in the school library. A table or trolley of relevant books and resources could be constantly at hand when teaching history. School library loan services can offer a wide range of material.

History around us – historic landscapes as a resource for history teaching

Britain offers a wealth of historic landscapes, townscapes, field systems, roads, tracks and routes, railways and canals, banks and boundaries, ancient woodlands, walls and hedges and old industrial sites, settlements which have been planned, settlements which have evolved over time. In recent years the historical value of these has come to be appreciated. At some stage the history teacher may want to tap into some of this.

Air photographs

Aerial photographs are often a useful way to start to approach these historic landscapes and townscapes. The overall view is an aid to understanding, for example, seeing the grid pattern of streets of a medieval planned town, for instance. Sometimes, too, features such as earthworks and cropmarks and patterns that are not easily visible on the ground become apparent from the air. Aerial photography is a technique that has revolutionised the study of archaelogy, leading to many new discoveries.

Walking and fieldwork

The local historian W. G. Hopkins once claimed that every historian worth his salt should get mud on his boots. Certainly fieldwalking is a valuable activity that can help pupils to appreciate the history around them. They can literally walk in the footsteps of people in the past, walking a section of Roman road or an old packhorse track, or following the route of an abandoned railway, or perhaps storming a hill-fort or castle.

Fieldwork and field survey can follow on (see Box 19). It might involve survey and dating of a length of hedge, by identifying and counting the shrub species it contains, a graveyard survey, or detailed survey work on an archaeological site or in a settlement. Historical resources are complimentary. Fieldwork in a historic landscape will often lead on to further research and document work to try to make sense of what has been found.

Box 19
A settlement survey

This was an enquiry which began with an exploration of a historic landscape, in this case a settlement. A group of fourth year pupils were doing historical survey work in a large village. Initally they were asked to divide the buildings in the settlement into three categories:

(1) pre-Victorian;
(2) Victorian;
(3) modern.

The teacher offered clues as to how small architectural details could help to date buildings. The Victorians, for instance, loved decoration – on iron work, bargeboards, ridge tiles, chimneys, and so on. They used a lot of brick, including decorative banding or the use of brick facings to doors and windows. The size and shape of windows offered further clues. Sash windows or bay windows were popular, and though these have often been renewed or replaced with double glazing, the proportions and large size and shape offer clues. Early houses often had very small windows. They often had distinctive big stone chimneys and low doorways. The steep pitch of a roof might hint that it had once been thatched. Pupils themselves were able to suggest some identifiers for modern buildings.

At the end of the fieldwork pupils decided that most of the buildings in the settlement were of Victorian date. They had also, in the course of walking around the village, noticed other things, such as a very large proportion of buildings that had formerly obviously been shops. These 'closed shops' aroused curiosity. Why were there so many of them and why had they closed? At this stage pupils needed further evidence and information and they were now ready to go on to look at documents, old maps, old photographs, oral history material. These sources confirmed their original impressions – that this was a village that had boomed in the Victorian age. Population figures and census records followed over time showed how it had changed from being a rural village to an industrial settlement with the growth of a local quarry. It had even become a small town, supporting a large variety of specialist shops. Trade directories and the census gave ample details of these.

Continued

Box 19 continued

> After the closure of the quarry, however, its main source of employment, the settlement had declined to become a village once again.
>
> This was an exercise firmly rooted in the use of a broad range of historical evidence that focused on key historical concepts such as change and continuity, and cause and consequence, and that encouraged and developed skills in using evidence.

The use of theatre in education

In recent years a number of theatre-in-education groups have made an important contribution to the teaching of history (see Box 20). Frequently the theatre-in-education group is associated with a historical site, although their workshops can stand alone and take place in school. Often the 'actors' are ex-teachers. A series of workshop sessions can be commissioned either by a particular museum, or by a local authority. These workshops are particularly valuable on a historical site that may be indistinct, puzzling and confusing, or extremely complicated. The sessions take many forms, but include short, dramatic representations of what happened on a particular site, or characters in role. Productions such as these should show a respect for evidence.

One advantage of the workshop approach, as opposed to a more formal dramatic presentation, is that the sequence can be stopped at any time. A key sequence, vital for historical understanding, can easily be re-run. The production can be halted at any point so that discussions and questions can take place. The sessions are also highly varied and interactive. Pupils are involved, answering questions, discussing a point, sometimes offering solutions to a problem, and usually at one point role-playing in the sequence.

Often in theatre in education there is a link person who has a number of key functions, in turn acting as presenter, teacher, questioner, comic relief, sometimes, indeed, pretending not to understand and needing to have points carefully explained. This person introduces things, and often links different sequences, sometimes imparting information, sometimes questioning the pupils, or the actors in turn.

Box 20
At the ironworks

A class of children are on a field visit to a foundry and ironworks which played a prominent role in the early industrial revolution. On a very difficult and confusing site, still under excavation and only partially understood, a theatre-in-education group of three actors have to make the site and the industrial processes that went on there meaningful to the visiting pupils. One of the team acts as the link person – sometimes as go-between, sometimes as presenter, sometimes in a teaching role, sometimes as a questioner of the other actors.

The session starts by investigating the history of the shed they are sitting in, starting with observation of the building itself, looking for evidence. This building it turns out has been used at different times for different purposes. In the nineteenth century it was used as a cowshed housing a milking herd, and still has the central drainage channel in the floor. What was that channel for? 'In the last group we had here, one person thought that channel in the centre was so the milk could flow down it', the presenter joked, 'But we soon put him right about that. You know what happens when you've got a herd of cows!' In the eighteenth century the shed had been used for one stage in the foundry process – fettling the iron castings.

Using simple visual aids (two sections of very modern plastic pipe), the link person confronts the children with a problem. The ironworks had made gun-barrels for cannons which were needed in the wars going on at that time. But being cast in two sections there was a problem – the barrels tended to blow apart when the cannons were fired. How then could you make gun barrels that did not blow apart in use? Then follows a dramatic sequence involving the ironmaster explaining his ideas for revolutionary new casting methods. He will cast the barrels solid in one piece and drill the centre out. Pupils listen as he details the revolutionary changes he will make at the foundry, using water power to assist in the drilling-out process, building a battery of eight furnaces to work simultaneously to produce the quantities of iron needed ...

The performance stops and starts. There are repeats of key sequences. Pupils are also required at one point to role-play – in the role of young children who are new applicants for work at the foundry. They are harangued and shouted at by the ironmaster, given their working orders, chosen for different tasks and sent off to different places in the works. The iron master warns them about the dangers of the site. It will be entirely their own fault if they have an accident.

Music

The National Curriculum recommendations made several references to the use of music as a resource for history teaching. This is an area together with art offering important cross-curricular links. Fortunately today recordings of period music are now widely available, much of it performed on authentic period instruments. There is no doubt that period music can enrich experience, add atmosphere and help to convey the experiences of people in past times. Music can be extremely memorable, and the involvement of all the senses is a well-tried expedient. Music allows pupils to appreciate the cultural contribution that different periods have made. The introduction of a piece of music also covers the cultural/religious aspect of the political, economic, social and cultural requirement.

Pupils can be introduced to short pieces of period music in a history lesson. Longer pieces might be played softly as background music on occasions to create atmosphere. Pupils will also enjoy performing simple period music (playing medieval music on recorders and percussion instruments, for instance, or perhaps performing negro spirituals in a lesson about slavery). Pupils will appreciate the distinctive elements of period music, if they are given opportunities to create their own music using elements/themes, rhythms from earlier music. Music can also be an important means of communication. One group of primary children were doing a pageant on the Celts and Romans. How to convey the battle scene posed a problem. Stage fights were considered but rejected. Instead the class used percussion music to convey the clash between the two armies. In primary schools learning will be seamless and music will fit naturally into the programme of activities. In secondary schools the cooperation of the music department might be enlisted, and the music department there may well have a wider range of recordings to offer, or may be able to advise on suitable pieces.

It is possible to use music at historic sites. (Just reflect how organ music playing softly can add to the atmosphere of a cathedral or religious building.) Appropriate period music can be played on visits to a historic building, and some groups have staged wholescale performances at historic sites (see Box 21). Many heritage establishments will be cooperative provided the matter is discussed in advance.

Box 21
A music workshop: South American instruments in a Victorian gaol

A primary school brought a small group of musicians with them on a field visit to a Victorian gaol in north Wales. After exploring and investigating the grim confines of the prison building, a music workshop was held. The instruments the musicians had brought along were mainly percussion instruments from South America. How could one link these with a Victorian gaol? And how could the visit be used to develop meaningful historical concepts? In the event a solution was found which linked past with present, which developed the concept of imprisonment onto a world scale, which explored the desire for freedom, and the experiences of imprisonment, and which provided a genuine creative musical experience.

The session started with a lively rhythmic piece of music 'to warm them up because the gaol was so cold!' Next the leader talked about prisoners in a gaol and developed on the concept of imprisonment. Through a reference to South African resistance leaders (this was before the ending of Apartheid), and prisoners under harsh South American regimes, he widened the theme of imprisonment to include prisoners anywhere in the world. Prisoners anywhere, he suggested, needed to communicate with one another, even though that was forbidden. They tapped out messages on the walls of their cells. Groups of children were located in different prison cells and tapped out their rhythms and 'messages' on the cell walls. The rhythms became the 'voices' of individual prisoners. This was quite an eerie, memorable experience which brought alive that historic setting. It enhanced the experience of isolation and confinement.

Next the leader introduced and demonstrated the musical instruments. The instruments had been brought to South America by slaves from West Africa, who were carried on slave ships to countries like Brazil. In captivity they had used their music to remind them of freedom and their home country. The 'prisoner concept' had now widened to encompass slaves (prisoners without prison walls). Smaller groups of children were tutored by the musicians, on different percussion instruments. They all had to learn to play a simple five-note percussion theme. When the class came together again, this developed into an impressive 'freedom theme' which was played in different ways by different groups as they marched in a long procession in a 'march for freedom' around the prison. The performance ended in a memorable climax.

Oral history

No one would claim that oral history is more free from bias than any other historical resources, and for the complete picture all the evidence must be weighed. But it does provide ... a human face behind the officialese, and for children, in particular, it can seem more real and relevant than any other historical source.[13]

The work of Sallie Purkiss in both primary and secondary schools has done much to highlight the value of oral history as a resource for schools. While it is especially useful with younger pupils, all pupils will benefit from contact with oral evidence. Older pupils may be using it in a more sophisticated way, for instance by comparing someone's reminiscences with another written account. Oral history offers the great advantage of allowing active participation in the collection of evidence. Pupils can collect oral evidence for themselves through interviews with the elderly. There are many benefits in the area of personal and social education.

A great bank of recorded oral testimony is also available. There have been many programmes in recent years for the systematic recording of the reminiscences of elderly people. A great deal of new evidence has become accessible which can be tapped by schools. Often this material is preserved in local record offices, museums or libraries. In some cases material can also be found in regional sound archives.

The value of oral evidence

Oral evidence has illuminated many areas of life that were previously poorly documented – many aspects of women's history, for instance, have been opened up through oral history. Oral history has also shed light on such things as family and community links – the importance of neighbourhood sharing in enabling many families to survive the experience of the depression has been highlighted, for example. Oral evidence is useful in redressing the inherent bias that exists in 'official' sources which often ignore important areas of experience or particular groups. For this reason the source has much to offer in the area of interpretations of history.

Like any other form of evidence, orally transmitted information needs careful evaluation. It is commonly recognised that people often transpose an occurrence from one date to another. Sometimes, too, people are less than truthful, either from reticence or embarrassment, or through a desire to put themselves or their family in a favourable light. The skills of the interviewer, and indeed the relationship between the interviewer and subject can also affect the quality of the evidence.

Using oral evidence in school

Oral history can provide a useful gateway to the past, which will be especially useful with younger pupils. The elderly in our own society have lived through unprecedented technical change, and oral history is now a major source of evidence for twentieth-century history. Initially teachers will find it especially useful for illuminating concepts of change and continuity, but it can also contribute to concepts of cause and consequence and two differing accounts can be used to examine interpretations of history.

Some work in schools may involve extensive use of oral sources, where pupils themselves will be involved in sorting and processing the oral data, and transposing it into other formats. At other times the teacher may use only a very short extract, lasting two or three minutes at most, perhaps to introduce a topic or to contrast with evidence of another type. A collection of short 'sound bytes' can be useful. Some tapes offering compilations of short edited extracts have been produced by museums, archives or oral history projects. In other cases written transcripts have been made of the sound recordings, and where these exist they will prove extremely useful to the busy teacher, as it is far quicker to scan through a written transcript, than to listen to a lengthy recording. Some archives and museums services have also produced publications based on their oral collections.

Using a tape extract can add variety to a lesson, and will be a useful leveller where a class includes pupils with reading difficulties. However it is often worthwhile using the material in a written form.

Myth, legend and the oral tradition

At earlier times in the past the tape recorder was unavailable, but occasional writers have sometimes recorded oral testimony. (Hearsay evidence, of course, needs handling with caution.) In the past folklore, early laws, myths, legends and rhymes, games and stories were passed down by oral means. Such things often reach back many centuries beyond the date when they were committed to writing. In some parts of the world, Africa or Australia, for instance, the oral record still has great importance.

Earlier myths and legends need especially cautious handling (many myths, for instance, are 'explanation myths' which try to account for some well-known feature; they are interpretations of history rather than direct evidence). Among all the embellishments there may lurk a few grains of truth.

All evidence needs to be cross-checked and carefully evaluated. Oral evidence is not exceptional in this respect. Pupils should be encouraged to look for several accounts wherever possible, and to check oral evidence against other forms of evidence.

Using historical resources

Many of the sources and resources outlined above complement each other. Best results will often be gained from using different types of resources together. A pictorial source and an artefact can often be used most effectively together. Documents can be used effectively alongside pictorial or statistical sources. Documents may help to illuminate a historical site. When using a computer database of census material, pupils should be shown examples of original census forms. They may use other relevant documentary sources in work away from the computer. Primary sources and secondary sources will often be used together.

Putting different kinds of sources alongside each other will help pupils to appreciate the particular strengths and weaknesses of different kinds of evidence. Pupils should also be constantly encouraged to cross-check the evidence of one source against another and to offer explanations for any discrepancies. This will be most important for Attainment Targets 2 and 3, on the use of evidence and on historical interpretation.

Reports of the National Curriculum committees for history have stressed the need to introduce pupils to a wide range of historical resources. Resources should be included in all schemes of work. At some point in the course planning process an audit needs to be made to ensure that a broad variety of resources has been included, and that a balance is achieved, over the year's work, although individual topics may lend themselves to particular types of resources.

Content	Activities to be carried out	Skills to be targeted	Resources to be used	Assessment

Safety

Matters of safety may not be the first thing that comes to mind in using historical resources, but, it is wise to carry out an assessment of the possible risks of any activity. Safety considerations must be paramount.

Handling artefacts

The teacher needs to be informed and aware of possible hazards in the use of particular resources, and to explain these to the pupils if necessary. The filters of many gas masks, of the type which children commonly bring into school, often contain asbestos for instance; certain types of early fire extinguishing equipment contain acid. When introducing archaeology, some museum educators delight the class by putting a modern plate into a plastic bag and smashing it with a hammer, afterwards going on to talk about archaeological finds of fragments of pottery. This is fine, except that any fragments of the plate handled afterwards by the pupils need to be vetted for sharp edges, as some modern ceramics break leaving a very sharp edge. Some old pottery (usually distinguished by its crazed surface) has a lead glaze, and it is wise not to consume foodstuffs or drink from it.

Recreations and experimentation

Certain activities involving the use of old-fashioned equipment may present hazards, if the exercise is not carefully planned and supervised (e.g. mangles, or heated box irons could cause injury or burns, in an old-fashioned washing activity). Today's children may be less aware than children of an earlier age about the hazards of using certain equipment.

Site visits

Historic buildings by their very nature do not always conform to modern standards or to safety requirements. Nor is it desirable that they should. The gloom, or steep staircases of a building, or the sheer drop from the battlements of a castle may be the very things that give the building its atmosphere and impact; but they can pose hazards. Other visits may be to a ruined site which lacks shelter and pupils may need appropriate clothing and footwear if they are to be warm, dry and comfortable.

Fieldwork

In fieldwork safety needs to be considered. An excursion to visit a hill-fort or certain field monuments could be a major undertaking. The distances to be walked, and any climbing, must be within the capacity of every member of the party. If the site is high up, there may even be a requirement for someone with a mountain leadership certificate. The weather can change rapidly, and will be worse a thousand feet up. Pupils need appropriate footwear and warm, waterproof clothing for fieldwork. Some pupils may have medical conditions which might pre-empt certain excursions, and a diabetic may need to eat at regular intervals.

Checklist

1. Safety matters should be a prime consideration in planning any activity or the use of any resource. What possible hazards might there be and how can the activity and the supervision be planned to prevent accident?
2. Safety must be recognised as the teacher's responsibility. The teacher has the final say on what the pupils will do or where they will go. A teacher may decide not to visit a certain area if the level of staffing is not adequate for close supervision.
3. Whenever possible a preliminary visit should be made to a site, with safety as one of the considerations. Advice can be sought from education officers or other staff.
4. Pupils may need to be briefed on safety matters and the need to take care. This is particularly important if pupils are to be sent off individually or in pairs for on-site activities.
5. Any safety equipment provided by the organisation your group is visiting must be worn at all times. (Safety helmets for a visit to a mine for instance.)
6. Clothing should be appropriate for the conditions. It is better to err on the side of pessimism.
7. Standards of behaviour can be negotiated with the pupils. They need to know what is acceptable behaviour for a site visit. Ordered, purposeful activity should be the aim.

For further consideration

(1) Devise an exercise to highlight the distinction between primary and secondary sources.
(2) Give a specific example of two document sources which could effectively be used together in an exercise, and state what skills or concepts might be covered.
(3) Give an example of another group of objects which could be used in a sequencing activity.
(4) Give one specific example of the way in which an object can lead on to further consideration of the people and society that produced it.
(5) List some clear objectives for a class visit to a museum or historic site of your choice. How would you assess whether the objectives had been achieved?
(6) Prepare a brief worksheet for use with an extract from either a video sequence, or an oral history interview.
(7) Review any piece of history software of your choice, and assess its potential for encouraging higher order thinking, and for developing historical skills and concepts. How would you structure the learning process to ensure that your objectives were actually achieved?

Notes and references

1. *Archives and Education*, Education Pamphlet No. 54, Department of Education and Science, HMSO, 1968.
2. For example 'History in danger', Mary Price in Vol. LIII *History* October 1968, p. 342, and 'Archives in schools', John Fines, in Vol. LIII *History* October 1968, p. 348.
3. 'Background to the History 13–16 Project', Schools Council, 1976.
4. Joan Blyth and Gill Aslett, 'History 5–9', Hodder and Stoughton 1988.
5. J. West, 'Frieze Frames', *Times Educational Supplement*, 17 February 1989.
6. With acknowledgement to Gail Durbin, Susan Morris, Sue Wilkinson, 'A teacher's guide to learning from objects', English Heritage, 1990.
7. This response came from a pupil at Talysarn School, Gwynedd and was quoted at a primary teachers' conference at Normal College, Bangor, in July 1990.
8. Mary Aris and Julia Burns (joint authors) of pamphlet 'Active learning in Beaumaris Gaol', publisher Gwynedd Archives and Museums Service, 1988.
9. R. W. Unwin, 'The visual dimension in the study and teaching of history', pamphlet published by Historical Association, 1981.
10. Research carried out by the National Foundation for Educational Research, 1991.
11. Alan Farmer, 'Video and History', *Teaching History*, Vol. 45, p. 9, 1981.
12. Peter Roberts, 'Some thoughts on the text book', *Teaching History*, Vol. 31, p. 28, 1981.
13. Sallie Purkiss, *Oral History in Schools*, pamphlet believed to be published by the Oral History Society, 1976.

CHAPTER 5

History 14–16: Key Stage 4

Ron Brooks

In the early years of the new National Curriculum it is worthwhile to recall the advice given to history teachers by Lord Eustace Percy who, as President of the Board of Education, finally laid to rest the first national curriculum in 1926[1]. Handing over the curriculum to the teaching profession he urged history teachers in particular to exercise their new classroom powers cautiously. 'Thought will, in the long run', he said, 'be valued only by those who have been discouraged early from jumping at conclusions and from letting imagination run too far ahead of knowledge.'[2] Sixty-two years later, Kenneth Baker's Education Reform Act restored central control over the curriculum. The first draft of the new history National Curriculum published in December 1990 carried a similar health warning. The programmes of study and attainment targets were designed to ensure that history teaching avoided the 'undisciplined use of the imagination' and was based upon 'a solid foundation of historical information'.[3] It is tempting to say that the more things change the more they remain the same but most pupils in our schools today, who have been trained by their teachers in the skills of subjecting such general statements to critical analysis, would recognise the difference in the positions. In recent years the acquisition of historical information and understanding has been undertaken as part of training in historical method. As the history working group pointed out in its recommendations to the Education Secretary in April 1990,

To have integrity, the study of history must be grounded in a thorough knowledge of the past; must employ rigorous historical method – the way in which historians carry out their task; and must involve a range of interpretations and explanations. Together, these elements make an organic whole; if any one of them is missing the outcome is not history.[4]

Planning for continuity across Key Stages 3 and 4

The present National Curriculum makes a more concerted effort to provide curriculum continuity than did that which was abolished in 1926. It offers several in-built features which teachers should exploit to ensure a smooth transition from Key Stage 3 to Key Stage 4.

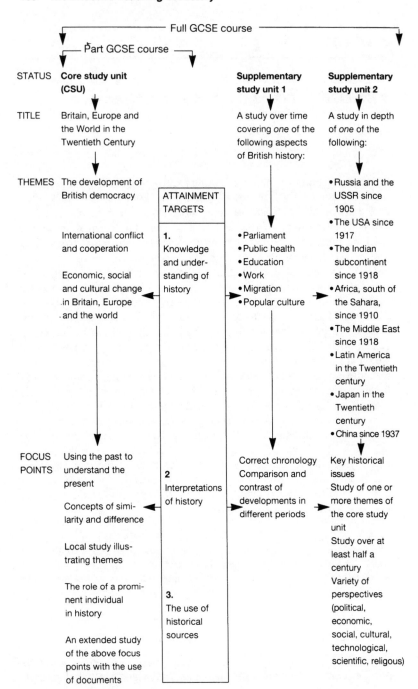

Figure 5.1   Key Stage 4: Integrating subject content and attainment targets

(1) Teaching methods and approaches will exhibit a great degree of similarity.

(2) The nature and range of resource materials used in Key Stage 4 will be instantly recognised by students moving from Key Stage 3.

(3) Students will be familiar with attainment targets (ATs) and their levels, some of the latter (levels 4–7) at Key Stage 4 overlapping with those of Key Stage 3. They will already have a baseline upon which to develop.

(4) Subject content has been carefully devised to assist curriculum continuity, particularly with the core study unit (CSU). Thus it is possible to sketch in briefly at Key Stage 3 some subsequent developments which are dealt with fully in Key Stage 4. For example, the subsequent expansion of the franchise in the twentieth century could be dealt with briefly as an appendix to the political developments covered in Key Stage 3.

Matching ATs and study units

Much of the teaching under the first national curriculum had limited aims and even more limited methods. Pupils were drilled in historical facts. Teaching was often confined to imparting information in the form of blackboard or dictated notes or through copying sections from books. Pupils were tested on their ability to recall information and not necessarily on their understanding of it.[5] The history curriculum of the 1990s requires pupils to process the prescribed content of the CSU and the teacher-selected content of the Selected Study Units (SSUs) in several ways, which means that teachers have to give more thought to planning than did their early twentieth-century predecessors. As in the case of the other key stages, consideration of and planning for the content and the ATs of Key Stage 4 should not take place as an afterthought. Consideration of and planning for the content and the ATs should take place simultaneously.

(1) Pupils should not simply be presented with historical information to digest and to regurgitate. For example, to be able to recall the provisions of the Acts of 1918, 1928 and 1969 is not a suitable test of whether or not pupils have understood in the CSU unit how and why the parliamentary franchise was extended.

(2) Teaching techniques and materials should be directed to the attainment of particular ATs and at Key Stage 4 to the achievement of particular levels in the 4–10 range of specific ATs. For example, the key concept of historical causation in AT1 could well lead the teacher of the Key Stage 4 compulsory unit to spend some time on the origins of the welfare state.

(3) Given that the time available is very finite this may mean that pupils can either be given an assessment task on causation in a different historical context such as in an area of history which links Key Stage 3 and Key Stage 4 (such as the diversity of British society), or on an area which links the SSUs to the CSU (such as the origins of the Cold War).

(4) This process of integrating, and not just linking, the ATs and the study units will mean that certain aspects of history will be treated with a broad brush to enable the more detailed study of areas and themes of history which blend naturally with ATs. For example in the CSU, the impact of the Second World War outside Europe may be examined briefly in order to concentrate more fully on the historical ideas and attitudes of people on the British home front.

(5) To attempt to treat all subject content in the same manner or depth is undesirable. It will not only take up more time than is available but will blur the focus of the unit or its parts. It is not intended that every part of every unit should seek to realise all of the ATs. Certain aspects of content lend themselves more easily than others to particular ATs and thus should provide its focus.

(6) It may be necessary to treat interconnecting aspects of history with a broad brush.

Planning Key Stage 4 for the single subject GCSE

The first requirement is to plan across the two Key Stage 4 years to ensure that adequate time is available to meet the requirement that 'the two supplementary study units should, together, make demands comparable to those of the core study units, in knowledge, understanding, and skills' (see Figure 5.2). This may mean giving the same time to SSU 1 and 2 together which is allocated to the CSU, although this may not be possible. SSU1 which focuses on change over time could well take longer to cover than SSU2 whose focus is a study in depth. Time may also have to be made available for a revision and an updating unit, the latter relating especially to 'the present day' requirement of the study-in-depth. Students should leave school with as up-to-date knowledge as is possible.

Planning Key Stage 4 study units

There are several general matters relating to the Key Stage 4 study units which need to be considered before smaller modules of work are planned. These are:

(1) The selection of unit themes to ensure a balanced coverage of political, economic, social, cultural, scientific, technological and religious aspects.

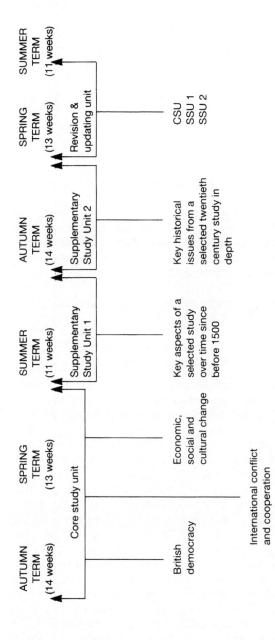

Figure 5.2 A basic planning model for Key Stage 4: single or combined subjects

(2) The integration of ATs into the teaching of themes which involves the careful identification of natural points of integration.

(3) The careful selection and wording of questions in the teaching and in the assessment process to maximise opportunities for students to demonstrate what they 'know, understand and can do'.

(4) Such questions at Key Stage 4 should maximise opportunities for students to demonstrate effective communication skills of a variety of kinds, to exercise numeracy skills and use information technology, to engage in problem solving (especially in evidential exercises), and to demonstrate an understanding of cultural differences and of the roles in history of women as well as of men.

(5) The careful selection, ordering and pruning of resources to avoid clutter and to point up ATs.

(6) The precise structuring and wording of tasks and activities to make explicit their links with ATs and to assist students to achieve the highest levels of response. Such tasks should pay close regard to time allocation.

(7) Implanting specific and natural cross-curricular links.

Applying these general points for consideration to a study unit would result in a planning schedule of the kind shown in Figure 5.3.

Key Stage 4 attainment targets in practice

AT1, knowledge and understanding of history, has three components, the nature of change, cause and consequence in history and situational analysis. Key Stage 4 is concerned with levels 4–10 of each of these components. The first question confronting anyone wishing to assess achievement in these areas is whether they should be tested separately or together. To avoid confusing students about the nature of the task and to ensure that schemes of assessment test what they are meant to, each component is best tested by a separate question or questions. That is not to say, however, that in order to save time and to be able to make assessment less intrusive, questions testing different components but relating to the same historical theme could not be grouped together. For example, when testing the Russian Revolution of October 1917 in the core study unit, separate questions could be based on the nature of change (covering the ideas and practices of the Tsarist government and the Soviet government), on cause and consequences (examining the relative importance of several consequences) and on situational analysis (relating to the different ideas of Russian people at the time about the war with Germany, the government of Nicholas II and the ownership of property). The five or six questions testing the three components separately could be preceded by a brief written

KS	KS4
Year	5th Year GCSE

SU TITLE	INTERNATIONAL CONFLICT	SINGLE SUBJECT/~~COMBINED SUBJECT~~	~~CORE~~/SUPPLEMENTARY STUDY UNIT

Theme		Points of integration with attainment targets (ATs)		Time allocation	Cross-curricular links
	AT	Questions to be considered	Resources/activities/assessment		
Superpower relations – the Cuban missile crisis	AT3	Examine Sources 1 and then answer the following questions: Who produced each of the sources? How might this affect their value to the historian? What does each tell us about the Cuban missile crisis? What does each not tell us about the crisis? Why do you think that this has been left out from the account? Which do you think is the most valuable source and why?	Resources: Textbook supplementary information sheet, collection of documents (US newspaper cartoons, Soviet newspaper account, US government statement, United Nations statement). Activities: Examine the textbook account of the Cuban missile crisis, and then answer the following question. How useful are the five sources individually and taken together in telling us about the Cuban missile crisis? Pay careful attention to the origins of each and what each tells us or does not tell us about it. Assessment: See levels of response mark scheme.	Teaching: 4 hours Assessment: 1½ hours	Cartoon production (Art) Maps (Geography) Weaponry (Design and technology)

Figure 5.3 A planning schedule for Key Stage 4

primary or secondary extract which highlights the three strands which are being tested. As it may be difficult to find a primary source or a textbook account to provide the focuses with sufficient accuracy, it may be preferable for teachers to devise their own half-page introductory account. A more precise guide of how this can be achieved in relation to AT1 for both full and part GCSE history students is given in Figure 5.4 although it should be noted that this is only one model. It does, however, have the merits of economising on teaching time and of providing coherent assessment tasks.

AT2 focuses on developing the ability to understand interpretations of history and as with the other attainment targets it is assumed that students will have developed this ability by Key Stage 4 so that at that stage it will be operative largely at levels 4–10. It is clear from the manner in which the National Curriculum defines these levels that the meaning attached to 'history' is not simply that of 'the past' but of the attempts made throughout the centuries to reconstruct and interpret the past and which continues today. It would be worthwhile to emphasise this point to students at the beginning of Key Stage 4 by using the following exercise which also links Key Stages 3 and 4.

The term 'history' can be used in three ways:

A   as a subject on a school timetable;
B   to mean the past;
C   to mean reconstructing and interpreting the past which people have been doing for a long time and which continues today.

Look at the way it is used in each of the following sentences and write the letter A to C on the dotted line according to which of the ways in which it is used in each of the sentences. You may wish to write more than one letter on the dotted line if you feel it has more than one possible meaning.

(1) We have to do coursework in GCSE history.   ....

(2) The history of towns in the nineteenth century
     was determined by the needs of industry and trade.   ....

(3) History is the work of great men such as Telford,
     Stephenson and Brunel.   ....

(4) That's old history; I'm more concerned with
     the present.   ....

(5) The television programme about the Black Death
     was very good as history.   ....

(6) I prefer listening to music to history.   ....

Figure 5.4 Practical examples of Attainment Target 1 at Key Stage 4

KNOWLEDGE AND UNDERSTANDING OF HISTORY

	Component One THE NATURE OF HISTORICAL CHANGE	Component Two CAUSE AND CONSEQUENCE	Component Three ANALYSING HISTORICAL SITUATIONS
LEVEL 4	Recognise that over time some things changed and some things stayed the same.	Show an awareness that historical events usually have more than one cause and consequence.	Describe different features of an historical period.
Example: franchise and politics	There have usually been more than two political parties but two have usually been dominant. Is this true of the years 1918–91?	Give more than one reason why women over the age of 30 were given the vote in 1918.	Describe the different features of political and social life in the 1920s.
LEVEL 5	Distinguish between different kinds of historical change.	Identify different types of cause and consequence.	Show how different features in an historical situation relate to each other.
Example: welfare state	Explain the political, social and economic changes which led to the Liberal Governments of 1906–15 to pass laws for the needy.	List the short-term and long-term consequences of the Liberal social reforms of 1906–15.	Explain how the political, social and economic changes in the years to 1906 helped to create a demand for reforms to help the needy.
LEVEL 6	Show an understanding that change and progress are not the same.	Recognise that causes and consequences can vary in importance.	Describe the different ideas and attitudes of people in an historical situation.
Example: mass-production	Show how mass production in the 1920s led to new but not necessarily better jobs.	Discuss in a group what you think were the most important consequences of the rise of the motor car and why.	Describe the different ideas and attitudes which people had about the mass-produced car in the 1920s and 1930s.
LEVEL 7	Show an awareness that patterns of change can be complex.	Show how the different causes of an historical event are connected.	Show an awareness that different people's ideas and attitudes are often related to their circumstances.
Example: Japan 1900–45	How far did Japan's economy, society and form of government change in the years 1900–41?	Explain how a number of different causes led to the Japanese attack on Pearl Harbour in 1941.	Explain why some people favoured while others opposed the dropping of atomic bombs on Hiroshima and Nagasaki.

continued

Figure 5.4 continued

LEVEL 8		Explain the relative importance of several linked causes.	Show an understanding of the diversity of people's ideas, attitudes and circumstances in complex historical situations.
Example: the Indian subcontinent in 1947		Estimate the effects on Britain's withdrawal from India in 1947 of Ghandi's campaigns, the Second World War and the election of a Labour government.	Explain why in 1946–47 some people favoured the partition of India while others opposed it.
LEVEL 9		Show an understanding of how causes, motives and consequences may be related.	Explain why individuals did not necessarily share the ideas and attitudes of the groups and societies to which they belonged.
Example: China, 1920–49		Present to the class an account of the causes of the revolution in China in 1949, making connections with the Second World War, other general causes, and the intentions and motives of Mao Tse Tung.	Explain why and how the ideas of Mao Tse Tung and his followers about how Chinese society should be organised differed from the views of many Chinese people in the 1920s.
LEVEL 10	Show an understanding of the issues involved in describing and explaining complex historical situations.		
Example: the EEC	Discuss why it is difficult to generalise about and explain changing British attitudes towards the European Economic Community.		

Having placed the emphasis upon interpreting the past the next point is to emphasise that interpretations can either be how people in past eras interpreted their own or other people's past or how people today interpret their own and other people's history. Again a Key Stage 3 example would be helpful where a recent television programme or interpretation of mid-Victorian towns could be compared with the view given by Dickens or in a Doré print. To understand the complexities of this attainment target it would be useful first of all for the teacher to list for her- or himself the different levels and how they cash out in terms of classroom activities and questions at Key Stage 4. The following is a list compiled by one teacher:

Practical examples of AT2 at Key Stage 4
AT2: Interpretations of history

LEVEL 4 Shows an understanding that accounts of the past may differ for valid reasons.

How does the Soviet account of life in the Soviet Union in the 1930s differ from that written by John Gunther, a writer from the West, and why?

LEVEL 5 Recognises that accounts of past events may differ from what is known to have happened.

Examine the account of Lloyd George's clash with the House of Lords over his 'people's budget', and explain how it differs from what is known to have happened. Consult the textbook and fact sheet for details of the latter.

LEVEL 6 Shows that the ways in which historical sources are selected can affect interpretations.

Look at the range of historical sources relating to the general election of 1945 and explain how a Conservative, Labour, or Liberal supporter might offer different interpretations of the result depending on the particular sources each selects.

LEVEL 7 Describes the strengths and weaknesses of different interpretations of an historial event.

Discuss the extent to which the newspaper and newsreel reports of the Depression in the United States give accurate, reliable and complete accounts of it.

LEVEL 8 Shows how attitudes and circumstances can influence an individual's interpretation of historical events.

Read the accounts of Ian Smith's unilateral declaration of independence in Rhodesia and the background notes about each of the authors. Explain how the attitudes and circumstances of each author was likely to have influenced his view of the event.

LEVEL 9	Explains why different groups or societies interpret and use history in different ways.	Show how and why different groups in the Middle East interpret the origins and development of Israel in different ways.
LEVEL 10	Shows an understanding of the problems and issues involved in trying to make history as objective as possible.	Explain the difficulties and problems in trying to achieve an accurate and balanced account of events in Northern Ireland.

AT3 focuses on the use of historical sources and in particular on developing the students' abilities to acquire evidence from sources and to form judgements about their reliability and value. These abilities will already have been developed to level 7 at Key Stage 3 and therefore it would be appropriate to ease transition to Key Stage 4 through a recap-and-development activity. This could involve the application of a student guidance sheet; part of one,[6] which could be used in connection with level 6, comparing the value of different historical sources for a particular task, follows:

How different are the sources in what they say?

Use the following clues to help you answer this:

Clue 1: Look at the author(s). This might give you a lead-in.

Clue 2: Note general similarities or differences in viewpoints and provide quotations in support.

Clue 3: Look closely for some differences in viewpoints that are similar, or similarities in viewpoints that are mainly different.

Clue 4: It may be that there are no similarities or differences that can be easily picked out. They may simply not overlap in what they are talking about. Together, they may provide a fuller picture but they may not contradict each other or repeat what other sources say.

How different are the sources in how they put across their message?

Use the following clues to help you answer this:

Clue 1: Look again at the titles. These may provide clues about how the message is likely to be put across. A government statement might use statistics and special terms. A cartoon seeks to poke fun at someone or something.

Clue 2: Look closely at the details. In written sources, look at the kind of words used. Look at the *language*. Is it personal? Is it very emotional? How might it convey a bias? Compare the language of the sources.

Clue 3: How are they similar or how do they differ in their *style*? This refers to the general way in which they try to put their message across. One might be full of unsupported statements, compared with another which provides statistics, and so on, in support. One might be highly personal in its style while another might be very formal.

Clue 4: Look at their tones. This may be very closely related to their styles. One might be light-hearted in the way in which it deals with a subject; another might be very serious in tone.

AT3 calls on a fuller range of skills and abilities than is illustrated above. Levels 4–10 are listed with appropriate kinds of practical activity in which students can engage.

Practical activities relating to AT3 at Key Stage 4

Level	Description	Activity
LEVEL 4	Puts together information drawn from different historical sources.	Using your textbook, the written accounts and the film material, estimate the damage done to the US fleet after the Japanese attack in December 1941.
LEVEL 5	Comments on the value of an historical source by reference to its content.	Discuss the value of the election poster of 1979 to the historian wishing to study party propaganda.
LEVEL 6	Compares the value of different historical sources for a particular task.	Examine the photograph, the cartoon and the written account about apartheid in South Africa in the 1960s. Compare the value of each with regard to its accuracy and point of view.

Level	*Description*	*Activity*
LEVEL 7	Makes judgements about the reliability and value of historical sources by reference to the circumstances in which they were produced.	Explain how and why the reliability of the information about the Nazi occupation of the Channel Islands derived from the following newspapers can depend on who wrote the account and for whom and who owned the newspaper and under what conditions the account was written.
LEVEL 8	Shows how useful information can be obtained from historical sources despite their inaccuracies and distortions.	Examine the range of party political propaganda produced for the 1929 election. Explain what light it throws on the issues of the time and means adopted by parties to persuade people to vote for them.
LEVEL 9	Shows an understanding that a source can be more or less valuable depending on the questions asked.	Look carefully at the following extract from the diary of Barbara Castle. (a) Write down the questions which it answers best, the questions which it answers least and the questions which it tells us something about. (b) Now show how it provides an answer to one of the questions it answers best.
LEVEL 10	Explains the implications of gaps in historical evidence, showing an awareness that conclusions based on historical sources can be provisional.	'The following source shows that collectivisation in the USSR in the 1930s was a success.' Look carefully at the sources and say why it is not possible to arrive at such a definite conclusion.

It is important in the planning process to ensure that all ATs at all levels are represented adequately in each study unit. The use of checklists or matrices of the following kind can help to ensure this, both across study units and within each of the principal themes or issues. An example is shown in Figure 5.5.

CHECKLIST A	THE SPREAD OF ATs ACROSS KS4																	
ATs	CSU SUBTHEMES (TITLES IN EACH COLUMN)						SS41 SUBTHEMES (TITLES IN EACH COLUMN)						SSU2 SUBTHEMES (TITLES IN EACH COLUMN)					
1. Knowledge and understanding of history	√	√	√ √	√	√		√	√	√	√	√			√	√	√	√	
2. Interpretations of history		√		√			√			√				√		√	√	
3. Use of historical sources	√	√			√		√	√	√					√	√		√	

Figure 5.5 An example of an Attainment Target checklist at Key Stage 4

A similar matrix can be devised for each study unit to ensure that each AT is represented at each level.

Strategies for differentiation at Key Stage 4

The brief analyses of the ATs and the provision of practical examples raise an immediate and vital matter for the teacher which affects the organisation of the classroom, activities, teaching techniques and assessment. That is the key issue of differentiation. Under the old-style GCSE, that which caused the greatest headache for teachers and examiners alike was the requirement that tasks, activities and examination questions should be the same for all students (not graded), so that pupils operated at their own level without any prior assumption about their level of ability. The same task (and the language level with which it was conveyed) had to be accessible to all students. Differentiation was to be achieved by outcome not by input (see Figure 5.6). The National Curriculum has broken away from what was, for many teachers and most examiners an impossible constraint. The constant danger was that the nature of the task and the level of language used to describe it would be so facile that the most able students would not be stretched. Freed from the requirement of planning all or most activities on a differentiation-by-outcome basis, teachers of Key Stage 4 can adopt a variety of assessment strategies to cover the wide range of AT levels. As Key Stage 4 has a wider range of levels of achievement than the other key stages it may be helpful to indicate the variety of tasks which can be employed.

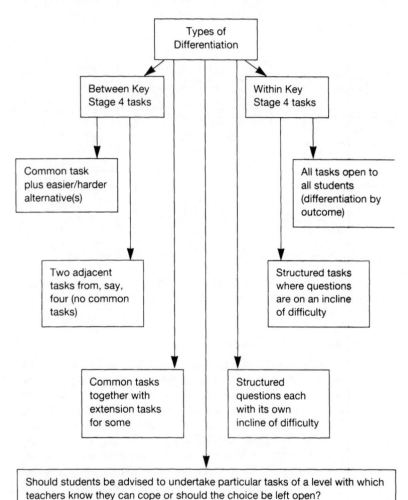

Figure 5.6 Identifying the kinds of differentiation

In terms of their application to the assessment of Key Stage 4 history, the basic considerations are indicated in Figure 5.7. What this

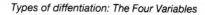

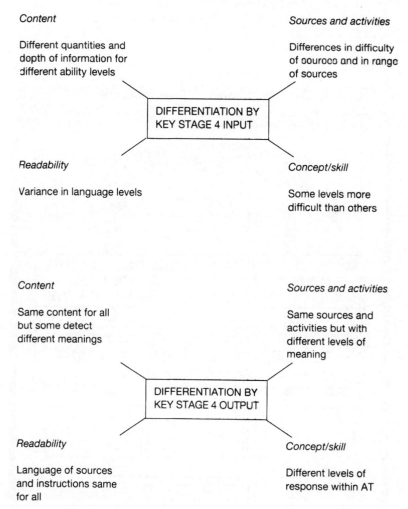

Figure 5.7 *Types of differentiation: the four variables*

figure indicates for teaching and learning strategies is that simply giving students extra time to complete a task is not always, or often, the best strategy for coping with the differences in ability level. The four dimensions (content, sources and activities, readability, concept or skill) can be varied to help ensure that the final stage of the National Curriculum leaves students with an active interest in history. Some means by which this can be achieved within the four dimensions are as follows. Content can be pruned or different aspects highlighted or special information briefings can be prepared to help students with particular learning difficulties. For example, some of the more difficult sub-themes of the core study unit on the development of British democracy can be presented initially in diagram form and discussed by

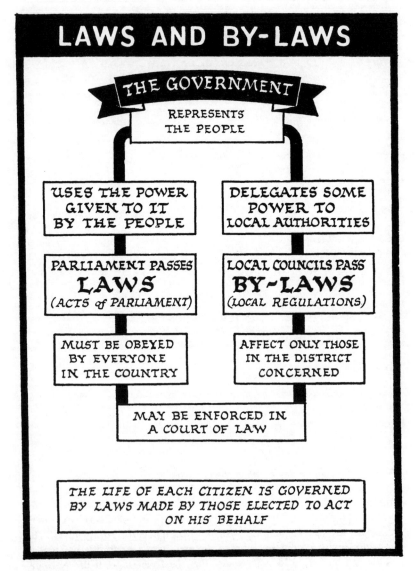

Figure 5.8 *History through diagrams: using older textbooks*

the use of particular examples. Some of the older textbooks[7] were particularly good at the diagrammatic presentation of political themes and their diagrams can be modified to serve some of the needs of the National Curriculum (see, e.g. Figure 5.8). In the case study unit at Key Stage 4 they can help in the explanation of concepts such as democracy or totalitarianism, but usually only after modification. History through diagrams is one way of approaching the teaching of Key Stage 4-isms which needs to be coupled with others.

The use of other visuals such as election posters and photographs, the employment of drama, film, artefacts and well-structured tasks which include oral history, should also help to make the more difficult areas of content more accessible to students. Group work and discussion, for example, on the British home front during the Second World War can greatly assist the learning process. If this is coupled with an individual practical task then the student's sense of achievement can be heightened. For example, Figure 5.9, a piece of Second World War propaganda presented to children in 1940 in the form of a paper folding exercise (which starts with four pigs and ends in a picture of Hitler's face)[8], can lead to a discussion of propaganda, its design and message.

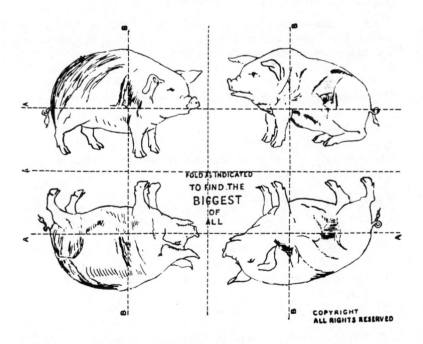

Figure 5.9 Wartime propaganda for children

Tasks such as the completion of sentences and diagrams, multiple choice and the annotation of visuals (including photographs) can be valuable in ascertaining whether students have understood the more intricate aspects of chronology or have grasped the meaning of key concepts. However, emphasis should be placed on encouraging students to communicate the results of their study in various ways and not just as a response to the more formal kind of examination question. This could include project work, a class presentation, or the use of IT. Very able students should not be expected simply to hand in more sheets of paper for marking than other students. They should be given a range of appropriate activities including discussion and further research. To preserve the focus of Key Stage 4 work, however, both students and teachers should be aware of the specific relationship between questions and ATs, and thus the generalised project where students just collect and compile material relating to a general theme should be avoided. It may thus be useful to have to hand a list of questions based on levels 4–10 for each of the ATs to help ensure that classroom activities are based on National Curriculum requirements.

Classroom questions at Key Stage 4

As in the case of other key stages, carefully devised questions can be used at Key Stage 4 to ensure precise links with the attainment targets. Examples of such questions are as follows:

ATI Knowledge and understanding of history

Chronology
(1) How long did . . . take?
(2) How does . . . relate to other developments of the time?
(3) Why did . . . take place before . . .?

Change
(1) Did . . . change considerably, moderately, little or not at all during this period? Give your reasons.
(2) Why did . . . change faster than . . . ?
(3) Why did . . . change and not . . . ?
(4) Do you think that the change in . . . could be considered as progress or not? Give your reasons.
(5) Did . . . change at the same rate as . . . ? Give your reasons.
(6) Identify the different ways in which . . . changed.
(7) Show how changes in . . . were linked to changes in . . .

(8) Explain why it is difficult to make general statements about the changes which took place in . . .

Cause and consequence

(1) What were the immediate and long term causes/consequences of . . . ?
(2) Which do you think were the most important causes and least important causes of . . . ? Give your reasons. Did you have any doubts? If so, explain why and what they were.
(3) Explain how the causes/consequences of . . . were connected.
(4) Explain how important in relation to each other the following causes/consequences of . . . were. (List causes/consequences.) Explain the reasons in full why you have placed them in this order of importance.
(5) Discuss how the causes and consequences of . . . were related in the case of . . .

Features of historical situations

(1) In what ways are . . . and . . . the same and in what ways do they differ?
(2) List the different features of . . .
(3) Write an account of . . . , linking together the following features . . .
(4) How did . . . and . . . differ in their views on . . . Explain these differences.
(5) How far do you think that the ideas of . . . and . . . were related to their circumstances and experiences?
(6) How far and why did the ideas and attitudes of . . . reflect their different . . . ?
(7) Matthew Arnold called those who did not share the ideas and attitudes of their group, class or society 'aliens'. Why do you think that . . . and . . . might be regarded as 'aliens'?

AT2: Interpreting history

(1) Show why interpretations of . . . may be restricted by the lack of evidence about . . .
(2) Why is there a difference in views about . . . between how people saw it at the time and how it is seen today?
(3) Explain how different ways of selecting sources about . . . can result in different interpretations of it/him/her.
(4) Read carefully the different accounts or interpretations of . . . and list what you think are (i) the strengths and (ii) the weaknesses of each account or interpretation.

(5) Examine the views of . . . as given in the film, the documents and the textbook and then list the strengths and weaknesses of each interpretation.

(6) Discuss how the circumstances in which . . . was written could have affected the view it presents of the event.

(7) How might the author's attitude toward . . . have been affected by his social class and political views?

(8) Show how and why . . . has been interpreted differently and used in different ways by . . .

(9) Can there ever be an unbiased and objective view of . . . ?

AT3: The use of historical sources

(1) Read carefully the following sources and use them to put together an account of . . .

(2) Read/look carefully at . . . and explain how useful you think it is in telling us about . . . Be careful to say what it does not tell us about as well as what it does.

(3) Examine the following sources about . . . and write down which you think is the most useful and the least useful. Justify your view by close reference to all the sources, taking care to comment on matters such as accuracy and bias.

(4) The following sources about . . . have obvious biases and inaccuracies. First of all, say what the biases and inaccuracies are and then explain why despite them the sources can still be useful to the historian.

(5) How far is the value of the following source(s) dependent on the questions which we wish to ask about . . . ?

(6) Examine the following sources about . . . and then explain why any conclusions about . . . we arrive at (just from using them) cannot be regarded as definite. What other kinds of evidence would you need to consider in order to arrive at a more reliable conclusion about . . .

The planning of SSUs

The kinds of question which need to be asked to elicit responses which relate subject content explicitly to the attainment targets are an important consideration in planning. In particular, they help teachers to decide which parts of the subject content of the CSU and SSUs can best be related to which ATs and to which levels of ATs. This means, as has been mentioned earlier, that not all aspects of the content of the programmes of study need to be treated in the same way or in the same depth. Planning should aim at identifying 'nodal points', that is at pinpointing aspects of content which naturally and peculiarly lend themselves to particular attainment targets. For example in the CSU the extension of the franchise in 1918, 1928 and 1969 provides an excellent focus for considering the nature of change. However, the CSU has been so designed to make the links between subject content and ATs appear natural and obvious. This is not so in the case of the SSUs where, for single-subject GCSE student teachers have to design their own units.

In the design of the SSUs it is helpful to think also in terms of nodal points rather than treating subject matter in equal depth for two reasons. First, it enables teachers to highlight and to give more time to aspects of content which dovetail easily with particular ATs; for example in the in-depth study a large body of documentary and other material is available for study in the case of the Russian Revolutions in 1917, the Arab-Israeli War of 1967 and the Chinese Revolution of 1949. The SSU which examines a theme over time (parliament, public health, education, work, migration or popular culture) also offers opportunities for identifying particular 'nodal points' during development which lend themselves to making comparisons and contrasts; for example, examining parliamentary elections before the secret ballot and after 1872 provides both links with the CSU and with earlier key stages and relates directly to the first of the compulsory attainment targets. The nodal points should then be further examined to see how well they facilitate the answering of the specific questions related to the ATs in the previous section. Secondly, it enables teachers to highlight those areas of the supplementary study units which link with the core units. Thirdly, it helps to ensure that students examine the full range of perspectives which are laid down in the National Curriculum, political, economic, technological and scientific, social, religious, cultural and aesthetic. Figure 5.10 provides examples of how this can work out in practice.

Study materials for Key Stage 4

The CSU and SSUs lend themselves to the use of a wide range of study materials. In view of the fact that many students may only be studying a part GCSE in history (and therefore the CSU only) it would be best not to confine certain categories of source material to the CSU and others to the SSUs. All attainment targets will apply to the CSU and therefore the full range of study materials which encourage students to achieve the highest levels in all of the attainment targets can be employed to good effect. It is therefore inappropriate to discuss study materials in relation to particular study units, although some may perhaps be more usefully employed than others. Perhaps the best general guideline is to use a mixture of study materials of a pictorial and written nature with perhaps the majority being of a primary nature if used as adjuncts to a textbook or information sheet.

A. *SSU CHANGE OVER TIME (EXAMPLES OF NODAL POINTS FROM SSU ON PARLIAMENT)*

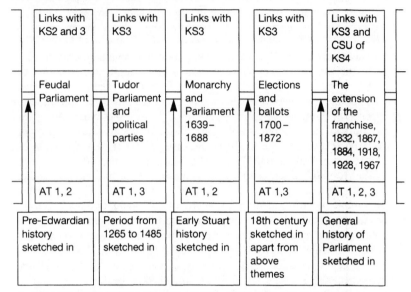

Links with KS2 and 3	Links with KS3	Links with KS3	Links with KS3	Links with KS3 and CSU of KS4
Feudal Parliament	Tudor Parliament and political parties	Monarchy and Parliament 1639–1688	Elections and ballots 1700–1872	The extension of the franchise, 1832, 1867, 1884, 1918, 1928, 1967
AT 1, 2	AT 1, 3	AT 1, 2	AT 1,3	AT 1, 2, 3
Pre-Edwardian history sketched in	Period from 1265 to 1485 sketched in	Early Stuart history sketched in	18th century sketched in apart from above themes	General history of Parliament sketched in

B. *SSU STUDY IN DEPTH (EXAMPLES OF NODAL POINTS IN THE HISTORY OF THE UNITED STATES OF AMERICA 1917 TO THE PRESENT DAY)*

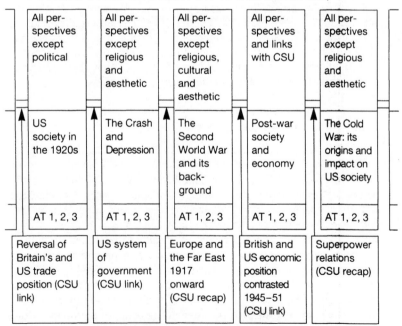

All perspectives except political	All perspectives except religious and aesthetic	All perspectives except religious, cultural and aesthetic	All perspectives and links with CSU	All perspectives except religious and aesthetic
US society in the 1920s	The Crash and Depression	The Second World War and its background	Post-war society and economy	The Cold War: its origins and impact on US society
AT 1, 2, 3	AT 1, 2, 3	AT 1, 2, 3	AT 1, 2, 3	AT 1, 2, 3
Reversal of Britain's and US trade position (CSU link)	US system of government (CSU link)	Europe and the Far East 1917 onward (CSU recap)	British and US economic position contrasted 1945–51 (CSU link)	Superpower relations (CSU recap)

Figure 5.10 SSU change over time and study in depth

Possibly one of the most difficult areas of the National Curriculum to teach is that which relates to forms of government whether these be in the CSU or SSUs. A range of materials and approaches could well be employed, including the following:

(1) Concentrating initially on one or two salient features with reference to Key Stage 3 concepts, reinforced with diagrammatic material.

(2) Broadening out the subject area by reference to comparison and contrast with other political systems (with documentary examples of the written constitution of the United States).

(3) Using anecdotal evidence from the past to highlight key areas, for example, accounts of life under a dictator.

(4) Using source materials such as newspaper accounts of elections, cartoon and electoral materials to highlight issues. Cartoons from *Punch*, where the language might be difficult, are not necessarily the best choice.

(5) Concentrating on the rhetoric and reality of party promises at election times and after.

(6) Using role play and group work to point up salient features of electioneering including canvassing and the presentation of arguments.

(7) Using oral history, particularly to improve communication skills (listening, interviewing, compiling results in various ways) and to encourage pupils to take a more active interest in political issues within their locality.

(8) Analysing party political broadcasts in terms of presentation and message.

(9) Examining the diaries and accounts of leading figures including the suffragettes and women war workers (1914–1918).

(10) Integrating the CSU study of British democracy with SSU studies over time or in-depth, to provide examples of practical insights into government attitudes and actions in the case of the former, and contrasts and comparisons in the case of the latter.

(11) Linking with other subjects, such as geography and social studies.

Whichever of these methods are employed the emphasis should be upon reducing the material to manageable sections. In the case of a single document such as that of the American Constitution of 1787, this can be done by dividing the relevant extracts into three and embedding them within a diagrammatic framework, as shown in Figure 5.11, overleaf.

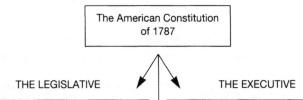

THE LEGISLATIVE

All legislative powers herein granted shall be vested in a Congress of the United States, which shall consist of a Senate and House of Representatives.

The Congress shall have power to lay and collect taxes, duties, imposts and excises, to pay the debts and provide for the common defence and general welfare of the United States.

To borrow money on the credit of the United States.

To regulate commerce with foreign nations and among the several States, and with the Indian tribes.

THE EXECUTIVE

The executive power shall be vested in a President of the United States of America. He shall hold his office during the term of four years, and together with the Vice-President, chosen for the same term.

The President shall be Commander-in-chief of the Army and Navy of the United States.

THE JUDICIARY

The judicial power of the United States shall be vested in one Supreme Court.

The judges, both of the Supreme and (lesser) courts, shall hold their offices during good behaviour....

Figure 5.11 The American Constitution of 1787: an example of deconstruction

Interlinking primary sources and developing a series of questions which become progressively broader or deeper is another method of teaching and assessing, as illustrated below on page 185.

Democracy in action

Source 1

Striking visual
(e.g. election poster
or cartoon)

Question on context
(using textbook), genre
and viewpoint

Source 2

Brief written account
(e.g. newspaper account)

Source 3

Lengthier account of
election, giving details
of views of political
parties or statistics.

This can be extended for the more able
students to include:

Source 4

More difficult cartoon
or prose material
(for written analysis
in terms of genre
and content)

Source 5

Autobiographical material
of a more difficult nature
(for discussion)

Cross-curricular links

The National Curriculum encourages cross-curricular links at each of
its key stages. At Key Stage 4 these may be particularly vital for at
this stage students may elect to combine history with other subjects.
For some students history may form one part of a GCSE course and
thus any links with other subjects which can help to make such a
course more coherent may well be more important at Key Stage 4 than
at any of the preceding key stages. It is thus fortunate that history, by
its very nature and its sources, encompasses most of the other subjects
on the school curriculum. National curriculum history with its
emphasis on the teaching of a wide variety of perspectives and sources
makes these links both explicit and essential. The cultural perspective
offers opportunities for studying the cultural products of various
groups of people within Britain and other countries. These may not
necessarily be restricted to 'high art' and certainly the SSU theme of
the development of popular culture over time encourages the study of
the popular culture of the masses. Folk songs, the decline of the music

A very popular traditional picture by Hokusai, 1830

A Japanese cartoon of the 1960s showing Japanese feelings against American naval strength

Figure 5.12   Cartoons and cross-curricular approaches

hall and the rise of twentieth-century popular music in its various forms offer rich opportunities for links with Key Stage 4 music. The cultures and cultural products of other countries also offer a wealth of material for discussion. Figure 5.12 shows how a traditional Japanese print has been turned into a cartoon of the 1960s directed against America's naval and nuclear strength.[9]

The close study of the design of cartoons to convey a clear message can be a rewarding aspect of Key Stage 4 teaching in view of the abundance of contemporary material for use with the CSU and SSUs.

The economic perspective can be used to foster numeracy skills, especially the understanding and presentation of statistical information. It can also be used to encourage the awareness and understanding of the various ways in which economic development can be measured and can make maximum use of information technology in both the CSU and SSU in order to do this. Graphs and graphics provide a particularly important set of links between history and mathematical skills. This could be combined with work in modern foreign languages if the material relates particularly to the EC.

The supplementary study units offer several opportunities for single-subject GCSE students to relate history to other aspects of the curriculum. That on public health provides natural links with health education and environmental education. That on work can relate well to careers education and can in particular show the changing career opportunities available to female students. The study of leisure in the CSU dovetails easily with physical education and recreational studies. Literature can provide a valuable historical source for studying each of these areas and many of the other themes in the CSU and SSUs.

Thus the range of content and the breadth of attainment targets offer immense opportunities at Key Stage 4 for offering students of history an interesting, relevant and challenging course which can lead to further study.

For further consideration

(1)   Compare the present National Curriculum with that in operation in the early 1920s.

(2)   Examine Figure 5.1 and the three attainment targets with their practical examples. Does the present National Curriculum provide a balanced and adequate course in history for (i) single-subject history students and (ii) students continuing history with other subjects at GCSE?

(3)   Discuss variants and other models for planning Key Stage 4 history to that given in Figure 5.2.

(4)   Using the format given in Figure 5.3 plan another work unit using each of the columns.

(5) Working as a group provide another example of practical activities for each component of AT1 at each level.

(6) Provide other examples of practical activities for AT2 and AT3 using the SSU one and two but not the CSU.

(7) Outline alternative activities to bridge Key Stage 3 and Key Stage 4 for each of the attainment targets.

(8) Discuss the difficulties of devising a question which the most able and the least able students can undertake.

(9) Distinguish between differentiation by outcome and differentiation by input by reference to particular tasks, activities and questions in history.

(10) Discuss the various ways of helping students to understand the political concepts of the core study unit.

(11) Apply the questions for directing teaching to the ATs to particular themes of the CSU and the SSUs.

(12) Plan part of another SSU on a nodal point model.

(13) Discuss other ways of developing cross-curricular links.

Notes and references

1. See R. Brooks, *Contemporary Debates in Education: An Historical Perspective*, Longman, 1991 (The Effective Teacher series), pp. 56–9.
2. Lord Eustace Percy, *Some Memories*, p. 108.
3. *The Final Report of the National Curriculum History Working Group*, April 1990, HMSO, p.1.
4. Ibid.
5. R. Brooks, op.cit., p. 55.
6. R. Brooks, *Modern World History*, Edward Arnold, 1989, p. 87.
7. The diagram is taken from R.W. Purton, *Our Democracy*, Collins, 1958, p. 151.
8. From R. Brooks, *Modern World History*, Edward Arnold, 1989, p. 109.
9. From R. Brooks, *Schools History Project*, Edward Arnold, 1989, p. 125.

CHAPTER 6

History in the sixth form

Irene S. Perry

Introduction

The sixth form has gone through many changes claimed and real in
the last few decades. During the early 1960s there was great pressure
for a review of the sixth form curriculum and examinations. The
Schools Council set up a series of enquiries which resulted in Working
Paper No. 5 which suggested a new pattern of provision based on the
following principles:

(1) That sixth forms now contain more and more pupils who are
    prolonging their secondary education but do not all intend to go
    on to any form of higher education, whose intellectual level may
    or may not have carried them beyond GCE ordinary level, and for
    whom A level courses in their present form may not be entirely
    suitable.
(2) That sixth form courses need to take into account changes that are
    happening within subjects and in the relationship between
    subjects; and also awaken the students' interest in ideas and
    problems which overlap and transcend their specialist studies.
(3) That the complaint of over-specialisation in the sixth form needs
    to be examined carefully, together with remedies which have been
    proposed and which some schools are practising.
(4) That in the face of these pressures, a review of sixth form
    curricula and examinations in the light of the staff resources
    available is plainly desirable.[1]

The Schools Council referred the paper to its subject committees
asking them to consider methods of examining other than external
examination and in particular oral assessments and teacher
assessments. The history committee was generally against a departure
from custom although it did feel that some form of teacher assessment
could be contemplated.

The 1970s saw attempts to address the findings of the Schools
Council Working Papers No. 46 and 47 with the formation of a
History Commissioned Group to prepare Normal (N) and Further (F)
Syllabuses with associated schemes of assessment and examination
papers. The group decided that they would cover British and European

history from 1450 to the present day but only develop selected aspects in detail. They identified their aims as follows:

(a) to develop an understanding of the nature and discipline of the subject;
(b) to emphasise that the study of history includes equally the discerning of longer term trends and short studies in depth;
(c) to encourage the use of a wide variety of sources;
(d) to encourage clarity of expression and historical imagination;
(e) to stress the skills involved in teaching and learning history by using a variety of assessment techniques. [2]

The outcome was a mixture of internal and external examinations with each using various forms of questions from multiple choice to the traditional essay. However the reform of the A level pattern as a whole was found to be politically unacceptable and the N and F models were dropped.

The early 1980s saw history decline in popularity as an A level and as a subject for study at university. Several factors accounted for this. At school level there was the introduction of new subjects competing for the academic options, e.g. economics and sociology. Also there was the onslaught of the Technical and Vocational Education Initiative (TVEI) which called into question those subjects whose immediate relevance to the employment market place was not obvious. Historians were slow to respond to criticisms of their subject's lack of contemporary study and any especial skills which it endowed in its students.

There was a growing fear that the fate of Latin would be shared by history unless there was an orchestrated fight back. This the various history societies and university departments had begun by the mid 1980s. The History at Universities Defence Group was established in May 1983 and in an article in the *Times Educational Supplement* on 21 February 1986 P. Beck showed that only one in nine history graduates failed to find employment which was no worse than average. These messages were passed on in the schools and sixth form colleges to try to counter the decline of the subject. Moreover there were various efforts in some authorities to show that history was relevant and provided an intellectual training which though not unique was appropriate to particular professions. More importantly, however, this challenge resulted in a reappraisal of traditional A level syllabuses and methodologies and an attempt to establish the value of sixth form history.

Simultaneously it was emerging that the different styles of assessment being pioneered in GCSE syllabuses were creating a mismatch at A level where all too often the traditional essay type answer was the only form of question. A few boards had introduced document questions but none had taken on board the principle of coursework in the same way as the GCSE examinations had done.

Although there was an attempt to resurrect the Higginson proposals for general A level reform and some exploratory talk of a British baccalaureate the Conservative government declared itself happy to retain the so-called 'gold standard' of A levels and begin reform from the bottom up with the national curriculum. There is still some uncertainty about the final nature of short course history at Key Stage 4 and its future attractiveness to schools and students. There has yet to be a discussion of a Key Stage 5 but since this is being suggested in other subjects there would appear to be no reason why moves in this direction should not be made in history. Several boards have already undertaken revision of their syllabuses and have introduced coursework elements as options along with seen and unseen document questions and in the case of the WJEC structured questions and case studies. With this greater variety of assessment techniques it is hoped that the subject itself will attract a greater audience.

The actual content of the syllabuses is also a factor in its marketing and it has been argued by writers such as Vincent A. Crinnion in his 1987 article that:

The syllabus must be firmly centred on historical problems rather than on periods of time, developing outwards from a single historical happening towards the temporal and spatial context that gives the event its historical meaning.[3]

The results of views such as this can be seen in the blend of chronological or outline periods and special subjects or studies in depth which most GCE papers now include. Given this more varied choice of study it is hoped that the decline of the subject can be stopped. Teachers must be ready to stress the place of their subject in the sixth form and its value.

The value of sixth form history

When a student chooses the subject at sixth form he or she is opting to be a historian with all the intellectual rigour which that implies. It is possible to apply the theoretical basis for this through a review of Coltham and Fines, 'Educational Objectives for the Study of History' produced as a pamphlet by the Historical Association in 1971. This publication provoked much discussion and is a useful starting point for the new history teacher. It sets out a framework within which the purpose of the subject is analysed thus:

Section A: Attitudes towards the study of history;
Section B: the nature of the discipline;
Section C: skills and abilities;
Section D: educational outcomes of study.[4]

This has relied heavily on an objectives approach to teaching history and as such has been criticised by those who believed that it was not sufficient to justify 'new history' simply through its use of evidence, rather one had to first analyse what was involved in historical understanding.

Professor Elton described the purpose of the study of history as threefold: to understand the past, to learn about human behaviour, and to search for the truth. The last he feels is its essence:

> Like all sciences, history, to be worthy of itself and beyond itself, must concentrate on one thing: the search for the truth. Its real value as a social activity lies in the training it provides, the standard it sets, in this singularly human concern. Reason distinguishes man from the rest of creation, and the study of history, regarded as an autonomous enterprise, contributes to the improvement of man, and it does so by seeking the truth within the confines of its particular province, which happens to be the rational reconstruction of the past. In this larger purpose it has no monopoly, for this it shares with every form of intellectual investigation, but it happens to have certain advantages in that it attracts a wide variety of intelligences, and does its work without too much demand on technical specialisation in the learner and can rest its capacity to train on its capacity to entertain.[5]

There are those who more recently have questioned that history can only be justified on the basis of its intellectual integrity at sixth form level. It is important to discriminate between the student who takes the subject along with others to gain qualifications and the undergraduate who has chosen to read the subject at university. While it should be recognised that history should not simply be a body of transmitted information and carefully rehearsed interpretations of that information neither should students be expected to behave as academic researchers. There is a middle road which leads to the heart of sixth form teaching and that is to teach the students to think historically.

This is not to imply that the value of the subject lies only in the ability to handle evidence or to enter into historiographical debate but rather it suggests that the effective teacher is the one who poses historical questions which allow progression from the factual event to the causes, motives, effects and results within a historical context. It is where students are trained in historical question-framing that the subject is imparting its best skills. V.A. Crinnion offered a list of these skills which though not exclusive to history do provide attributes of key social relevance:

(i) *The skills of communication* :
  (a) an ability to write fluently and concisely, organise ideas and information in an ordered and logical manner, marshall evidence in support of cogently constructed argumentation;
  (b) a willingness and facility for oral discussion and debate, to listen and to persuade;

(ii) *The attributes of rational enquiry:*
  (a) a willingness to always view information in an open-minded and critical way;
  (b) a capacity not to be imprisoned in familiar ideas or viewpoints or to accept habitually statements of authority (personal, political or scholarly);
  (c) an ability to expand upon what is given, to attain new levels of thought, more subtle or profound, which go beyond first impressions and instincts; acquiring different ways and techniques of looking at a question, idea or event;
  (d) a tolerance of ambivalence, uncertainty and contingency.

(iii) *The ability to appraise and use evidence:*
  (a) an acquaintance with the importance and nature of the relationship between explanation and the concept of proof (especially, but not only, in the sense of empirical evidence and inductive thinking);
  (b) a discriminatory attitude towards the concept of 'Facts' and types of opinion or degrees of bias;
  (c) a familiarity with basic statistical ideas and quantitative methods whenever such discrimination as to data is significant.

(iv) *The awareness of important aspects of social change:*
  (a) some understanding of man's capacity for improvement and decline, together with an appreciation of the contemporary values (democracy, scientific rationalism, materialism etc.) that help shape such viewpoints;
  (b) an insight into the logical and methodological problems involved in discussions of causation (primary and secondary, necessary and sufficient, long and short term, etc.);
  (c) an acceptance of the co-existence of social elements of continuity and discontinuity in those periods usually characterised in terms of one or the other.[6]

The teacher new to A level teaching would do well to study this list and use it both to explain the value of the subject to aspiring sixth formers and to guide the pedagogical techniques which need to be developed to achieve these skills.

Classroom approaches

The syllabus

It will be rare indeed for a newly qualified teacher (probationary teachers no longer existing) to be able to select which syllabus he or she would like to teach. This will normally have been decided by the Head of Department and all too often on the basis of that person's own preference and expertise and the resources which are available in the school. However the pace of change is so fast in education today that new syllabuses are due to appear in the next few years and given due consultation all department members should share in the selection of new syllabuses.

Inevitably there will continue to be limited funding and this means that costs will have to be borne in mind should a department decide to change from say Tudors and Stuarts to nineteenth-century Britain and Europe. However teachers should have some criteria by which they judge the examination courses offered by the various boards. Three are suggested here.

First, there is the question of period. The chronological length of some periods of study can lead to a content overload which almost invites a didactic and superficial approach. Few history syllabuses suffer from brevity but teachers should examine the demands of one period as against another in the light of the approaches they wish to use. It is also important that where in-depth studies are offered the selection should in part at least be motivated by the need to intrigue and stimulate the interests of sixth formers while providing sufficient depth to enable genuine contrast and comparisons to be drawn.

Secondly, there is the question of form of assessment. Again this needs to be matched to the approaches used in the classroom. It will depend on how much use is made of the range of techniques available as to which examination format is best suited to the students.

The choice includes:

(1)   oral assessment;
(2)   multiple-choice questions;
(3)   short answer questions;
(4)   single-source questions;
(5)   multi-source questions;
(6)   case studies;
(7)   structured questions;
(8)   historiography questions;
(9)   essay questions;
(10) school based assessment encompassing critical bibliographies; or book reviews or prepared essays or dissertation.

It will be vital that students are trained for the correct assessment procedures and given ample opportunity to practice the necessary skills.

Thirdly, there will be the question of resources. Despite funding problems it is essential that students are given access to a wide range of materials. Teachers should prepare extensive reading lists for students to negotiate with their local library or with which to scour the second hand book shops.

Where there are difficulties over basic textual supplies prepared notes by the teacher are often used to plug the gaps. Documents are increasingly published in ready-to-order packs, but because of the limited A level market it is likely that only a selection will be appropriate for each syllabus. Therefore the conscientious teacher must set to in cut and paste exercises with many a begging letter for photocopying permission to prepare a school based document pack. Fortunate are those who can, through their LEA or local teachers centre enter into a shared endeavour working group where more may be produced for less individual effort. Additional stimulus material should be provided through audio-visual and video resources which can be built up over time.

Given that a syllabus has been selected and the department has opted for a chosen period and/or in-depth study, it is then important that the exact wording of the syllabus is studied and clearly understood. The effective teacher will supply students with the syllabus in as full a fashion as possible. This allows senior classes to develop a sense of direction and aid independent learning among students. Any rotational changes of question focus need to be closely monitored and copies of the syllabus updated annually.

New teachers to A level should also read examiners' reports. These are an invaluable source of guidance. Not only will they outline faults committed by candidates but they will commend good practice, recommend texts, guide teacher approaches and offer further advice on the interpretation of the syllabus. These reports will also deal with the way in which the paper was marked. The assessment procedure must also be carefully studied to ensure that candidates are properly prepared for the final examination. This should entail the identification of each form of assessment and the topics associated with each. Past papers will further support teachers in their preparations to teach the course.

Methods of delivery

Just as history examinations at A level held on longer to traditional forms of assessment so the teaching methods used to deliver sixth form history have shown a remarkable resistance to change. In a survey conducted in 1985 of 200 lower sixth history students the following results were recorded:[7]

Feature	Percentage of lesson time taken up			
	0–25	26–50	51–75	76–100
(1) Dictated notes	29	49	11	11
(2) Class discussion	58	36	5	1
(3) Individual reading and making own notes (excluding essay preparation)	64	27	9	0
	0–5	6–10	11–15	16–20
(4) Slides, television, tapes	73	13	9	5
(5) Primary documents	86	11	2	1

While this is a relatively small sample, it is probable that it is fairly typical of the range of teaching approaches used at sixth form level. It is worthwhile dwelling on each of these to consider their strengths and weaknesses as effective methods.

Dictated notes

Dictated notes in the sample took up more than half the lesson time for 78 per cent of the respondents. This is understandable when one accepts that most schools or colleges find it difficult to provide a sufficiently wide range of reading materials for all students. Teachers therefore usually prepare their own notes on topics which are either poorly covered by the set course textbook or on interpretations of aspects which are different. The hard pressed teacher cannot always have these notes duplicated for large groups and there is a valid argument that given the nature of lectures in higher education establishments students need lots of practice in note taking but this is not quite the same as dictation. The amount of time which can be consumed in dictation must be measured against the benefits of having additional materials presented in this way. A prepared lecture would be more realistic as practice but could be supported by giving students a skeleton outline of the content from the outset and an opportunity for review at the conclusion. If these notes were later checked over this would ensure accurate as well as sufficient coverage.

Class discussion

As with the previous method the sample recorded a significant usage of this in lessons but its frequency rapidly diminished as the percentage time increased. It is arguable that since the sample concentrated on the lower sixth form perhaps the emphasis had to be skewed towards transmission of information until the students were aware enough to make a reasonable contribution to discussion. However too often lessons can take the form of passive reception of information. There should be a balanced approach in order that students can feel actively involved in their learning. This can vary between an organised debate with adequate preparation, a mini-tutorial with differing contributions from participants or a series of group sessions with a plenary reporting back. Students can often learn a great deal from each other in this way especially in the interpretation of questions.

Individual reading and making own notes

Inevitably this will form a major part of an A level course. It is not enough to stress the need for active reading to students, they must be encouraged to develop specific skills according to the type of reading they are undertaking. The obvious starting place is with the general history book. L. G. Brandon in his guide to advanced level study offers these suggestions as to how to proceed:

(1) select a chapter or a section which deals with a particular topic and read it fairly quickly in order to form a general picture of the sequence of events and ideas;
(2) read the same part again, more slowly and have two separate pages for notes. On one page put references to any ideas or words which you do not understand, and the names of any people about whom you know little. On the other page give very brief notes about the sequence of events and about any statements which you regard as especially important. (Later sections will suggest other references which you may wish to include in these notes when you have become accustomed to critical reading);
(3) work carefully through your first page of notes, using the index of your textbook and any other available help, until you have found the necessary information;
(4) find an examination question which deals with your topic and sketch out a brief answer to it in note-form.[8]

There are many ways in which an effective teacher at A level can advise students to make their reading more purposeful. Strategies can be adopted to improve concentration and speed of reading both of which are invaluable aids. When students move from general histories to monographs it is important that they realise that they must be more critical in their reading since this is a more specialised form of writing based on front-line evidence. Articles can be particularly useful to students since they are usually more brief and succinct and offer an interpretation of major historians' work. There are several publications now aimed at the student of sixth form history and if teachers can at least arrange for their libraries to have an institutional copy this would be an asset.

Slides, television, tapes

It is little wonder that the use of such audio-visual aids is notably slight in sixth form teaching. Since this is a smaller and more specialised market few companies provide a comprehensive range of software for use. It is also very important that such aids are carefully previewed by the teacher looking in particular for a bias on the part of the producers or unsubstantiated comment. These can highlight for students the need always to question evidence. Some tapes are available of discussions of eminent historians on major figures and issues in history but teachers need to set the scene and use their judgement to intervene at times with provocative questions if the interest and concentration of students are to be maintained. Television can be a double-edged sword in the teaching of modern history syllabuses. While there is much benefit in the viewing of documentary footage it is also possible to convey a distorted image because of lack of clarity in the purpose of the programme makers. It is important that the teacher explores this fully with students. Although not mentioned in the survey the use of computer programs is still negligible at A level confined mainly as it is to factual revision tests.

Primary documents

This is one element of the survey which may well have changed since 1985. Every examination board now has some form of document question included in its paper. In some cases it can be a document selected from a previously specified pack, i.e. a *seen* document, in other cases it could be an unseen document. Since this is a growing element in examinations the effective teacher will be one who carefully prepares the work for the students and guides them through the use of documents. Several texts are available for sixth formers to aid their understanding of the methods to use when handling documents. One of the most useful is John Fines' 1988 publication, *Reading Historical Documents – A Manual for Students*. This manual cautions students that documents must be handled with care. Indeed in the interests of correctness 'document' is a term which should be reserved for 'a complete item of primary material in continuous prose'.[9] Most material would therefore be *source material* and what we get out of these sources is our *evidence*.

John Fines suggests how to tackle a document in eight easy steps which are summarised below:

Stage one   What is it? Describe your document – diary, letter, etc.

Stage two   Break it down into sections, e.g.:
  • information about people;
  • information about time;
  • information about places;
  • information about ideas.

Stage three What do you not understand? Look up these things.

Stage four   What things in the document mark its period? It may be something obvious such as language but look also for attitudes.

Stage five   Evaluate the reliability of the document. Is there anything which raises your doubts?

Stage six   Is there something else you would like to know as a result of reading the document?

Stage seven What use is the document to the historian? What is its worth?

Stage eight How are you going to record your findings?[10]

These steps are reproduced here not only to commend the manual and its methods but to show new teachers to A level the sort of process they will need to go through with a document before setting it for their students. It is important to be thoroughly prepared yourself before launching students on such exercises.

Where a syllabus has prescribed documents the teacher must ensure that all of these are covered but where the choice lies with the examiner then the teacher has to prepare a sufficient selection of documents to cover various interpretations of a topic or period. This can be a major task. If, for example, students were studying Nazism 1933–45, the teacher must seek to cover the most significant official documents, selections from the notable historical works, e.g. Alan Bullock's *Study in Tyranny*, a range of eye-witness accounts and perhaps a few extracts from memoirs. The syllabus should give some guidance but the teacher needs to research carefully his or her programme of study and collect suitable documents as illustrations.

Where the period of study is considerably earlier, let us say the sixteenth century, there are further considerations of the difficulty of language. The purist historian would say that one cannot 'doctor' sources but it has to be acknowledged that teachers will have to provide explanatory notes at least on some occasions. It is not necessary to prevent access to an understanding of certain documents by students for want of some key to the terminology or a typed replica of a copperplate written work.

Would the following extract be rendered more accessible by providing some guidance on language?

Costs of the Reformation
The following extracts are taken from the Churchwarden's accounts of Leverton, near Boston in Lincolnshire. How might they help an historian to write about the effect of the various changes in religion

upon the common man? (Volume of Accounts, 1492–1625, deposited in the Lincolnshire Archives Office.)[11]

1526: 'Recevyd of Janet ffranckyshe for the legacye of William ffranckyshe hyr husband to the biynge of ymages of Alybaster to be set in the forsyde of the rode lofite: xlvi s viiid'
1549: 'Item payd to the peintor for penntyng over the Rod Loft: iiis viiid'
1555: 'payd to John lynne for a pyxe : viis viiid'
1561: 'item paid for removynge the Alters out of the chyrch: xiiid' [11]

This extract was reproduced in an Historical Association pamphlet, No. 54 in the *Teaching of History* series (1984) entitled Source-based Questions at A-Level, and written by John Fines. In this selection of sources the author identifies the three major skills required with such materials – handling, evaluation and application. For the source exampled above he identified the handling skill as:

Questions about *period*: can you apply period and time sense to this source – can you empathise in a properly detached way, can you visualise both the time and conditions?

He also identified four forms of application:

1. Can you sort out what *questions* the source raises, as well as the answer it gives?
2. Can you estimate the *significance* of the evidence?
3. Can you *extrapolate* from the evidence to provide a conclusion, or an hypothesis?
4. Can you provide a *description*, a *comparison* or an *interpretation* as a result of using evidence that conforms to the pattern of what we call History.

This extract serves to show that when teachers select documents to work on with their students they have to address several different aspects. First, of course the document should be relevant to the period or topic being studied. Secondly, there must be sufficient meat in the document to justify its selection, i.e. its actual content must be significant. Thirdly, the teacher must be able to formulate various types of questions to set which will ensure that students use a range of skills. Finally, it can be argued that a 'good' document will provoke further posing of questions and so lead on to more detailed study.

Reference so far has perhaps inclined more towards the use of written material as documents but visual sources such as photographs, paintings, cartoons, posters or engravings can all serve to test students' ability with evidence. With these the range of skills may be more constricted but interesting exercises can be set where comparisons of written and visual sources are invited. This introduces a further refinement which a few boards encompass at A level – the multi-source question. In the Appendix there is an example taken from the WJEC A level paper of 1992 on the special subject of fascism. Students were asked to study all the sources and answer the questions which are printed below. The objective of such questions is to encourage students to test the reliability of accounts against one another to try to find the truth. Where two or more sources agree, there may be confirmation but where there are contradictions students must try to unravel this through further study of more sources or by reaching valid conclusions based on the available evidence and their own knowledge.

Thus when dealing with several sources teachers have to develop the skill of synthesis in the candidates.

Synthesis is the process of blending a number of pieces of evidence together into one coherent account. It requires an element of direct involvement because of the need for selection and weighing of evidence, but the whole product should be no more than the sum of the parts. . . . . Where eminent historians argue, the student can do little more than be aware of the conflict of ideas. A famous example concerns the origin of the Second World War.[12]

When students are being trained to judge the reliability of documents it is important that the teacher has selected interpretations such as those below which have inherent contradictions. They can be used to encourage the student to reach higher level skills in sorting the evidence presented and drawing on internal knowledge to achieve an evaluation. ·

The settlement at Munich was a triumph for British policy, which had worked precisely to this end; not a triumph for Hitler, who had started with no such clear intention. Nor was it merely a triumph for selfish or cynical British statesmen, indifferent to the fate of far-off peoples or calculating that Hitler might be launched into war against Soviet Russia. It was a triumph for all that was best and most enlightened in British life; a triumph for those who had preached equal justice between peoples; a triumph for those who had courageously denounced the harshness and short-sightedness of Versailles. Brailsford, the leading socialist authority on foreign affairs wrote in 1920 of the peace settlement: 'The worst offence was the subjection of over three million Germans to Czech rule.' This was the offence redressed at Munich. Idealists could claim that British policy had been tardy and hesitant. In 1938 it atoned for these failings. With skill and persistence, Chamberlain brought first the French and then the Czechs, to follow the moral line. A.J.P. Taylor, (*The Origins of the Second World War*)[13]

Hitler's prestige rose to new heights in Germany, where relief that war had been avoided was combined with delight in the gains that had been won on the cheap. . . .

Abroad the effect was equally startling, and Mr. Churchill described the results of the Munich settlement in a famous speech on 5 October 1938:

'At Berchtesgaden . . . £1 was demanded at pistol's point . When it was given (at Godesberg), £2 was demanded at pistol's point. Finally the dictator consented to take £1 17s 6d and the rest in promises for the future. . . We are in the presence of a disaster of the first magnitude.' Austria and Sudetenland within six months represented the triumph of those methods of political warfare which Hitler had so sedulously applied in the past five years. His diagnosis of the weakness of the western democracies, and of the international divisions which prevented the formation of a united front against him, had been brilliantly vindicated. . . . The fact that the Prime Minister of Great Britain had twice flown to Germany to intercede with him, and on the third occasion had hurried across Europe with the heads of the French and Italian governments to meet him at the shortest possible notice, constituted a personal triumph for Hitler. (A. Bullock, *Hitler, a Study in Tyranny*)[14]

The preparation of documents for such classroom work can be very time consuming. Where texts of prepared documentary materials are available they should be purchased but they will rarely be completely adequate, it may therefore be beneficial to prepare your pack of documents as you plan your programme of study. Although many teachers may feel that students have a grounding in the use of evidence at GCSE level, there is still adequate justification for using the first few weeks of lower sixth as a transitional period when the approaches to be used at A level can be practised. This is particularly true in the handling of documents and a self-supported study module could be prepared for students to work through as preparation.

Marking students' work

At first thought the marking of A level work may appear no different from that of any other level at school. It is important that work is promptly marked and returned to encourage prompt submission of work. It should also be marked constructively to avoid repetition of technical errors. However, more should be considered by the effective A level teacher. It is vital at this level that students receive clear indications of how they performed if standards are to be raised. When an essay has been set, submitted and marked, time must be laid aside for its subsequent analysis. The main points can be identified on the board, the key words in the question re-examined for their significance and possible variations in interpretations highlighted. There should also be occasions when students can question the question – What was the teacher/examiner really after? Is there another way to approach a question which will give sufficient quality in the answer? Too many sixth form essays can be damned by comments such as 'poor analysis', 'insufficient depth' or 'too short'. The effective teacher should offer much more guidance than this.

It must be remembered, however, that in secondary schools there are other classes whose work will need to be prepared, resourced and marked. Sometimes the teacher of the sixth form will find it hard to write in detail on every script and this is where a general report back in lesson time can be valuable for all. Going hand in hand with this technique can be an opportunity to share with students the language of examiners who use guide words to denote which operation is required. Here are some examples, extracted from *History: a Guide to Advanced Study* by L.G. Brandon:[15]

Discuss – Consider – Comment upon = candidates are free to express their own opinions and to make any observations which are appropriate to the main wording of the question.

Explain = show that you have understood why things were as they were or happened as they did.

Examine = test or enquire into.

Assess, estimate, to what extent, how far? = here there is a clear indication that something is to be measured, even though the answer cannot be expressed in numbers. The topic to be considered concerns achievements, influences or other matters which can vary widely in importance or amount. The candidate is asked to weigh up his evidence and to reach a conclusion which shows the significance of certain aspects of the topic.

What is the significance of? = this invites consideration of the important consequences of a man's political, economic or artistic work. It suggests the questions: What did he do? What was its value? How has the value been judged? Who benefited from it? It may also be used to ask for the results of actions and events over a short or long period of time.

What were the principles underlying. . . ? = candidates are asked to think about a whole series of things and see if there is a pattern.

Compare and contrast = this instruction is clear enough. The important matter is to decide how the answer is to be arranged; whether to make the comparison step by step or whether to deal totally with one and then with the other. The first method is usually the better but one thing to avoid is a mixture of the two.

What were the problems facing . . ? = this demands careful thinking about the problems as they would have been understood at the time, not as we have come to think about them since.

What considerations influenced . . ? = this is a question about thoughts and motives and is very difficult to answer with assurance.

Sharing these examples with students in the course of their study can only serve to improve at least the relevance of their answers to questions if not the quality of content.

Another way in which teachers can use their marking to improve the work of students is to maintain a consistency of format. While it cannot be assumed that all A level history students will go on to read the subject at university, two years studying the subject should establish certain practices in the presentation of their work. They should include quotations not in a spurious sense but with perspicacity. The pithy quote can often raise the interest level of an answer.

The intelligent use of quotations . . . requires skill: too often quotations are thrust into answers in such a way that they distort argument or lead candidates into ever-increasing irrelevance . . . It may be worth mentioning that some candidates achieve grade A without mentioning any historian or writing down a single quotation.[16]

Similarly, students should always provide a bibliography in prepared work for the teacher. It may be that students rarely read anything which their teacher has not but that does not negate the practice of acknowledging the sources of information used. It also enables the teacher to prompt further discussion to establish what level of understanding has been achieved of other historians' work. The inclusion of an essay plan should also be encouraged for two reasons. It allows the teacher to see the structure the student sets for himself or herself and if there is some problem it may be here that it can be quickly solved. Secondly, when students are in the habit of writing a plan, they will do so in an examination and should their timing go wrong an allowance can be given for a plan which is appropriate.

It may appear simplistic to state but the effective teacher will also correct bad grammar, punctuation and spelling. With the return of penalties for such faults in external examinations the teacher must try to improve standards through regular correction of class work errors. In history there is a range of words which appear more often than others and it is vital that these are well learned, e.g. parliament, government. It creates a very bad impression on examiners if students spell wrongly the names of important statesmen whom they have been studying for a considerable time.

Preparing candidates for the examination

Although students often see the examination as something separate from the course it is of course only the conclusion to this stage of their studies. As such teachers will have been preparing them for this from their first day in lower sixth. There are however certain ways in which their final performance can be enhanced with timely advice.

Revision is a process which we often take for granted without actually examining what it involves. It is a way of reviewing work at regular intervals in a variety of ways in which to stimulate the recall of certain information which will provoke further recall. Students need to practice this and be encouraged to draw up adequate revision schedules. There are several publications available which offer very useful advice for students and a new teacher to A level would do well to go through some of these with the class. Below is an example of a revision schedule taken from *The Modern History Manual* which is highly commended.[17]

AN EXAMPLE OF A REVISION CYCLE FOR
A TWO A LEVEL STUDENT

	Week 1	*Week 2*	*Week 3*
Monday	History E 30 m	English 30 m	History E 30 m
Tuesday	English 20 m	History PS 30 m	English
Wednesday			
Thursday	History E 25 m	English	History E 20 m
Friday	English	History PS 15 m	English
Saturday		English	Hist/Eng A 30 m
Sunday	Hist/Eng A 30 m	History M 10m	

Key: M = morning, A = afternoon, E = evening, PS = private study, m = minutes.

This manual contains many other useful elements of advice which can be passed on to students to improve their personal preparations. Where the teacher can promote good study methods the students will find the examination less of a hurdle and can approach it as a challenge and not a threat.

Since September 1989 the *Modern History Review* published by Philip Allan Publishers has introduced a new section into its triannual magazine, the 'Examiner's Report' which provides excellent feedback and advice from experts in A level marking. So far the series has looked at several essay questions, document questions and examiners' advice. In the issue of September 1989 it also carried an article by Eric Evans, Professor of History at the University of Lancaster and Chief Examiner of A level History for the Joint Matriculation Board, entitled Doing it right. In it he stated:[18]

A-level History is assessed overwhelmingly through essays. most candidates are required to do eight pieces of work in two three-hour papers. Six or seven of these will be essays. Candidates facing the exam should therefore be *trained essay writers*, yet many plainly are not. They underperform because they cannot write essays properly, and the essay medium actually obscures the historical message they are trying to convey.

The message for the sixth former teacher is clear.

Later in the same article is some thought provoking information on document questions.

Firstly candidates tend to get rather higher average marks on their document questions than on others. This is not surprising. The tasks required here are often more precise than an essay which begins with an open-ended injunction like 'Comment on the view that. . .' . The questions are often broken up into component parts, with separate marks for each part. . . . Cumulatively, therefore, the marks can add up encouragingly. Secondly the specific marks covering those all-important grade boundaries in A level History are very tight. A specially good performance on a documents question can easily push you up into a higher grade.

The message is clear: pay special attention to document questions. They are 'nice little earners'. . . . Badger your teacher during the upper sixth for plenty of practice in refining the specific skills they aim to test.

Here again the advice is as relevant to the teacher of A level as to the student.

A critic once observed that good history teaching produces informed, literate sceptics who know both how to ask the awkward question and how to refute the inadequate or mendacious answer.

The effective teacher of history could not have a better remit.

Conclusion

The teaching of A level classes is still seen in some schools as a perk which the young teacher must earn. In others, however, as the implications of local management of schools begin to bite it may result in newly qualified teachers being popular appointments many of whom can be asked to teach the entire 11 to 18 age range. It is important that sixth form teaching is not seen as mainly the transmission of information but that history at this level is as varied and challenging as it can be in the junior years of secondary.

Resources must be carefully selected not only for the delivery of content but to extend the horizons of study. Many of the recent publications directed at the sixth form market are very worthy and it is always surprising that students will heed more readily advice presented from a journal or magazine than that which the teacher has often said to them based on his or her own experience.

Finally teachers themselves must determine to keep their own knowledge fresh. Gone are the days (we all hope!) when a teacher could prepare a series of dictated notes knowing they would last ten even twenty years: 'the teacher who has ceased to take part in the work of exploration, discovery and restatement is very unlikely to remain a useful instructor.'[19]

New interpretations have to be taken on board and new assessment methods mean that syllabus changes are more frequent. If standards are to be raised students need to be trained to meet the new assessment criteria and that means that teachers have to update their knowledge of these criteria. The advent of the National Curriculum is hailed as the new age of historical training. If this is so then A level syllabuses will have to be reviewed in this light. Despite the ever-increasing demands on teachers' time and energy, the effective teacher will be the one who tries to keep in touch with the changes and thinking in education and in particular in the subject. Several associations exist to help and their journals and conferences are an obvious means through which to gather the knowledge which will make you even more effective.

Further questions to consider

(1) Are you fully conversant with the syllabus for your school/college?
(2) What proportion of time are you going to devote to discussion?
(3) Which journal or magazine are you going to subscribe to?
(4) Are you aware of the professional associations which you are eligible to join?
(5) Have you drawn up a programme of study for the two years of sixth form?
(6) What detailed preparations are you going to share with candidates for external examinations?
(7) In your marking do you have clear symbols explained to students so they can identify and rectify stylistic errors?
(8) What criteria will you use in the selection of documents?
(9) What variety of techniques can you embody in your teaching programme?
(10) Often teachers share the teaching of A level, how can you ensure that candidates do not get contradictory messages and at the same time advice is not needlessly repeated?
(11) Are 'mock' examinations set at the appropriate level and marked to standard? Have you asked an experienced colleague to check?
(12) Do you regularly review your own notes?
(13) What are the implications for A level syllabuses of the National Curriculum to Key Stage 4?
(14) Do you consider that only modern history (post-1918) should be taught at A level?

Notes and References

1. Schools Council Working Paper No. 5
2. History Commissioned Group Report on N and F syllabuses, Schools Council 18+ Research Programme, November 1976.
3. V. Crinnion, 'Some problems and principles of sixth form history'. In C. Portal (ed.) *The History Curriculum for Teachers,* Falmer Press, 1987.
4. C. Coltham and J. Fines, 'Educational objectives for the study of history', Historical Association, 1971.
5. G.R. Elton, *The Practice of History*, Collins, 1967.
6. V.A. Crinnion, op. cit.
7. Ibid.
8. L.G. Brandon, *A Guide to Advanced Study*, Edward Arnold, 1976, p. 4.
9. John Fines, *Reading Historical Documents – A Manual for Students*, Basil Blackwell, 1988.
10. Ibid.
11. John Fines, 'Source-based questions at A level', *Teaching History Series*, No. 54, Historical Association 1984.
12. J.A. Cloake, V.A. Crinnion, S.M.Harrison, *The Modern History Manual*, Framework Press, 1987, p. 117.

13. A.J.P. Taylor, *The Origins of the Second World War*, Penguin, 1964, p. 234.
14. A. Bullock, *Hitler, A Study in Tyranny*, Penguin, 1952.
15. L.G. Brandon, *History: a guide to Advanced Study*, Edward Arnold, 1976, pp. 46–9.
16. London University Examiners' Report: A Level History, University of London, 1981, p. 361.
17. J.A. Cloake, V.A. Crinnion, S.M. Harrison, op. cit.
18. Eric Evans, 'Doing it Right', *Modern History Review*, September 1989.
19. G.R. Elton, *The Practice of History*, Collins, 1969, p. 179.

APPENDIX

WJEC: A level History 1992, S S 4, Syllabus A, Paper A2

SECTION B

*Answer **either** Question 3 **or** Question 4.*   [30]

3. *Study the following sources carefully, and then answer the questions based upon them.*

Source A

"I believe in Rome the Eternal, the mother of my country, and in Italy. . . . I believe in the genius of Mussolini, in our Holy Father Fascism, in the communion of its martyrs, in the conversion of Italians, and in the resurrection of the Empire."

[The Balilla Creed]

Source B

"Article 19: The Holy See shall appoint Archbishops and Bishops. . . .

Article 20: Bishops before taking possession of their dioceses shall take an oath of loyalty at the hands of the Head of State . . . 'I shall not participate in any agreement or take part in any discussion that might be injurious to the Italian state. . . .' "

[The Concordat of the Lateran Treaty (1929)]

Source C

"The Italian State recognises the organisations connected with the 'Azione Cattolica Italiana' (Catholic Action) in so far as these shall (as provided by the Holy See) carry out their activities outside any political party, and under the immediate direction of the hierarchy of the Church, for the diffusion and practice of Catholic principles."

[Article 43, the Lateran Treaty]

Source D

"A conception of the State which makes the young generations belong entirely to it . . . cannot be reconciled by a Catholic with the Catholic doctrine. . . .
We have not said that we wished to condemn the party as such . . . (only) that much in the programme and in the action of the party which we have seen and have understood to be contrary to Catholic doctrine and the Catholic practice."

> [Pius XI, 'Non Abbiamo Bisogno' ('We have no need')
> (29 June 1931)]

Source E

". . . prepared souls for the redemption of Ethiopia from the bondage of slavery and heresy and for the Christian renewal of the ancient empire of Rome."

> [Cardinal Schuster, Archbishop of Milan,
> supporting the invasion of Abyssinia in 1935)]

(a) (i)   What does Source A. reveal about the relationship
            between Church and State in Fascist Italy?   [5]

    (ii)   To what extent do Sources B, C and D provide
           evidence of the manner in which Mussolini could
           undermine the authority of the Church after 1929?   [5]

(b) (i)   Can you reconcile the comments made in Source E
            with those in Source D? Explain your answer.   [5]
    (ii)   How far do the sources illustrate an inconsistency in
           the Church's attitude towards Fascism?   [5]

(c) How far do the sources contribute to an understanding of the
      problems facing churches in a totalitarian
      state?   [10]

BIBLIOGRAPHY

Adams, A. and Jones E. (1983) *Teaching Humanities in the Microelectronic Age*, Open University.

Blyth, J. (1988) *History 5–9*, Hodder and Stoughton.

Brandon, L.G. (1976) *A Guide to Advanced Study*, Edward Arnold.

Brooks, R. (1989) *GCSE Coursework in Action : British Social and Economic History*, Edward Arnold, 1989.

Brooks, R. (1989) *GCSE Coursework in Action : Modern World History,* Edward Arnold, 1989.

Brooks, R. (1989) *GCSE Coursework in Action : Schools History Project*, Edward Arnold, 1989.

Brooks, R. (1989) *GCSE Coursework in Action : British and European History,* Edward Arnold, 1989.

Cloake, J.A., Crinnion, V. and Harrison, S.M. (1987) *The Modern History Manual*, Framework Press, (Curriculum Council for Wales, Non-Statutory Guidance for History, 1991).

Department of Education and Science (1968), Archives and Education, Education pamphlet No. 24, HMSO.

Dickinson, A. and Lee, P. (1983) *History Teaching and Historical Understanding*, Heinemann.

Durbin, G., Morris, S. and Wilkinson S. (1989) *A Teacher's Guide to Learning from Objects*, English Heritage.

Edington, D. (1982) *The Role of History in Multicultural Education*, London.

Fines, J. (1984) 'Source-based Questions at A level', Historical Association.

Fines, J. (1988) *Reading Historical Documents,* Basil Blackwell.

Goodhew, E. (1988) *Museums and the Curriculum*, Area Museums Service for South East England.

Greenhill, E. H. (ed.) (1989) *Initiatives in Museum Education*, Department of Museum Studies, Leicester.

Jones G. and Ward L. (1978) *New History, Old Problems*, University College of Swansea. Faculty of Education.

Morris S. (1989) *A Teacher's Guide to Using Portraits*, English Heritage.

National Curriculum Council (1990) *History Orders – National Curriculum.*

National Curriculum Council (1991) *Non-statutory Guidance for History*.

Nichol, J. (1984) *Teaching History*, Macmillan.

Purkis, S. (1987) *Oral History in Schools*, University of Essex.

Steel, D. J. and Taylor, L. (1973) *Family History in Schools*.

Tames, R.L.A. (1973) *Exam Guide for A level Modern British History*, McGraw-Hill.

Williams, M. (1983) *Teaching European Studies*, Heinemann.

INDEX